KINGS AND PROPHETS

CONTEMPORARY COLLEGE THEOLOGY SERIES

GENERAL EDITORS: J. FRANK DEVINE, S.J.
RICHARD ROUSSEAU, S.J.

KINGS AND PROPHETS is one of the volumes in the Biblical Theology
section of this series.

Kings and Prophets

Dennis J. McCarthy, S.J.
ST. LOUIS UNIVERSITY

THE BRUCE PUBLISHING COMPANY / Milwaukee

IMPRIMI POTEST:

    Leo J. Burns, S.J.
    Vice-Provincial

NIHIL OBSTAT:

    Richard J. Sklba, S.S.L., S.T.D.
    Censor librorum

IMPRIMATUR:

    ✠ William E. Cousins
    Archbishop of Milwaukee
    March 3, 1968

Library of Congress Catalog Card Number: 68–24581

Copyright © 1968 The Bruce Publishing Company

MADE IN THE UNITED STATES OF AMERICA

EDITORS' INTRODUCTION

THE CONTEMPORARY COLLEGE THEOLOGY SERIES

This series begins with the presupposition that theology is necessary. It is necessary if Christian intelligence is to search for meaning in its dialogue with God, man, and the world. Since Christian intelligence is not the exclusive possession of the theological specialist or the cleric, the search must be carried on in all those areas of life, secular as well as religious, including the college situation, where meaning is to be found.

This search is a peaceful one, for in some mysterious way it has already achieved its goal: the vision of faith and the fullness of love. Still it remains a relentless and universal search. Its inner certainty must radiate out not only to the edges of the mind but also into the farthest recesses of the world. We could call it "lay" theology, but this word seems too pale a description for such an exciting enterprise of the Christian life.

In view of this, the editors of this series are convinced that new ques tions had to be asked, new structures created, and new books written. These books would be neither catechetical nor apologetic. They would be purely and simply theological. The primary audience would be believers, but all thinking men would find them useful. In scope they would be broad enough to ensure perspective. They would be scholarly enough to be intellectually relevant. They would avoid pedantry. In short, they would try to present a rich and deep understanding of Christian revelation in such a way that today's college students would be able to respond with a Christian faith and life that are both culturally mature and scientifically precise. Finally, the authors of these books would be, for the most part, teachers in colleges and universities where much of the contemporary theological dialogue is now going on.

The series falls into four parts: biblical, historical, ecclesial, and ethical. The divisions were not predetermined by the editors. They follow the shape of the most vigorous theological work now being done.

The books in the biblical section are intended to go beyond the traditional treatment of Bible history and the now familiar perspectives of salvation history. They concentrate on various books of the Bible. Their method has been especially designed for college work. Tentatively it might be called "exegetical theology." Every verse is not considered after the fashion of a commentary, nor are narratives developed as a biography, nor is there any attempt to create large theological syntheses. Rather the individual books are studied in chronological sequence; key passages are treated in detail and the rest are summarized. At the same time some attention is paid to the growing theological synthesis.

Since scholastic theology is already represented by individual works and sets of textbooks, the books in our historical section study dogmatic questions from a developmental point of view. In this way the editors hope to make the college students more aware of the great wealth of theological thinking that recent historico-theological studies have uncovered. This method, which is more inductive than deductive, should happily coincide with the thought processes of the college student. The three basic poles for synthesis are: God, Christ, and Man. In each area the historical development will be studied and a significant number of basic source texts presented. The problems raised in these studies will range all the way from Augustinian pessimism to Teilhardian optimism.

The textbooks for the third part of the series will deal with issues of great contemporary importance. They will examine questions discussed by the Second Vatican Council. As the name implies, ecclesial theology must first concern itself with the Church, what the Church knows herself to be, as expressed in the insights of the new *Constitution on the Church* and with the more significant of the Church's allied concerns: other world religions, American Protestantism, its history, its motivating forces and spirit, and finally the new sacramental theology so enriched by the many magnificent liturgical advances. All of this growth has brought a wider and deeper appreciation of the nature of the Roman Catholic Church and her relationship, rooted in understanding and love, with the whole world.

The fourth and final section of the series is devoted explicitly to Christian moral response. The editors subscribe to the position that the proper place for the Catholic college or university to examine ethical questions is in a revelational rather than in a purely philosophical context. In addition to the "virtue" divisions of the *Summa* or the classic moral theology text, designed primarily for confessors, there is a need and a place for a "Christian ethics" that reflects the new insights which both biblical and dogmatic theology can provide. These books will strive to be openly Christian in spirit, eclectic in approach, up to date in scholarship, and will address themselves to those ethical problems which are most real to the modern American mind.

Finally, the editors would like to express their thanks to all those whose interest, advice, and cooperation have made this series possible. They are especially grateful to Mr. William May of The Bruce Publishing Company, who not only initiated the project and sustained it through the inevitable disappointments and complications, but contributed so much of his editorial skill to its final shape. To the individual authors who so graciously added to their heavy burden of academic responsibility by undertaking these books, we can only express the hope that their share in the shaping and influencing of the American Catholic community of today and of tomorrow will be far more meaningful to them than any meager thanks of ours.

The Editors,
REV. J. FRANK DEVINE, S.J., Boston College
REV. RICHARD W. ROUSSEAU, S.J., Fairfield University

Contents

PART I: KINGS

INTRODUCTION

A short introduction seems called for in order to acquaint the reader with the aim of this book and help him toward its proper use. There are also some small explanations with regard to vocabulary which seem necessary. Beyond this, it is hoped that the book will explain itself.

The purpose of the book is to introduce the reader to the meaning of the story of the kings, and to the message of the prophets of Israel. It should, therefore, be accompanied by a careful reading of the pertinent books of the Bible, 1–2 Samuel and 1–2 Kings and the books of the prophets. This is not so formidable a task. In an ordinary edition of the Bible which lies before me all this material adds up to no more than 430 pages. However, admittedly this material from a very ancient and very different culture can be difficult at a first reading. Hence, through this book we will suggest various readings to accompany its various divisions. In most instances these are selections from the books just named, but the reader should not be deceived. Having read the selections, he has not finished the pertinent biblical material. The selections suggested are not substitutes for the whole books. They are rather introductions to those books. Hopefully, reading the selections first will make it easier to understand the whole books. In any case, easy or not, the reader should be sure to read all of the Old Testament books in question.

So much for procedure. There are certain difficulties in vocabulary which face anyone dealing with the period of Old Testament revelation which is the subject matter of this book. Chief among them is the word "Israel." In biblical usage this is the most common term for the *whole community* of the worshipers of the true God, Yahweh. However, it is also the name of one of the two political units into which that community

xiii

divided after the death of Solomon; the Kingdom of Judah in the south and the Kingdom of Israel in the north.

This double use of the same name can cause immense confusion. Is one speaking of the religious whole or the political part? In order to avoid this ambiguity we have generally restricted Israel to name the political unit, the kingdom. When we are speaking of the religious community or of the whole Yahwist population in contrast to others who did not serve the one God, we have used the term "Hebrew." This is not an ideal solution because "Hebrew" had no special religious connotations. In fact, the name seems to be sociological in origin. The Hebrews who appear as Habiru in many texts from the second millenium B.C. seem to have been "displaced persons" of some kind who often banded together for mutual help. However, even though the word is not the standard biblical term for the sense we give it, it does offer a practical alternative to the accurate but hopelessly ambiguous "Israel." Furthermore, there is some justification for our usage in the Bible. The Old Testament tends to restrict the name "Hebrew" to contexts where it is consciously setting the whole of the chosen people off from alien groups. This is essentially what we use the word to do, though we do imply religious overtones not always present in the original use of the word.

The reader should note that in the period covered in the latter part of the book, the era of the Babylonian exile and afterward, the old political divisions had disappeared. There were no kingdoms. The only chosen people were those who held firmly to Yahweh no matter where they were or who ruled over them. Hence the danger of confusion no longer exists. "Israel" can only mean the community of the worshipers of Yahweh. Therefore, in this latter part of the book we return to the biblical usage and call that community Israel.

The words "Jew" and "Jewish" are also confined to this latter part of the book. This is in accord with the practice of modern scholarship which sees in the exilic and post-exilic communities the beginnings of Judaism, a religious phenomenon continuous with but quite different from the religion of the monarchical and premonarchical eras.

Finally, we often speak of "Davidids," which may sound like odd English. This is simply the adoption of a convenient, if unfamiliar, ending borrowed from the Greek: "-id" simply means "descended from" or "belonging to the family of." Hence a Davidid is no more than a legitimate successor within the family of David.

Books of the Bible

(Following the order and spellings of the Revised Standard Version; Confraternity variations in parentheses)

OLD TESTAMENT

Gen	Genesis	Wis	Wisdom of Solomon
Ex	Exodus		(= Wisdom)
Lev	Leviticus	Sir	Sirach
Nm	Numbers	Is	Isaiah (= Isaia)
Dt	Deuteronomy	Jer	Jeremiah (= Jeremia)
Jos	Joshua	Lam	Lamentations
Jg	Judges	Bar	Baruch
Ru	Ruth	Ezek	Ezekiel (= Ezechiel)
1 Sam	1 Samuel (= 1 Kings)	Dan	Daniel
2 Sam	2 Samuel (= 2 Kings)	Hos	Hosea (= Osee)
1 Kgs	1 Kings (= 3 Kings)	Jl	Joel
2 Kgs	2 Kings (= 4 Kings)	Am	Amos
1 Chr	1 Chronicles	Ob	Obadiah (= Abdia)
	(= 1 Paralipomenon)	Jon	Jonah (= Jona)
2 Chr	2 Chronicles	Mic	Micah (= Michea)
	(= 2 Paralipomenon)	Nah	Nahum
Ezr	Ezra (= 1 Esdras)	Hab	Habakkuk (= Habacuc)
Neh	Nehemiah (= 2 Esdras)	Zeph	Zephaniah (= Sophonia)
Tob	Tobit (= Tobias)	Hag	Haggai (= Aggai)
Jdt	Judith	Zech	Zechariah (= Zacharia)
Est	Esther	Mal	Malachi (= Malachia)
Job	Job	1 Mac	1 Maccabees
Ps	Psalms		(= 1 Machabees)
Prov	Proverbs	2 Mac	2 Maccabees
Ec	Ecclesiastes (Qohelet)		(= 2 Machabees)
S of S	Song of Solomon		
	(= Canticle of Canticles)		

NEW TESTAMENT

Mt	Matthew	1 Tim	1 Timothy
Mk	Mark	2 Tim	2 Timothy
Lk	Luke	Tit	Titus
Jn	John	Phm	Philemon
Acts	Acts of the Apostles	Heb	Hebrews
Rom	Romans	Jas	James
1 Cor	1 Corinthians	1 Pet	1 Peter
2 Cor	2 Corinthians	2 Pet	2 Peter
Gal	Galatians	1 Jn	1 John
Eph	Ephesians	2 Jn	2 John
Phil	Philippians	3 Jn	3 John
Col	Colossians	Jude	Jude
1 Th	1 Thessalonians	Rev	Revelation (Apocalypse)
2 Th	2 Thessalonians		

CHRONOLOGICAL TABLE FOR KINGS AND PROPHETS

N.B. The dates given are those most widely accepted by modern scholarship. There are some problems; for instance, the reigns of the kings of Israel and Judah do not correspond perfectly, but in the case of the kings most of the dates are close to exact. The same is true of the dates given historical events.

It is impossible to be so precise about the prophets. However, we can be sure of the period of the prophet's activity in most cases.

KINGS		PROPHETS	NOTABLE EVENTS
The United Kingdom			
Samuel, Saul (c. 1040–1000) David (c. 1000–860) Solomon (c. 960–922)			
The Two Kingdoms			
Israel: Jeroboam I (922–901)	*Judah:* Rehoboam (922–915) Abijah (915–913)	Ahijah	918: Pharaoh Shishak (Sheshonk I) invades Judah.
Nadab (901–900) Baasha (900–877)	Asa (913–873)		900: Baasha murders Jeroboam's family, usurps the throne of Israel.
Elah (877–876) Zimri (876)			876: Zimri usurps the throne, but Omri replaces him, founding Israel's greatest dynasty.
Omri (876–869)*			
Ahab (869–850)		Elijah	858–824: Shalmaneser III restores Assyrian power, begins the drive to the west.
			853: Battle of Qarqar: Israel and Syria turn the first Assyrian thrust.
		Elisha	
Ahaziah (850–849) Joram (849–842)	Jehoram (849–842)		
Jehu (842–815)	Athaliah (842–837)		842: Jehu murders the kings of Israel and Judah, replaces the Omrids in Israel.

Kings	Prophets	Notable Events
Joash (837–800)		837: In Judah the usurping Queen Athaliah is slain and the Davidids restored.
Joahaz (815–801) Joash (801–786) Amaziah (800–783)	Amos (c. 760–750)	745–727: Tiglath-pileser III renews the Assyrian drive to the west.
Jeroboam II (786–746) Uzziah (783–742)		
[Jotham: regent (750–742)]		
Zechariah (746–745) Shallum (745)		745: With Shallum's murder of Zechariah begins a series of palace revolutions ending only with the end of Israel.
Menahem (745–738)		
Jotham (742–735)		
Pekahiah (738–737) Pekah (737–732)		
Ahaz (735–715)	Isaiah (c. 742–700)	
Hoshea (732–724)		734, 732: Assyrian campaigns reduce Israel to Samaria and environs.
	Micah (c. 720–700)	721: Samaria falls to Sargon II; Israel disappears.
The Kingdom of Judah		
Hezekiah (715–687) Manasseh (687–642) Amon (642–640)		
Josiah (640–609)	Zephaniah (c. 630–620) Jeremiah (c. 624–585) Habbakuk (c. 625–600) Nahum (c. 612)	626–612: Decline and fall of the Assyrian Empire.
Jehoahaz (609) **Jehoiakim** (609–598)		605: At the Battle of Carchemish Nebuchadnezzar establishes Babylon's

KINGS	PROPHETS	NOTABLE EVENTS
		hegemony in western Asia.
Jehoiachin (598–597)		597: First deportation of Judean notables to Babylon
Zedekiah (597–587)	Ezekiel (from 593, in Babylonia)	
		587: Jerusalem falls, the Babylonian exile begins.
		559–529: Cyrus II the Great creates the Persian Empire.
	Deutero-Isaiah (c. 550–535, in Babylonia)	
		539: Cyrus conquers Babylon.
The Community of the Return		538: Cyrus' decree permits the return of the Jews.
		520: Work on the second Temple resumed.
	Haggai (520) Zechariah (520–518)	
		515: Second Temple dedicated.
	Trito-Isaiah (c. 500)** Malachi (515–445)	
		445: The successful efforts of Ezra and Nehemiah to reform and consolidate the Temple state begin and continue through most of the rest of the century.
	Jonah (c. 440–400)**	
	Joel (after 400)** Obadiah (after 400)**	
		333: Alexander conquers the Persian Empire.
		312: Seleucus I Nicator founds the Greek dynasty of Syria (continued until 64 B.C.
		301: Ptolemy I Soter founds the Greek dynasty of Egypt (continued until 30 B.C.) and rules Palestine.

KINGS	PROPHETS	NOTABLE EVENTS
	Isaian Apocalypses: Is 24–27; 34–35 Zecharian Apocalypse: Zech 9–14 (3rd century?**	
		198: Antiochus III the Great takes Palestine from Egypt for the Seleucid Empire.
	Daniel (167–164)	168–142: Maccabean wars against the Hellenizing policy of the Seleucids.

* Boldface indicates kings specially important in the history of prophecy.
** For most of the post-exilic writings any very close dating is impossible. The dates given in this list and marked by asterisks give the probable time *about when* or *during which* the material in question originated.

PART I: KINGS

CHAPTER 1.   KINGS AND PROPHETS

Readings: Dt 31:1–23; Jos 1:1–9; 12:1–8; 23; Jg 2:11–23; 1 Sam 12:6–25; 2 Sam 7; 1 Kgs 8; 2 Kgs 17:1–20

The combination in this title may seem strange. Why lump together the prophetic and institutional aspects of God's revelation? What about the tendency of an enduring and sometimes rigid institution like a monarchy to conflict with the free spirit which is typical of prophecy? Hebrew history often shows serious conflict between king and prophet. However, this need not be the case, and in fact it often was not. In many ways Hebrew kingship depended upon the prophetic movement and vice versa. Strikingly the era of vital Hebrew prophecy is roughly the era of the original Hebrew monarchies.

To understand something of this we must be clear about the nature of prophecy. It is not primarily concerned with the prediction of coming events, although the English word has come to mean this. Among the Hebrews, as in religion in general, the true claim of prophecy is that the prophet speaks for God, and he does so not merely about the future but about the past and especially the present. His function is to communicate the divine will and so guide the people. This function gives us

3

a first clue to the relation between prophecy and kingship among the Hebrews. The monarchy arose when the people were hard pressed by the efficient military machine of the invading Philistines. They needed stronger leadership than they had had under their original tribal organizations. Thus they sought a king, for monarchy was the only form of central government known to them. But it was not enough that the people of God need a king. The nation belonged to Yahweh alone, and it was only he who could designate its true leader. Since prophets were his spokesmen, it was natural that he should use them to point out the chosen king.

Moreover, once the monarch was established the Hebrew kings were accustomed to consult prophets as regular members of their court, trusted and reliable advisors. In fact, many of the great prophets of whom we learn in the Old Testament are associated one way or another with the kings. To the men of the time there was nothing surprising about this. In so relying upon prophets the kings of the chosen people were imitating the best practices of the governments of the age. Quite apart from the phenomenon of mantic practices among primitive peoples and in areas cut off from the Near East, which was the cradle of the Hebrews, prophetic activity was not confined to the chosen people. The Bible itself accepts the validity of the directions given by pagan Philistine diviners (1 Sam 6:2–9), and the gentile Balaam is treated as an authentic prophet (Num 22–24). In prophecy as in other matters ancient Israel, though the possessor of a supernatural revealed religion, lived and expressed itself in the forms familiar to the men of the time, the only forms they could understand without extravagant miraculous intervention on the part of God.[1]

Thus Israelite prophecy was not an oddity in its time and place. Its visionary character, its concern with the whole life of the people including the political, the very forms in which its message was couched, are paralleled in and often borrowed from Israel's environment. Moreover, when in the later Persian period and Hellenistic era prophecy ceased to play an important role in the public life of the ancient east, it also disappeared from Israel. Seemingly God used prophecy as long as it was an accepted form of communication in normal society, and abandoned it when it was no longer so accepted. This readiness to talk to man in man's terms, the only terms he could understand, characterizes most of revelation in the Old Testament and the New. The revelation itself goes far beyond

---

[1] The most complete survey of extrabiblical prophetic texts seems to be André Neher, *L'éssence du prophetisme* (Paris: Presses universitaires de France, 1956).

the forms and ideas which it borrows for its expression, but to be understood it must begin with these things which men know.

THE ORIGINS OF THE MONARCHY:
THE SOURCES OF OUR KNOWLEDGE

We have many sources which say something about the monarchy in Israel, its nature, its meaning, and the situation in which it was evolved. There are psalms which deal with the king. The prophets often refer to the kingship. There are even a few references to Hebrew kings in records from other ancient nations. However, these sources are scanty compared to all that we can learn from the books of Samuel and Kings (in the older Catholic versions called the four books of Kings) and the parallel history contained in 1 and 2 Chronicles (called 1 and 2 Paralipomenon in older Catholic versions). Note that these books are divided quite arbitrarily in our Bible; originally they went together, Samuel and Kings forming a single literary unit, 1 and 2 Chronicles another. The reason for the present separation is simply mechanical. In ancient time writing was conserved on rolls of a kind of paper thicker than ours. After a certain amount of paper had been rolled up, it became so unwieldy that a long piece of literature had to be broken in order to accommodate it to several rolls of convenient size. The divisions are purely arbitrary and we should not pay any attention to them in our study of the books, except to note that the divisions into rolls sometimes attracted additions to the texts. The end of a roll was a place where a scribe would naturally attach material related to the subject of a book which he felt should be preserved. Chapters 21–25 of 2 Samuel represent such additions.[2]

Furthermore, both Samuel-Kings and Chronicles are each parts of larger histories. To take the simplest first, the history in Chronicles is continued in the books of Ezra and Nehemiah. As things stand in our Bibles, the conclusion of a larger book has been separated from its introduction and made into the books of Ezra and Nehemiah. So also Samuel-Kings are but two-thirds of a longer whole which includes everything that we find in our Bibles beginning from the Book of Joshua down through 2 Kings, originally a single history of Israel from the time of its entrance into the promised land until the fall of the kingdom of Judah.

It will help us to read this history intelligently if we understand the

---

[2] For detailed studies of the dates and authenticity of biblical texts one should refer to the *Introduction* to the Bible under the appropriate biblical heading. For references see the Bibliographical Notes. The standard Old Testament introduction is Eissfeldt, but Tos or Ellis are easier to use.

nature of this long history of Israel in the promised land. It is the work of a scholar or scholars (this modern title really is suitable in this instance) who gathered together what there was to find about the ancient and the recent history of the people and attempted to interpret this history. Since the interpretation of the history so collected was guided by the theology of the book of Deuteronomy, we call the history as a whole the Deuteronomic History. This is not to claim that the book of Deuteronomy and this history are all from one pen. The core of Deuteronomy (5–28) is the older book. It is a theological document providing a restatement of the law of Moses. In this restatement the law is clearly acompanied by conditional threats and blessings; if Israel is faithful, it will prosper; if Israel is faithless, it will be punished. This, much over-simplified, is the theology of the book of Deuteronomy. Well after the time in which the core of Deuteronomy was written, the history of the Israelite people was interpreted in the light of this theology.

The motivation for this attempt at the theological interpretation of history is clear. Even though the kingdom of Israel, that larger of the two kingdoms into which the Hebrew nation was divided after Solomon's death, had been destroyed in 722 B.C., in the smaller, southern kingdom of Judah the Hebrews retained a hold on a portion of the promised land. But early in the sixth century B.C. this kingdom too was conquered by Babylon and its people exiled. It is hard for us to imagine what a shock this was for the men of the Old Testament. Possession of the promised land was the sign and fulfillment of their special relationship to God. The loss of any hold on the land eventually caused them to reflect on the nature of that relationship itself, but it raised more immediate questions. How could this happen? Were not the Hebrews the people of God? Had Yahweh not guaranteed the safety of Judah? (Is 37:35) These were the problems to which the Deuteronomic History addressed itself, and it is obvious how the theology of Deuteronomy helped answer them. The chosen people had been unfaithful and so had brought down on themselves the curses threatened against such unfaithfulness.

So bold a statement is a fair summary of a basic attitude of the History, but it is nothing like a complete picture. The theology of the Deuteronomic History is richer and more complex than this. This is truly a book of theology, a profound searching out of God's ways with men. However, it is theology told in a special way. It is not abstract in the sense that it theorizes about history and God's role in it. Rather, it tells the story of what happened, but in such a way as to show forth the meaning of the story. This means that, if we are to see something of the meaning beneath the stories, we must look with some attention to the sources the History used, the principles (apart from the general idea of retribution drawn from Deuteronomy and already mentioned) which dictated the use made of these sources, and finally the structure which was given the materials collected according to these principles.[3]

What, then, were the important sources at hand to the historian? For the period of the Judges the material was largely stories of unusual men and great events, the sort of thing people always love to tell about and which easily turns into legend. There is some of the same sort of thing in the books of Samuel and Kings, but it is largely confined to the stories of Samuel, Saul, and the prophets Elijah and Elisha. However, for the period covered in these books the historian had the use of annals and archives as well. Already with the advent of David, although the popular element does not entirely disappear, more formal sources came to hand. The account of the succession to David's throne running from 1 Samuel 9 through 1 Kings 2 (except of course 2 Sam 21–25, which are later additions) is the clearest example. None of the malice or weakness or folly of the national hero, David, is passed over or palliated. There is little of the marvelous either; yet the hand of God is clearly seen, guiding the history of his people through what seems an ordinary, even sordid, human story (2 Sam 18:28). Such respect for the truth, even when unpleasant or obscure, marks truly objective history writing of a high order.

Apart from continuous histories like this, the archives of the kings of Israel and the kings of Judah contributed to the Deuteronomic History. Most probably these annals of the kingdoms had already been edited into a concise and organized form before the Deuteronomic History was written. We believe this to be so because the work was composed about 550 B.C., almost forty years after the destruction of Judah and one hundred and seventy years after the fall of Samaria. It seems unlikely that full official archives survived the plundering of the capitals by the conquering armies. Hence we conclude that some kind of summary had already been made and was available to historians after the fall of the

---

[3] There is no adequate study of the Deuteronomic history in English. The basic study is Martin Noth, *Überlieferungsgeschichtliche Studien I* (Halle: Niemeyer, 1943). Some information can be obtained from M. Noth, *History of Israel*, Part I, C.I., no. 4, plus the references in the indices of this book and of John Bright, *A History of Israel*, under "Deuteronomic History," and Gerhard von Rad, *Studies in Deuteronomy. Studies in Biblical Theology* 3 (London: S.C.M. Press, 1953), chap. 7, "The Deuteronomic Theology of History in the Books of Kings."

Hebrew kingdoms. Such excerpts from official archives were, of course, contemporary with at least part of what they recount, a fact which increases their claim to credibility.

Nevertheless, faithful recorder though he is, the historian was also an editor. Obviously a great deal happened over the four-hundred-year history of the Hebrew monarchy, and much of it must have been recorded; yet our Bibles offer only a selection from all this material. We will understand the history better if we understand why this selection was made. Clearly the basic aim, which was to explain Hebrew history in terms of Deuteronomic theology, dictated much of the selecting. The historian ignores data which were not relevant to his theological purpose, though in fact there is hardly anything which might not serve this purpose in certain circumstances. For instance, he largely ignores economic matters, but when he is concerned to show the success of Solomon which fulfilled the promise made to David (2 Sam 7) he does record that king's trading ventures.

Beyond this general aim, there were particular things which were of special concern to him: the temple at Jerusalem, and the prophets. He was eager to conserve anything about the relationship of the kings to the temples. Thus he carefully recorded those kings who repaired the temple and those who for one reason or another took away its treasures. This interest leads him to make David's desire to build a temple and Solomon's accomplishment of this desire the high point of his account of their reigns and the key to the explanation of the persistence of the Davidic dynasty. His great interest in the prophetic movement seems to have led him to retain from the royal records every reference to prophets who, because they had business with the kings, are mentioned in these sources. He also turned to sources which probably came directly from the prophetic groups and so supplemented the data he drew from the royal records. The great example here is the cycle of stories about Elijah and Elisha. It is significant that this interest in the prophets and in particular this use of the stories about Elijah and Elisha has resulted in giving us a full account of the reign of King Ahab, King of Israel, and his queen, Jezebel. The fact that Ahab was a capable king and made his country a respected and prosperous power does not interest the author, and we learn it only because Ahab was a king who had trouble with the prophets.

All this business of sources and selection indicates the nature of the history as a literary structure. Essentially it is a collection. The bulk of the matter is taken bodily from older sources, histories, official archives, and stories. The historian's work was to take the data so gathered, organize them into an intelligible scheme, and interpret them. The organization has been done in a number of different ways, dictated largely by the nature of the material the historian had at hand. Thus, for the era of the judges he found himself with a collection of stories about heroes who had led Israelite tribes against attacking neighbors in the unsettled era before the monarchy, and a list of men who were judges but not heroic war leaders (Jg 12:7–15). This latter has all the marks of a list of office-holders who succeeded one another. Now one of the names on this list is Jephthah, and one of the heroes in the stories was also named Jephthah. One might assume that but one individual was involved. Jephthah, there-fore, would be a judge as well as a heroic war leader. But if Jephthah was a judge as well as a hero, then the other heroes might also be called judges. Thus emerges a picture of successive hero-judges who led Israel against oppression. The historian need only place his stories of hero-judges in this picture.

So far all is a question of source material. Everything the author has to say is taken from the "authorities" he has consulted, written or oral. He repeats what was in the sources without editorializing or changing. But note that sources here is a true plural; he did not find this material all in one place or completely organized. It is he who created the final organization. Still, it is usually not enough simply to arrange stories one after another. To have intelligible history we need interpretation. The Deuteronomic Historian provides this. He takes each of his stories of the Judges and provides it with a frame which explains it theologically. Each unit begins with the notice that Israel has sinned, by its sin called down punishment in the form of a foreign oppressor, repented and called on God for help, and so God raised up a savior who drives the oppressor away. Then the unit is closed with the notice that as long as the hero-judge lived Israel stayed true to Yahweh and prospered, but when the judge died Israel fell away again and the process of punishment, repentance, and salvation begins again [4]

The interpretative technique is especially clear in the book of Judges because the sources provided short narratives which had been given a fixed overall arrangement neither by tradition nor by the nature of their content. The historian had to provide the arrangement and, because the stories were short, he was able to provide also an explanatory introduc-

---

[4] For example see Jg 3:7–11.

tion and conclusion for each unit. Essentially this is the interpretative technique used in the whole Deuteronomic History, but in many instances the sources provided such long, connected narratives that the historian was not able to intervene as regularly as in Judges. Nevertheless, his work is always essentially the same; he repeats the content of his sources and explains it theologically.

We should look for a moment at this process as it operates in the books which especially concern us, Samuel and Kings. Here the narrative is often a long story because the sources provided the author with considerable information covering a long period of time, and the material is naturally ordered because it relates the events under a leader or a succession of leaders. Hence the author is not able to intervene just as he might wish, but he still expresses his interpretation of the history satisfactorily.

Thus, in the cases of Saul and David, the sources provided several relatively long narratives. Often these stories were such that there was little need of explanatory intervention. However, the author could, when necessary, indicate subtly the direction God was taking history, as is illustrated by the story of the fall of Saul and rise of David beginning in 1 Samuel 13.[5] In the case of the other kings the succession from father to son provides a natural framework for the stories. The historian announces the advent of the king, dates him in relation to the other kings, relates what may be of interest in his reign, and tells of his death and burial. This scheme— announcement of king, narrative, announcement of death, and introduction of the successor — forms the backbone of the books of Kings. There is one element of interpretation in this. The author makes a judgment upon each of the kings as he goes along, a judgment based upon the king's success in living up to the demands of the Deuteronomic theology. Few of them did. Only David, Hezekiah, and Josiah merit unequivocal approval.

This much for interpretation in detail in Samuel and Kings. More important is the overall view of history which the document teaches. The historian is concerned to show how God has directed the history of his people, not merely in this or that crisis, but on a large scale and with an end in view. He does this as far as possible by means of speeches made by the actors in the events in which they interpret history. Here an excellent example is 1 Samuel 12 where Samuel explains that Israel's

---

[5] See D. J. McCarthy, S.J., "II Samuel 7 and the Structure of the Deuteronomic History," *Journal of Biblical Literature* 84 (1965), pp. 131–138, for the details by which the author directs his story.

choice of a king before God had chosen him is a sin. Further examples of this technique are Nathan's promise that David's dynasty will endure forever, which thus explains the remarkable continuity of the kingship in Judah (2 Sam 7), and Solomon's speech at the consecration of the temple which renews and reapplies Nathan's promise and outlines the hopes for the future (1 Kgs 8). Where the author cannot easily use a speech to his purpose he simply gives us an essay which accomplishes the same thing. Here the explanation of the fall of Samaria in 2 Kings 17 is a perfect example. He sees history not as a series of disconnected episodes but as a developing whole directed by God and very much influenced by man's reaction to God. He presents this interpretation as far as possible by means of speeches by the actors in the events. When the author cannot easily use a speech for this purpose he resorts to an essay which accomplishes the same thing. There are nine such speeches or essays (Dt 31:1–23; Jos 1:1–9; 12:1–8; 23; Jg 2:11–23; 1 Sam 12:6–25; 2 Sam 7; 1 Kgs 8; 2 Kgs 17:1–20). These interpretative passages give a structure to the whole history, and they point up its dramatic development. Three of them give programs: Deuteronomy 31 for the conquest of Canaan, Joshua 23 for living in the newly conquered land, and 2 Samuel 7 for the newly instituted monarchy. Another three tell of the first implementations of these programs: Joshua 1 is the introduction to the conquest, Judges 2 to the life in the Promised Land after the conquest, and 1 Kings 8 to the monarchy and its temple-centered religion. The last three tell of the end of the action: Joshua 12 the successful conquest, 1 Samuel 12 closes the difficult period of the judges, and 2 Kings 17 explains the end of the monarchies. With these last two sets of passages an element of drama, of opposition, begins to appear, for Judges 2 is pessimistic. God has been faithful to his promise and has given the people the land of Canaan, but the people will misuse the gift by turning to the gods of Canaan rather than to Yahweh alone. However, this dark note is not the end of the story. Though the passage in Judges forebodes ill and 1 Samuel 12 shows that the foreboding is correct — the era of the judges was indeed one of backsliding — this is not the end of the story; for, as we have seen, 2 Samuel 7 presents a new hope, a new divine program, and 1 Kings 8 shows this program in its glorious beginning. Still, in the end man fails again to respond, and 2 Kings 17 tells why God's new intervention, the monarchy, ended in failure.

Thus the history of the people of God is seen as a real event, a real movement. There is drama, for there is struggle. The first period (Dt 31;

Jos 1, 12) is pure success. The second (Jos 23; Jg 2; 1 Sam 12) is a failure, or rather a setback. In the last period (2 Sam 7; 1 Kgs 8; 2 Kgs 17) hope is renewed with a new promise and a new institution. Perhaps the setback can be retrieved. The new hope is thus dramatized, but it, too, ends in failure.

We should not be dismayed by all this interpretation mixed right into the history and even put into the mouths of the historical personages who act in that history, as though this procedure were simple falsification. Interpretation is essential to any real historical writing. The most objective and scientific of historians is an interpreter; if he were not, he would not be scientific, for only the careful interpreter can sift out misleading evidence. Hence the mere fact of interpretation in the Deuteronomic History does not make it unreliable as history. As a matter of fact, there are few if any who have any serious doubts about Samuel and Kings as sources for facts about the first half of the first millenium B.C. Thus they are of great use to the historians of the era. However, we must be clear on this point: our interests are not the same as the historian's. We are dealing as theologians with a theological book. This is a theology about history, but as such it does not ask the historian's questions about probability, evidence, and confirmation. The historian struggles with the location of Tarshish and the land of Punt, the number of chariots Ahab controlled, and all the rest. These are matters of importance, and they are often helpful toward the proper understanding of what the theologian is trying to say. For instance, we may well believe that Ahab's deep involvement in the politics of his time and place led him to accept a compromise with the worship of the gods of the nations, and that this in turn stimulated the great outburst of prophetic inspiration under Elijah. However, this does not really answer our questions, which concern God's part in history. This is matter for revelation, not the object of the historian's researches.

So much for our primary sources concerning the Hebrew monarchy. We can deal with the other important source concerning the era, the books of Chronicles, more briefly. By and large these books depend upon the books of Samuel and Kings. However, the Chronicler did have access to other information and can occasionally supplement what we know from the books of Kings and Samuel. Like his model, the Deuteronomic History, the Chronicler is careful of his sources, and his own personal interests are very clear so that it is easy to separate them out from his facts. Once again we have a good historical source book, but once again we have much more. Essentially the Chronicler was a theologian preoccupied by the temple and its liturgy. Hence his interest in the establishment of the temple, and his desire to show the legitimacy of its worship and its priesthood. Since David is his great hero and model king, he wishes to make David as much as possible the originator of the temple and its liturgy. David gives all the directions for building the temple, David collects the materials for it, David has the design made, and David designates the priestly families who are to serve in it. Solomon is simply his agent in carrying all this out. This may not be accurate to the smallest historical detail, but it is the Chronicler's manner of expressing an immensely important insight: the whole life of the people of God is determined by its duty to praise God.

There is one final point one must consider in the study of any biblical books, namely, that of the quality of the texts. These books were written thousands of years ago. How could all mistakes be avoided as the text was copied and recopied over so long a time? Then, in the course of this long history the books were liable to additions and other significant changes which could alter meanings. Hence, in biblical studies we must always check to be sure that we have as true a text as possible and not a corruption. Fortunately, we are relatively well off in regard to the historical books of the Old Testament. The Deuteronomic History has, it is true, suffered some additions. The separation of the original book into rolls, to which we have already referred, occurred very early in the history of the text, and the ends of the rolls attracted additions, as we have seen. But these are not real corruptions of the text, even though the additions did not come from the hands of the Deuteronomic historian they are canonical and inspired just as the larger literary works. Moreover, they often contain valuable data in their own right. Thus, though the literary purist might find these changes painful, we must be grateful for them. The real problem concerns the correct transmission of the words and smaller textual units. They are so easily miswritten or dropped or repeated or something of the sort. Reflect upon your own experience in typing from a copy and you will realize how easy it is to skip words and so on. This sort of thing can be a serious problem. In poetical books such as the psalms and the prophets the text at its best could be difficult to understand so that the poor copyists easily made mistakes in transcribing what must often have been for them no more than letters, not words and sentences which they understood. Naturally, they made mistakes doing this. Often we can only guess at what the original must have been.

We are fortunate in that the text of the historical books is in good shape. It is largely prose, clearly written, and hence more easily understood and copied. There are difficulties with this, that, or the other text, but in general we can be confident that we get back to the original meaning.

We must, for the sake of accuracy, add one qualification to this. The basic text of the Old Testament is the Hebrew text which is called the Masoretic (commonly abbreviated MT). Early in our era this text was standardized by the rabbis and since then it has been transmitted with amazing fidelity, truly a remarkable effort of devotion and will power. We can hardly find a difference among many different copies written by many different hands so that we cannot appeal to one manuscript against another to support changes in the text as we commonly can with other ancient works. The only important independent source of information about the original text is the Greek translation of the Old Testament called the Septuagint (commonly abbreviated with the Roman numerals LXX), which was produced before the Christian era. Since our Hebrew text was fixed only in the sixth century A.D. this Greek translation may represent a text much older than MT, and it is sometimes of great value in bringing us back to the original. In Samuel especially the LXX sometimes represents a Hebrew text quite different from MT. The study of these variations can be important, and some of the famous Qumran discoveries indicate that we will have to give closer attention to the LXX text. Thus there are problems about the exact text in places even in the historical books. However, these difficulties usually are related to details which, though not unimportant in themselves, are not the kind of things we are concerned with here.

Chapter 2. The Origins of the Monarchy

Readings: 1 Sam 8–12; 1 Sam 13–2 Sam 6

To understand how the Hebrews came to have kings we must look briefly at the era of the conquest and the judges. The people were a loosely organized confederation of tribes. By and large these tribes took care of their own affairs. They farmed their own lands and raised their own herds, judged themselves according to their own version of the common law, and even fought their own wars. In time of great need several neighboring tribes might get together to resist oppression.

Beyond this there was little organization. The Hebrews probably formed what has been called an amphictyony, that is, a group of tribes held together by a common center of worship. The contact of the tribes with one another was largely confined to their coming together to worship Yahweh at his great shrine on certain stated occasions. This shrine itself moved. The important thing was the Ark of the Covenant, the symbol of Yahweh's presence. In origin the Ark was a kind of portable throne, the symbolic seat of the tribal god. Since the Hebrews were nomads by origin, it was natural that they had a portable cult object and not a temple as the major sign of God's presence. Even after they entered the promised land the Ark was often moved. We know that it was settled for a time at Gilgal, Shechem, Bethel, and Shiloh. The Hebrew tribes, or more probably their official representatives, convened on the great feast days at the shrine where the Ark currently reposed. There they would join together in worship, renew their pledge of loyalty to Yahweh, and hear anew the essential elements of the religion of Yahweh and the demands it made upon men.[1]

Another thing which drew the Hebrew tribes together in those days was the holy war. From the beginning Yahweh was "the God of Armies" (the *Dominus deus sabaoth,* "Lord God of Hosts," of our liturgies) who had brought his people out of Egypt by destroying the Egyptian army. He continued to fight his people's battles, and the Ark was not merely an object of reverence, it was the palladium, the "battle flag," of the people. It symbolized Yahweh's special presence with the fighters, and men believed that it was Yahweh, not human arms, who won the victory. This is well illustrated by the story of Gideon's battle with the Midianites where the Hebrew forces were deliberately reduced to a ridiculous number so as to show that Yahweh and not the might of Hebrew arms brings victory (Jg 7:2–7). The concept of God the Warrior (Ex 15:3) may seem crude, but it is one of the many examples of the way the God of history has taught mankind using the means at hand, the customs and ways of speech men could understand. Out of the idea of the war with its emphasis on total dependence on Yahweh and not on self grew gradually the idea of divine grace, God's free and loving gift (Dt 9:1–4).

Unlike the periodic liturgical gatherings around the shrine of the Ark of the Covenant, the holy war was not a regular occasion. Rather, when oppression or attack threatened the people, a leader summoned the men of the tribes, usually only those nearer the danger point (Jg 4:6), to war in the name of Yahweh. This was like the gatherings at the great feasts, an experience of the unity of the people, and this was a unity which existed only because they all served the one God. So important was this experience of the holy war as a unifying element that taking part in such a war seems to have been the proper way to earn the title of "people of Yahweh" (Jg 5:11).

Such forms of organization, loose and casual, were congenial to the early Hebrews. They had been nomads. They had but recently settled down, and they were jealous of their independence. Moreover, because

---

[1] See Martin Noth, *History of Israel,* Part 1, chap. 3, and John Bright, *History of Israel,* Part 2, chap. 4, section B, for more details on the amphictyony.

these institutions were more religious than political, they emphasized that it was the common belief in and worship of Yahweh which constituted the people. However, such loose organization was a danger before a well organized enemy. As long as Israel had to face only the original Canaanites who were split into a number of small city states, each with its petty king and jealous of the others, it had a foe which was not a danger to Israel as a whole, even though an occasional Canaanite group could achieve an important success against one or another Israelite tribe.

With the coming of the Philistines the Hebrews faced quite a different enemy. The Philistines were strangers to the Semitic world. They were part of the movement of what were called "the sea peoples" which overwhelmed the ancient near east at the end of the thirteenth century B.C. Some ancient kingdoms like the mighty Hittite empire of Asia Minor were destroyed. Egypt managed to repel the invaders but at such a cost that it never resumed its former power. These invaders were felt in areas where they did not penetrate. The disturbance and the migrations which they caused affected even Mesopotamia (Iraq).

It is not unlikely that the movement of the sea peoples was connected with the wandering of the Greek Achaeans who conquered Troy. The Philistines spoke a non-Semitic language. Their settlements on the coastal plain between Judea and the sea were promptly organized into city states which seem to have been governed like the early Greek cities. This was a warlike people, well organized for the time, knowledgeable in military tactics, and well equipped. Their iron weapons made the bronze of the Israelites obsolete, almost useless.

Furthermore, though these people were organized into city states, they managed to work together. Against this military power Israel could set only an ancient tribal organization with a haphazard army organization and without a pretense of central government. Hence the Philistines quickly conquered not only the Canaanites but also all the Hebrews west of the Jordan, that is, all the area which really counted. The situation was desperate. Instead of the followers of Yahweh gradually taking over from the Canaanites as their power increased and that of the degenerate Canaanites weakened there was a very real threat that they would be replaced by these invading Philistines. Hence the call for a king "like all the nations" (1 Sam 8:5). The people saw that they must have a central government to prosecute war against these organized invaders, and in those times this could only mean a king. Theoretically, states can organize in various ways. There can be presidential government, a cabinet, a parliament, and so on. But the ancient Semites knew only one organization which went beyond the loose forms of clan and tribe — monarchy.

THE BEGINNINGS OF A MONARCHY

We are relatively well furnished with data concerning the choice of the first Israelite king. However, the sources are not without their problems. We must turn to the earlier chapters of 1 Samuel, and these chapters are very complex constructions. They are made up of materials drawn from various sources representing different points of view. We must sort some of this out, if we are to search out the origins of kingship in Israel.

Briefly, from both the literary and theological points of view the king is represented as the successor to the judges. In 2 Samuel 7, in the promise spoken by Nathan on behalf of God, the troubled period of the judges is contrasted with that of the monarchy because the kings bring that which the judges aimed at unsuccessfully, lasting peace and quiet. This same concept of the king as the last of the judges is attested from another source with a very different point of view. In I Samuel 12:5–12 we have Samuel's account of the history of Israel through the Exodus and the troubled, sinful era of the judges culminating in the kings. Furthermore Samuel persisted in addressing the king by the old title *nagîd* ("prince," "leader," or the like), and not by the word *melech*, "king," which he wished to reserve to Yahweh. Thus he sees the king as much the same sort of thing as the judges, and the self-willed popular demand for a king as a kind of ultimate sin (1 Sam 8:7–9; 12:19).

This ambiguity in the testimony about the kingship, the admission that there was a king and that he had power but along with this a doubt about the legitimacy of his position, is deeply embedded in our sources. Note that in 2 Samuel the kingship is approved without reserve while in 1 Samuel 12 the kingship is a sin. One story of Saul's accession does not like kingship. The much more pragmatic objection to kingship was that it meant the draft and taxes. Some scholars hold that such a reference must reflect conditions as they developed later, when kings like Solomon had imposed heavy levies on the country. Lately this has been called into question since the people of Israel need not have waited for their own experience. They saw about them the Canaanite people subject to kings who levied a draft, taxes, and the rest.[2] This is true but hardly conclusive.

---

[2] I. Mendelsohn, "Samuel's Denunciation of Kingship in the Light of the Akkadian Documents from Ugarit," *Bulletin of the American Schools of Oriental Research* 143 (1956), pp. 17–22, presents the data for this argument.

The people were asking for a king precisely to build an effective state which could defend them. They must have been willing, if not happy, to submit to the necessary conditions for this, including a draft and taxes, or their wish is meaningless.

Still, it does seem that there was opposition to the monarchy in Israel from the beginning. Samuel's objections to the monarchy are not based simply on these pragmatic arguments that the king would tax and draft his subjects. He is especially concerned because the demand for a king is a rejection of Yahweh (cf. 2 Sam 8:7–18; 12:12, 17). If, indeed, the very fact of having a king is a sin, there is a grave theological difficulty, for the truth is that the institution of kingship was of immense importance in Old Testament religion and very fruitful in developing revelation, especially that concerning the Messiah. This fact, among others, makes it more than ordinarily important that we check our sources of information. Are the anti-monarchical passages in Samuel very ancient? Do they represent a basic theological objection to kingship?

Generally this is denied. In the first place Chapter 8 and especially Chapter 12 are judged to be later writings because of their style. They reflect the terminology and ideas of the book of Deuteronomy, which was written toward the end of the eighth century B.C., so that the passages reflecting its ideas must be several hundred years later than the time of Samuel and Saul. This judgment about the date of the anti-monarchical passages in Samuel has even greater weight in view of other evidence. They reflect the attitude of the prophet Hosea, who repeatedly condemns the misdeeds of the kings he knew, who were in fact not models for a true Israelite, and they show the same suspicion of kings as the law of Deuteronomy 17:14–20. This is the only Old Testament text which actually tries to legislate the duties of kings, and it does seem very restrictive. The sole positive duty of the kings is to copy and learn the content of the law of Moses. Negatively, they are forbidden to establish an army (Dt 17:16, "multiply horses" for chariotry, the decisive arm in the wars of the era), a harem, and a treasury. In short, the king may not be a Solomon. Surely such a law is the result of experience of kings who tended to think themselves above the law which guided the ordinary Israelite.[3] Thus the attitude of the anti-monarchical passages of Samuel are so similar to those of the Deuteronomic school that they could easily

---

[3] Not everyone thinks that the law of kingship is so restrictive. George Fohrer, "Der Vertrag zwischen König und Volk in Israel," *Zeitschrift für Alttestamentlichen Wissenschaft* 71 (1959), pp. 1–22, believes that there was a kind of contract, almost a constitution, defining extensive royal powers, while Geo. Widengren, "King and

be derived from it. Since these ideas are much later than the events recounted in Samuel, we may assume that the Deuteronomic historian has attributed later ideas about kingship to ancient times. This is in accord with his established technique of interpreting his history through words put in the mouths of the actors in that history. If we accept this point of view, and it seems correct, what we have in Samuel is not a condemnation of the very idea of kingship but rather of the way the institution worked out in Hebrew history. In itself the institution remained theologically acceptable.

However, it must be admitted that important scholars think not only that the objection to kingship was antique in Israel but also that kingship was incompatible with Yahwism. First of all, they assert that the Deuteronomic language in the anti-monarchical parts of 1 Samuel is no more than annotation added to ancient texts which condemned the institution of kingship because it was not only oppressive but pagan. These scholars, therefore, see kingship as a rejection of Yahweh, a kind of idolatry. They feel that the only possible organization for the covenanted people of God was the loose organization of tribes united only by a common center of worship. This left no room for a human leader who by virtue of office stood at the head of the covenant people and so between them and God. The only permissible leadership for such a people was that of the occasional hero moved directly by God to act in the hour of need.

Thus there remains the theological question. Does the inspired text condemn the monarchical institution in itself and from its beginning? This is not quite the same as asking whether some Hebrews opposed it early. It is natural that the new institution aroused some opposition. A radical change almost always does. There must have been sincere followers of Yahweh who opposed the kingship. The question is, did their opposition receive official canonical expression from the very beginning as it is presented in 1 Samuel? On balance it would seem that the arguments against the antiquity of the anti-monarchical texts of 1 Samuel are decisive. In other words, they represent an objection to kingship based not on principle but on pragmatic experience interpreted by the Deuteronomic school. This is important because it leaves the *principle* of monarchy free of theological taint. It can be accepted among God's people and so be the source of important theological developments.

Covenant," *Journal of Semitic Studies* 2 (1957), pp. 1–32, even finds the Deuteronomic law positive: the king is to be the custodian and source of law, a view he finds confirmed in other texts.

In fact, the older texts accept the kingship. The pro-monarchical accounts of the beginnings of Hebrew kingship, 1 Samuel 9:1–10; 14; 11, seem more ancient in their popular manner and matter. Often they sound like folklore. Since they favor Saul, they probably were fostered especially in the very old shrines in the areas near his own tribe of Benjamin such as Gilgal, Bethel, and Shiloh. However, we cannot simply say that the anti-monarchical attitude was late and concerned with particular abuses, not with the institution as such, while the pro-monarchical is older, and so forget the theological problem. Samuel is represented as condemning the kingship of Saul because it was a basic rejection of Yahweh, and this condemnation is as much a part of the work of the inspired Deuteronomic historian as are his sources favorable to the king. How did he, and how can we, reconcile the two attitudes he does present?

The answer seems to be that the objection is to the kingship of Saul because he is the choice of the people, not Yahweh. There is nothing wrong in itself with the king's being popular with his subjects. The trouble was that the choice of Saul came from the people in the first instance before divine approval. To be a true leader in Israel one had to be chosen from the beginning, before any human choice, by God. This was not the case with Saul according to the anti-monarchical tradition, and hence, Saul had ultimately to be rejected. Paradoxically, this basic idea is confirmed in the pro-monarchical sections. Their whole point is that Saul was God's chosen one, a point made through a collection of stories which differ in detail, but all insisting that Saul was chosen by Yahweh to be king. In one version Yahweh reveals to Samuel that Saul is God's choice (1 Sam 9.15 10); in another it is Saul's divinely given stature which seems to have marked him out (1 Sam 10:23); in another he is chosen by lot, a traditional way of determining God's will (1 Sam 10:19b–22); finally, Saul is represented as being seized by the spirit of Yahweh and so moved to lead the fight against the gentile invaders (1 Sam 11:6). All this is confused and confusing. To take but one example: Saul can scarcely have been chosen by lot, that is, by pure chance, and also because he stood head and shoulders above the people! But amidst the confusion, we repeat, there is an agreement in all the stories: to be a true king of the Hebrews one must be chosen by God.

Incidentally, the very confusion in the details of Saul's becoming king in the stories favorable to him is the proof that our historian is handing on sources as he found them. A single writer would surely be more consistent, and a less reliable historian would have smoothed out the discrepancies. This one passes on what he knows without forcing it into conformity with his own opinions or even into entire consistency. We may find the method confusing, but it is honest, and upon consideration, not so unfamiliar as seems at first sight. We expect a competent historian to report the divergences in his evidence, but we find his report in footnotes. The author of Samuel did not know this convenient device so that he has to give his divergent evidence right in the text.

In conclusion, we may look at the whole which has been constructed out of this profusion of sources. It turns out to be an adroit historico-theological document. The author has taken pragmatic objections to kingship and used them to give expression to an uneasiness which many surely felt when a radically new institution was introduced into the Yahwist community. He has built these objections into the account of Yahweh's choice of Saul to be king. He could do this because the basic problem is the setting of one's own will above God's and it was not Saul but the people who sought the kingship. Notice that all through the story of the setting up of the monarchy (1 Sam 8–12) Samuel condemns the people for taking it upon themselves to seek a king (1 Sam 8; 10:17–19; 12), never Saul.

This is good history writing. It gives the facts from the sources: the need for a king and the rise of Saul. It is psychologically accurate: many welcomed the new institution, but the old leader, Samuel, was being displaced, and conservatives in general looked askance at the novelty so that it was right to represent a dissatisfaction with the royal institution, even if this was done in terms borrowed from a later age. But most important, it establishes a basic theological principle: God's people must be ruled by his will, not theirs. Finally, there is a neat literary touch. Even though Saul himself is not condemned, by ending the story of his becoming king with the strong condemnation of the people's sin in 1 Samuel 12:17–25, the story of his beginnings is given a darksome atmosphere. We are prepared for his rapid fall.

THE RISE OF DAVID

Saul had hardly become king when he was rejected by God. He was an imposing figure and an attractive one. To some extent he succeeded in his task. He fought the Philistines and occasionally beat them and so brought some measure of order and independence to the Hebrews. Nonetheless he lost his position because he lost the favor of Yahweh.

The personal story of Saul is revealing. He seems to have been an unstable personality. He was susceptible to some kinds of outside influence to such an extent that he might give way to hysterical phenomena, as when he got near the ecstatic prophets (1 Sam 10:10–13; cf. 1 Sam 19:18–24; we must remember that these prophets resembled nothing more closely than whirling dervishes). He was moody and impulsive, liable to violence, and he would not accept advice. But we must not let these personal details obscure the true significance of the story. It was not Saul's attractiveness or unattractiveness which determined his position as king. Yahweh was ready to put up with far worse characters than Saul and did not inflict upon them anything like the punishment of Saul and his family. Why, then, must Saul suffer?

Essentially it is because he had been raised to a responsible position and then failed in the basic obligation of a member of the chosen people. He disobeyed the clear voice of God. This was not the mark of the true Hebrew. From Abraham on, the Hebrew was the one who followed God, even though God's instructions seemed ruinous, as they did for Abraham when he was asked to sacrifice his only son. The great leaders, of whom Moses is the classic example, were men who took up the tasks given them by God despite natural reluctance. Saul failed in this obedience.

On this point our sources are embarrassing in their richness. He is represented as having failed twice. He performs a sacrifice when Samuel should have. Notice that it was not usurping the place of a priest that was wrong. In the early days any Israelite could sacrifice, and royalty certainly did (2 Sam 8:18; 1 Kgs 3:4, etc.). Saul was rejected, therefore, not because he violated the later law which limited to the Levitical priesthood the power to sacrifice. He was rejected because he failed to follow the instructions given him by Yahweh's spokesman, Samuel (1 Sam 13:2–14). In another tradition Saul's failure to slay the king of Amalek constitutes his disobedience. Amalek had been "devoted," that is, all its people and all of its possessions had been given over to Yahweh and so must be destroyed to remove them from the profane sphere. Saul failed to do this. He spared Agag, king of Amalek, perhaps because he respected another king, perhaps because he was humane. Whatever the reason, good or bad, he disobeyed and was rejected.

In contrast, the central fact about the successful king, David, is the steady affirmation that he was a man after God's heart. This certainly does not mean a plaster saint. David was a guerrilla leader, a covetous man, wily, unscrupulous, overindulgent with his sons to the point of endangering the body politic. He had his full share of human weaknesses, but he was a devoted Yahwist, ready to try again to walk in the way of the Lord. Still, David's character is not the major point. He is the man after God's own heart, because he is God's choice. Unlike Saul, he was not first chosen by popular acclaim. He was an obscure youth chosen not because of merit but simply because God wanted him. The presentation of David's coming to power is magnificent literature and theology. Saul is not simply dismissed and David introduced. Rather we have something in the nature of a tragedy. Saul with all his splendid characteristics and goodwill grows ever more difficult and less obedient while David rises gradually and with difficulty to his destined place. If we consider him dispassionately, David appears as the typical guerrilla leader, a notable warrior who broke away from the armies of Saul to live a near-bandit life in the wilderness of Judah. According to the stories, he did not break away because he was ambitious. The details are not clear because popular tradition has molded the stories into forms which made them interesting, but it is clear that David was in danger of Saul's jealous rage. He fled to save his life, and being a successful war leader and an attractive personality he brought with him a devoted band of warriors. The picture of David the guerrilla in 1 Samuel 21–30 is realistic. He lives by expediency. He imposes levies upon peaceful farmers. He even deals with the Philistines, and though the stories show him avoiding attacks upon Israelites, this is somewhat less than the purest Israelite patriotism. Still, David's conduct during this difficult time could not have been too self-seeking, for he kept and even improved the good reputation which made him an acceptable successor to Saul when his time came.

Once more, the historian's use of sources is informative. He is dependent on varied traditions: he has different accounts of Saul's sin (1 Sam 13; 15), different stories of David's introduction at Saul's court (1 Sam 16:14–23; 17:12–22), and a double version of the story of David's respect for the anointed king (1 Sam 24; 26). These show the effect of popular storytelling on traditions. A further sign of this popular character of the sources is the account of David's secret anointing as king by Samuel in 1 Samuel 16. It reflects the ever popular folklore motif: the unexpected triumph of the youngest son. The historian has kept close to his sources, but he produces a vivid and meaningful narrative. We learn of Saul's fall. We meet his successor, a winning and courageous young man, but, more important, one sought out by God to lead, not one appointed by the people or pushed forward by ambition. We are taught the respect due to those close to God, such as the anointed

king, even when they are in the wrong. All this material is united into
a tale moving to a climax: David's active exercise of his kingship. Moreover, the meaning of it all is kept prominently before us. There is more
than the tale of David's anointing. There are allusions to a lasting dynasty
to come (1 Sam 13:13–14; 24:20; 2 Sam 3:9–10, etc.). It will last
because its enemies are to be destroyed (1 Sam 20:15). The new king
will finish the work left undone by the judges (2 Sam 3:18), and he
will be the good shepherd of God's people (2 Sam 5:2). These little
touches tie the story together and build the picture of the true king.

Such details are worth noting, for they illustrate something which is
true of the Bible in general: One cannot separate literature and theology.
Often a certain careless way of speaking and writing leads one to think
of separating the kernel, God's true message, from the literary forms, the
niceties of expression which cover the message. This is simply not the
case. The literary expression, the medium, *is* the message. And so it is
here; the organizing of stories from various sources and the insertion
of editorial notes into the history to build the carefully developed climax
in 2 Samuel 5 to 7. These are literary devices which unify and give
interest to the story. They are equally theological because through them
we learn the meaning of the history. God's grace works where he wills.
He chooses the weak and makes them strong to guide history to his ends.
And in the end exclusive election becomes a blessing for all, for through
David the people will flourish (2 Sam 7:10), and the promise to David's
dynasty (2 Sam 7) is the first step on the road leading to the Messiah
Savior.

So much for sources and meaning. We must return to the actual account of events. For Saul things grew steadily worse. At first he was able
to hold off the Philistines and also pursue the fugitive David, but his
troubles increased. His personality deteriorated and he could not hold
his forces together. In the last analysis, even from the natural point of
view, Saul never had a chance. As the first of the kings of Israel he was
too close to the days of the ancient tribal federation and so unable to
count on any tradition of loyalty to the king and his government. In any
event he did not create a central administration or, more important, a
real standing army. He always depended on the tribal levies, all the able-
bodied men of Israel, amateur soldiers whose service must be short since
they had to return to take care of home and farm. In the circumstances
he was utterly unable to cope with the Philistine menace in the long run,
and he was eventually destroyed by it.

On the other hand, David had his guerrilla band. He started out an able warrior, and the experience of guerrilla life developed his abilities until he was a warrior of talent and a diplomat of skill. At the same time his growing band of loyal guerrillas was becoming the nucleus for a truly professional army. The very locale of his activity was shrewdly chosen. He stayed near the territory of Judah, no doubt because this was his own tribe and the population was friendly, a factor indispensable to any guerrilla activity. Furthermore, he proved able to protect the people from the desert tribes who periodically raided Judah from the south. In this way he constructed not merely military strength but also a political power base which was really solid, rooted in the loyalty of a large tribe with a certain tradition of self-reliance.

Hence, when Saul finally fell, a victim of his own weakness and ultimately of God's disfavor, and when his son Jonathan, the best hope of succession in his line, fell with him, David was the obvious man to take over. For a time Saul's general, Abner, attempted to maintain a shadow kingdom by appointing one of Saul's remaining sons, Ishbaal,[4] king. However, Abner soon turned to David, and the last remnants of Saul's kingship disappeared. Abner brought the northern tribes over to David of Judah and even though Abner himself was treacherously murdered soon after, they remained united to David. Why not? He accomplished exactly what had been hoped for from the king. He beat off an attack by the Philistines, and then carried the war to their territory. From then on, the Philistines were a source of annoyance to the Hebrews but they were never again a real threat. Moreover, David conquered Moab and Edom. He even reduced Syrian kingdoms, Damascus for example, to tributaries. His was a true empire, a kingdom with power far beyond anything Israel had ever hoped.

David, of course, could only achieve all this because the time was propitious. There was an interregnum in the middle east at the time. The great powers such as Egypt and Assyria were in decline, leaving a no-man's-land between them, Palestine and Syria, at peace for a time. David made use of the opportunity to construct his empire.

David's was a special kind of kingdom. He was not simply king of all the Hebrews. He was king of Judah (the south) and of Israel (the north),

---

[4] 2 Sam 2:8. In the Hebrew Saul's son is called Ishbosheth, but this is a scribal alteration of the original Ishbaal to avoid using the word *baal*, "Lord," which had become too closely associated with the worship of false gods addressed by the title *Lord*.

two political units under a single ruler. He deliberately conquered Jerusalem, a Canaanite city up to that time, with his personal troops (David maintained a mercenary army of foreigners loyal to him rather than to the old tribal traditions) so that he could have a capital which was his own personal possession and not part of the Hebrew nation as such. He thus created a personal union of states. There was not one kingdom of the Hebrew people. There were separate entities united under one monarch.

This elaborate setup demanded an elaborate bureaucracy. However, we have little record of how David organized his kingdom and we may leave this matter for discussion under Solomon, the king under whom the administration of the kingdom was worked out to its last detail.

Of more lasting importance than David's political acts were certain of his religious ones. He arranged to have the Ark of the Covenant brought to his new royal city. The Ark was the symbol of Yahweh's presence, the object around which his worship centered. Thus it was an extremely important unifying factor for the Hebrews and an object of great devotion. By bringing it to Jerusalem David made himself and his family custodians of this most holy object. The king could supervise the worship centered around the Ark, and he himself soon became a symbol of unity by association with that worship. Jerusalem also became automatically a center of pilgrimage. All this helped keep king and capital before the people as symbols of unity. The king even shared some of the awe given the holy object and cult.

This bringing of the Ark to Jerusalem is directly connected with the other great religious aspect of David's kingship: the promise given him and his dynasty through the prophet Nathan (2 Sam 7). In the very old and basic verses 11b and 16 of 2 Samuel 7 it is said that rather than David's making a house for Yahweh, Yahweh will make a house for David. This prophecy, so full of possibility of theological development, is actually built on a pun. "House" in Hebrew (as in English) can stand for a building (here, David's intended temple) or for a dynasty. It is from this double meaning that the promise was formulated. This use of punning is a serious characteristic of Hebrew prophecy. However, the nature of prophecy and the importance of Nathan's promise must receive fuller attention later.

God's promise through the prophet Nathan that David and his line would reign forever marks the high point of David's success. He had not only gained a substantial kingdom; he had acquired a central place in the religious life of God's people. He remained the man after Yahweh's heart in the essentials: the purity of Yahweh's religion and Yahweh's worship, but he could also fall victim to his human weaknesses and he did. He could commit adultery and stoop to murder to cover his crime (2 Sam 11–12). He repented this, but the sin had been committed, and it revealed a weakness, self-indulgence, which extended to his family and caused infinite trouble.

As was natural in the eastern world he used his family to administer his kingdom. Such use of one's family was not simple favoritism. In that world one's own family was, practically speaking, all that one could trust. However, David was unable or unwilling to exercise the severity necessary to curb the royal family. He allowed Joab, his cousin, to murder Abner treacherously (2 Sam 3:22–30). Worse, he spoiled his sons. In the ancient kingdom, where the oldest son did not automatically succeed to the throne, the orderly control of the succession was very important. The king had to choose a successor and make clear that the succession was regulated to avoid disturbances and even civil war. David so loved his sons that he could not exercise this necessary severity. He allowed now one now another to build up a following and pretend to the succession. It was only through the instigation of the prophet Nathan and the favorite queen Bathsheba that Solomon finally was proclaimed and anointed king. Only then was the succession clear so that it could take place without grave disturbance.

Chapter 3. Solomon and the Divided Kingdoms

Readings: 1 Kgs 1–2; 11–12; 16:29–22:40; 2 Kgs 9–12

David's successor, Solomon, symbolizes the glory of the Hebrew kingship both in the Old Testament and in Jewish legend. He did not entirely deserve this reputation. Yet he did accomplish two things. First of all, he organized the administration of the kingdoms of Judah and Israel, arranging Israel and Judah into manageable districts. He established a more or less equitable principle of taxation. He modernized David's standing army, by collecting horses and charioteers which he quartered at strategic points, Gezer, Megiddo, and Hazor. The chariots were the armored force of the age so that Solomon was actually providing for the proper defense of his people.

All of this work of improving the civil and military administration had important side effects. No one in the new kingdom had experience in such matters. From king to clerk the Hebrews were inexperienced administrators. They had to turn to the experts, and these were necessarily foreigners and scribes. The scribe in the ancient world, despite his name, was not simply a man who knew how to write, a kind of public letter writer such as still exists in some parts of Asia and Africa. His training in writing also included an introduction to fiscal, judicial, and political administration. Hence, to staff their administration the first Hebrew kings had to import foreign scribes, mostly Egyptians.

These Egyptian scribes brought with them ideas of absolute monarchy, ideas which were foreign to the free spirit of Israel and its religion. They also brought the extravagant terminology and ritual which went with these ideas. In Egypt one spoke of the king as a god's son in the literal sense. This idea, of course, was unacceptable in Israel, but the terminology does appear in a coronation ritual, e.g., in Psalms 2:7. The terminology was an important influence on the development of messianic thought, but it could be dangerous. A king or a people without a strong mind and firm Yahwist convictions could be misled by such lofty talk.

In addition to ideas about kingship the foreign scribes brought the traditions of their own learning into Israel. This is called Wisdom in the technical terminology of ancient near eastern studies. In its beginnings Wisdom was concerned with instructing the young scribe in the courtly arts as well as in those which would make him an efficient and fair administrator. However, Wisdom very early went on to general instruction on leading the good life. It delighted in the proverb, the sententious saying, often rather prosy but containing a good deal of common sense. Another aspect of this Wisdom tradition was more scientific. It collected long lists of things belonging to a category — stones, animals, trees, and so forth. This began as a practical necessity, for the first scribes wrote in ideograms (writing with a different sign for each idea). Such forms of writing have a great number of characters and hence are difficult to learn. The lists with all members of a category along with the signs proper to them were of great help in learning such a cumbersome method of writing. However, these lists soon became something more, attempts at a kind of "scientific" classification of things and their usefulness, both practical and magical. Without a doubt Solomon's association with the scribes he brought in to administer his kingdom, and with their "Wisdom" earned him the reputation of being the model wise man. Thus, according to 1 Kings 4:33 he knew all that there was to know about trees and plants and stones and their properties, a typical element of Wisdom in its most technical character.

However, beyond organizing the royal administration and introducing ancient oriental Wisdom in Israel, Solomon's greatest achievement was the construction of the Temple. As a matter of fact the Temple was actually the palace chapel of the kings of Jerusalem. It was included within the precincts of the royal palace and protected by the royal guard. The priests also were the king's appointees (1 Kgs 2:35). David even made his sons priests (2 Sam 8:18; the law restricting the priesthood to Levites came into force only later). The construction of the Temple climaxed David's brilliant stroke of bringing the Ark to Jerusalem. The Temple, as it were, nailed down the Ark. It gave the Ark a splendid setting and a place worthy of pilgrimage. The Temple rapidly became the center of Israelite religion so that control of the Temple gave the king of the Davidic line an important hold over the people.

THE FAILURE OF SOLOMON

Despite his wisdom, despite the care in which he organized his administration, despite his modernization of the army, despite his devoted construction of the Temple, in sum, despite all Solomon's good beginnings his reign turned into a failure. To some extent this was inevitable. Circumstances were changing; the power vacuum which had enabled David to build up his kingdom had changed. Egypt and Assyria were renewing their power and that meant renewing their interest in the lands of Syria and Palestine which lay between them. This confronted Solomon with opponents of a stature he could not match. Apart from this, Solomon was vainglorious. He was indeed a splendid monarch, he knew it, and he spent a great deal of money to demonstrate it to others. His splendid court, his huge building program, his ambitious trading projects all demanded capital, too much even for the heritance which he had received from David. He had finally to cut down on his armies and he lost control over the outlying parts of the empire he had acquired from David. He even had to trade away Israelite cities to pay for his building adventures (1 Kgs 9:11).

Worse yet, his vast projects were expensive. He increased the taxes of the people and, worse, increased their obligations to work for the king for a certain period of time each month or each year, a practice called *corvée*. This was an invasion of the traditional rights of the Hebrews. By the end of Solomon's reign his kingdom was boiling with indignation. Trouble was sure to come.

Most of all, Solomon appears to have been a religious failure. There is no reason to doubt the sincerity of his Yahwism. Oddly, from our point of view, it was possible for an ancient Hebrew to believe firmly in Yahweh and still believe in and worship other divine powers. However, when we consider the superstition of many believing Christians who practice astrology and the like, perhaps it will not seem so strange. In any event Solomon did not remain true to the exclusive worship of Yahweh. He was a cosmopolitan who dealt with many foreigners and saw the beauty of their culture and the attractions of their religions.

As a result of all this the prophets turned against Solomon. His syncretism, that is, his willingness to admit the worship of other gods besides Yahweh, had lost the adherence of these steadfast followers of Yahweh, who were not merely practitioners of religion. They were a real force in the whole life of the Hebrew people. The prophetic call officially designated Jeroboam a true king chosen by Yahweh (1 Kgs 11:27–40). However, this did not deprive Solomon and his successors in the Davidic family of the legitimate position of those chosen by the promise of Yahweh. No matter what they did they were always the heirs to the promise Yahweh had given through Nathan (2 Sam 7:14–16; Ps 89:30–37), which guaranteed that, though the dynasty be punished by the loss of part of the kingdom, it would still have a lasting reign.

THE DIVISION OF THE KINGDOM

We must remember that Judah, the Hebrews of the south, had always lived a life of its own. In the days before the monarchy the cult center where the Ark was kept was always in the north central part of the country, and we have seen that this cult center was the real unifying force among the Hebrews. Not only was it never in Judah, but until David took Jerusalem the Hebrews of Judah were kept apart from the northern tribes by a foreign power which stood squarely on the road which should have united the tribes. Hence there was a real tradition of separation: the tribes of the north on the one hand, Judah on the other. The monarchy united the two, but even then it did not make the people one state. The king of Judah, David, had become king of the northern group of tribes also. So in his person he united all the Hebrew people. He ruled his two kingdoms from a capital which was his personal property, Jerusalem. Under Solomon this union of the two separate Hebrew groups in the person of the king continued, as we can see in the very organization of the kingdoms. Each of the two parts, Judah and Israel, was divided into twelve districts for administrative purposes. Thus each had its own separate and parallel administration; but, especially under Solomon, Judah was favored. Its people did not have to submit to labor forced upon loyal subjects as much as did those of Israel. This imprudent policy, favoring the king's own tribe and so arousing jealousy in the others, led directly to a split into Hebrew states along the old divisions. The tribes of the area north of Jerusalem formed the kingdom called Israel thereafter, while the tribe of Judah formed the kingdom of Judah. The personal fief of the Davidic king, Jerusalem, went to Judah, of course.

In addition to this religious unrest and this political resentment there is the fact that when Solomon died after a long reign the prestige of David was a thing of the distant past and did not carry the weight it had. The Philistine enemy had been crushed and no other threatened immediately. The people could look to their immediate grievances. They could feel free to air them when occasion arose, as it must, since each king of the united monarchies needed to be accepted by the people of the northern and southern states. Solomon's son Rehoboam was accepted by the people of Judah. He was, after all, the son of David and one of their own. However, when he went to Shechem to receive the acknowledgment of the ten tribes of the north, they laid certain conditions upon him. The young king refused to accede. He would not alleviate the taxes and other oppressive measures under which the people of Israel suffered. At once the ten tribes of the north rejected the Davidid (member of the Davidic family) and formed a kingdom of their own under Jeroboam. The Hebrews were divided into two kingdoms, a division which lasted as long as there was kingship in the land.

THE KINGDOM OF JUDAH

This was the southern of the two Hebrew kingdoms. It was constituted by the tribe of Judah and its hangers on (the Calebites, the Kenites, and other obscure groups) with the addition of the small tribe of Benjamin which occupied the territory immediately north of Jerusalem. The boundaries of this kingdom varied a good deal in the course of history. Usually Benjamin was under its control, but it tended to turn to the north, the new kingdom of Israel, when it could. The desert tribes and kingdoms were sometimes under the control of the king of Judah, but often they broke free and raided even the territory of Judah itself However, Jerusalem remained permanently the capital of the kingdom of Judah, and its importance increased immensely as time went on.

This tiny kingdom, only some thirty-five miles wide and one hundred and twenty miles long, was not even fertile nor rich in minerals.[1] It was

---

[1] The Judean "heartland" of the kingdom was even smaller, covering only the area from Jerusalem to Hebron and from the Dead Sea to Philistia, perhaps 40 by 60 miles.

mountainous, and, because as one goes south and east in Palestine the rain decreases, much of it is correctly called the Desert of Judah. Thus the kingdom of Judah was poor and consequently weak in the military and political sphere. Its poverty and weakness meant that this kingdom was less cultured. It was a backwater, but this was not an unmixed evil: a certain pure though primitive Yahwism persisted in this backwater.[2]

In part this happened because Judah did possess certain concrete advantages. The centralization of the cult in the later sense of the Old Testament, that is, the demand that the worship of Yahweh through sacrifice take place only in Jerusalem, was unknown under the monarchy. Nonetheless the Temple with the sacred object it enshrined, the Ark, was a liturgical center which far overshadowed any other in the land. The worship of God symbolically present on his throne, the Ark, had formed a principle of unity in the earlier days of the Hebrews. This worship continued to be immensely important for the religious unity of that people even though they had acquired a more sophisticated political organization which brought them under separate governments. Moreover, the Ark was the symbol of Yahweh's presence as leader of the people, assuring success in war and prosperity in general. Thus it remained an important object of pilgrimage. Moreover, the "house" which Solomon had prepared for this sacred object, the Temple, acquired a great respect in its own right. It was a holy place, looked upon with awe. It was the place where God was present and so could be expected to appear in a special and effective manner.[3]

It is difficult for us to appreciate what all this meant. The kingdom of David gave the Hebrews a political organization which enabled them to stand up to the attacks of their neighbors. Even this unity, however, had a religious basis. Remember that the king must be the chosen one of Yahweh and that the Davidids were the objects of a special and enduring promise mediated from God by the prophet Nathan. Even when the people were unified politically, therefore, religion played a supremely important part in their life as a people. They were one people not as subjects of a single king, but because they worshiped one God and this God had given them this king. With the subsequent division of the kingdom of David into the separate kingdoms of Israel and Judah this reli-

---

[2] The country people ("people of the land") remained especially loyal to Yahweh and the Davidids; note their help in restoring Joash after Athaliah's usurpation (2 Kgs 11:18).

[3] For instance, in 1 Kgs 8; Is 6 Yahweh appears in the Temple, and in 2 Kgs 20:6 he protects his special place.

gious element became even more important.

Once again the Hebrew people lacked political unity. They were not fragmented as in the old tribal system where it had been pretty much a matter of each man for himself. The kingdoms were able to perform the proper functions of the state, maintain order, encourage economic growth, and engage in a more or less successful foreign policy. Still, the people were disunited. But there remained a realization that they were one people because they alone worshiped Yahweh in the way in which he wished. Thus the Ark and its house, the Temple, remained symbols of Yahweh's special presence and the centers of the worship to which all the tribes subscribed. Consequently they became even more important for through them the people asserted their fundamental unity, though disunited politically. The people continued to come in pilgrimage to the Ark in Jerusalem, to enter into the worship carried on in the Temple, and to hear the doctrine proclaimed there, for the worship should include instruction.[4] Thus the Ark and the Temple were symbols of unity in a divided people. They made a center where traditional doctrine was conserved and taught. A prophet like Amos simply assumes that the worship in the Temple is the legitimate worship of Yahweh (Am 1:2). Amos was from Judah, and this fact may have given him a special interest in the Temple. Still, he chose to preach in the northern kingdom of Israel; this means that he recognized both its greater importance and its true Yahwism. In light of this, his assertion of the supremacy of the Jerusalem Temple must have been a consciously religious claim, not a show or simple local pride. On a less lofty religious level we must remember that the Davidid kings in Jerusalem had a great power over the Temple, the palace chapel. At the beginning at least the kings chose the high priests, and the Temple was always much in their power since the palace guard also protected the Temple precincts. Hence they were able to control much that went on in the Temple and, human nature being what it is, we may assume that they used the opportunities offered by the gathering of the people from Israel as well as from Judah in the Temple for worship to further their claims to be the only true kings of the Hebrews.

The kingdom of Judah possessed another important advantage, religious in nature but significant in its political aspects. This was the promise given by God through Nathan guaranteeing that the Davidids would reign

---

[4] Pss 15 and 24 show the priests giving instruction on the requirements for proper participation in the Temple liturgy; Hos 4 condemns the priests for a general failure to instruct the people. Clearly teaching was part of the priestly office.

forever. There was no questioning of this promise; even when Solomon's infidelity merited punishment the promise remained: only part of the nation was taken away from the Davidids. Thus we see that so religious a thing as a prophetic utterance had political aspects. This is not surprising. The Hebrews lived in a culture where there was no distinction between the secular and the religious. Through the words of the prophet God made a religious covenant, binding himself to the family of David in a matter which seems to us purely political. He guarantees the rule of David's dynasty.

The closer interpretation of the promise will concern us later. Here we should only note that 2 Samuel 7 as it stands is made up of several sayings which repeat and explain the basic promise. Most important here, the formulation of the promise in 2 Samuel 7:14–15 (paralleled in Ps 89:30–39) takes into explicit account the problem raised by the infidelity of Solomon. It makes clear that if the Davidids fail to keep the law of Yahweh, they will be punished, but the dynasty will continue.

This covenant between Yahweh and the Davidids gave the kingdom of Judah a tremendous stability. The king already had Yahweh's approval through a prophet. Simply because he was a descendant of David he was God's choice to be king. This, we have seen, was the basis for any legitimate rule among the Hebrews. It aroused great respect among the people of Judah, great enough to assure loyalty to a king even when he was personally a man of little worth. He was still the anointed decendant of David, Yahweh's choice, and so not to be replaced. To emphasize this it seems that the promise of Nathan was proclaimed anew at the coronation of a new king and often in the liturgy (as in Pss 89 and 132). The different formulations of essentially the same promise in 2 Samuel 7 are probably liturgical variants on the basic words of Nathan which have been gathered together here. The result of all this was that Judah enjoyed remarkable stability. The dynasty of David reigned for all the four hundred years of the life of the kingdom of Judah with but one short interruption under Athaliah, the daughter of Jezebel. She, widow of a Davidic king, attempted to usurp the throne, but even under her a Davidid, Joash, survived and was recognized as true king so that the the continuity of the dynasty was unbroken. Thus the kingdom was guarded against changes in dynasty, palace revolutions and all the upsets these disorders brought on other kingdoms, Israel included.

THE KINGDOM OF ISRAEL

The kingdom of Israel included the ten northern tribes. It held the lion's share of the population and the territory of the old monarchy. It contained the rich agricultural land of Galilee, the timber and grazing land of the Gilead in trans-Jordan, and it had in the mountains of central Palestine a rather easily defended power base. Furthermore, it was closely connected with the great trading kingdoms of Syria and Phoenicia. It commanded the so-called Royal Road running from Damascus through Galilee and down the coast. Thus it was in a very favorable position to profit from the trade passing between the great kingdoms of the Nile valley and the Euphrates-Tigris valley. Thus the kingdom of Israel prospered economically to a degree forbidden to Judah.

This, however, was not pure gain. The best agricultural lands were easily invaded, and the Royal Road carried armies as well as traders. The result was that Israel was often at war, especially with its traditional enemy, Damascus. The story of the kingdom is one of constant fighting between the two powers, now with one dominant, now with the other. As long as these struggles involved the small states of Syria and Palestine Israel held its own or better. However, involvement in international politics eventually brought Israel into a conflict with the Assyrian empire, and that was its end.

The religious problems of the kingdom of Israel were much more significant than these political ins and outs. These were directly connected with the international situation. For reasons of state the kings of Israel had to marry princesses from neighboring kingdoms, and these princesses brought in their own religion with them. The typical example here is the famous Queen Jezebel. She constructed temples to Baal and organized a priesthood and bands of prophets to serve him. She was not unique in this, although her ability and forceful personality enabled her to have special success in achieving her aims. This was all the easier because of the nature of the kingdom. Before David the Hebrews were able to occupy, practically speaking, only the highlands of Palestine. The rich cities located in valleys, Galilee for instance, remained Canaanite. David conquered these cities and made them part of his kingdom. They were incorporated into the provinces of the kingdom on a par with the original Israelite tribes. This meant that a pagan population of great power because of its wealth and cultural advancement was incorporated into the Hebrew state. Doubtless these people were ready to worship Yahweh, but in the fashion of the time they were quite ready to worship their own gods too, the gods called Baal (a title, "lord," not a proper name). In the circumstances the temptation for the Hebrews was great. Even before they had

had Canaanites as fellow citizens the Hebrews had found the worship of
the Baals tempting. Baal worship was the work of a people much superior
to the Israelites in culture and so it was naturally attractive. Moreover,
as the Hebrews settled down to agriculture they were tempted to turn to
the Baals as the gods of agriculture since the ancients tended to attribute
different functions to different gods. Thus the Baals would seem more
appropriate to farmers than the God of their nomadic wanderings, Yahweh.

The facts seemed to support this attitude. The Canaanites had wealth,
and the ancients attributed success to the gods. Therefore it was natural
for the Hebrews both to attribute the success of the Canaanites to their
devotion to Baal and to adopt this worship themselves. Finally, the cult
of the Baals was essentially a fertility cult, and its worship was sensuous
and licentious. It must have been tempting to indulge the appetites in the
guise of religion. Now, after David, the Hebrews found that their erstwhile enemies, the Canaanites, were their fellow citizens. Thus political
circumstances enabled contacts with foreign powers to reinforce the
already strong temptation to add the worship of the Baals to that of
Yahweh. Notice that there was little true apostasy among the ancient
Hebrews. They did not desert their old God entirely to profess the new.
They simply added worship of the Baals and the other gods who came
to their attention, such as Tammuz (Ezek 8:14–15) or the divinities of
the Assyrians (2 Kgs 16:10–16), to the Yahwist practices.[5]

Apart from all this, however, the kings of Israel were confronted with
what was really an insoluble problem. Those among their people who
were true Yahwists, and these were many, recognized the Temple and
especially its sacred object, the Ark, as the center of their religious loyalty
and devotion. Thus they made pilgrimage to Jerusalem which, as we have
seen, was closely connected to the Davidic king. Such devotion to and
contact with Jerusalem created a constant danger of subversion in the
northern kingdom.

The first king of Israel, Jeroboam, attempted the only possible answer
to the problem. He set up rival sanctuaries. One was at Bethel, the other
at Dan. These were both ancient cult centers, already familiar places of
worship and of pilgrimage and so suitable places for a new worship. Note
carefully that they were to be rivals to the Temple of Yahweh at Jerusalem
and not pagan shrines. In our sources Jeroboam is condemned for having

---

[5] Hence the probable meaning of the First Commandment: "Thou shalt not have
other gods in my sight"; i.e., it calls for exclusive worship of Yahweh without denying completely the existence of other gods.

set up the golden calves,[6] but even they do not claim that this was strictly idolatry. The calves were not intended as idols to be worshiped. Rather, the golden calves were supposed to be pedestals, symbols of the presence of Yahweh who was imagined to stand invisibly upon them. This, of course, parallels the significance of the Ark in the Jerusalem Temple, the symbolic throne upon which the invisible Yahweh was specially present.

However, the books of Kings are essentially right in condemning Jeroboam for setting up the golden calves. They may have been intended as symbols of Yahweh's presence, but given the propensity of the ordinary Hebrew to add other gods to Yahweh, and especially the tendency to worship the Baals whose symbol was a bull, it was inevitable that the calves become objects of idolatrous worship. Hence the evil in setting them up, and the condemnation of all who allowed them to exist.

Despite the power and prosperity of the kingdom of Israel, then, the government of that state was essentially unstable. Part of the problem here was its leaning toward a false form of Yahwism and even open service of false gods. Such practices naturally alienated the group who were devoted to Yahwism in the strictest sense, a Yahwism which would allow no dealing with other gods. Such people naturally did not feel loyal to kings who violated their basic religious obligations.

There was another religious source for the instability of the northern kingdom. The Davidids had the promise of God given by Nathan. Such a prophetic pronouncement guaranteed to the kings of Judah the character essential to legitimate Hebrew kingship, God's prior choice. The kings of Israel enjoyed no such promise. They had, indeed, prophetic approval. Jeroboam was called to be king by Ahijah, but this was a call to Jeroboam himself, not his dynasty. In fact prophets often intervened in the choice of a king for Israel. The typical situation was that the reigning king failed to fulfill his religious duties, in that he did not supress Baalism. Therefore, the prophets announced that the king who had failed had been set aside by Yahweh and that another had been chosen. Thus the new man became the legitimate king, the one with the necessary mark of God's prior choice, and revolution followed. The best example of this is the revolution under Jehu, who was appointed king through the prophet Elisha (2 Kgs 9–10). The dynastic principle was never really established. The eldest son of the preceding king was not automatically the king chosen by Yahweh; prophetic approbation was necessary.

---

[6] The "calves" were really bulls, which were commonly associated with divinity as symbols of power.

Even apart from religious factors the kingdom of Israel had its share of problems with unity. For one thing, there was rivalry among the tribes which made it up. In general the very large Joseph tribes, Ephraim and Manesseh, were the leaders, but this was not always accepted without cavil by the others. Then there was the problem of a suitable capital city. Israel had no city with the prestige of Jerusalem. At first the capital moved around. It was simply the city of the reigning king, usually the most important settlement within the bounds of the tribe to which he belonged. Eventually a king of greater ability, Omri, found the same solution as David. He bought Samaria from the Canaanites and established it as his capital. Like Jerusalem this city was the personal possession of the king and hence a safer refuge against tribal intrigue.

If we were to stop at this point we would have an entirely false picture of the significance of the Hebrew kingdom of Israel. It would appear a fair success as such things go in the political and economic spheres, but religiously the picture would be negative. We have already discussed the problems of prophetic intervention in politics and the tendency toward idolatry, but this is far from complete. There was a positive side to which the prophetic activity gives the clue. The energies which the kingdom called forth were in part directed toward true Yahwism, and if there was much in the realm that threatened the ancient religion, there was also force to reinterpret it and strengthen it for new tasks. In fact, it is in the northern kingdom, with its greater wealth based on agriculture and trade that Hebrew life, including religious life, flourished and developed. It was in the north that the prophetic movement became strong according to the stories about Elijah and Elisha, very great men indeed, even though they did not leave prophecies in writing. Even a Judahite like Amos, the first prophet whose sayings form a separate book of scripture, went to the north to proclaim his message. It would seem that only here was Yahwism ready to accept this relatively new form of divine expression.

Besides prophecy, theology proper flourished in Israel. Of the important documents of the Pentateuch, the oldest, the Yahwist source (J), was written in the time of David or Solomon in an effort to explain how Israel had acquired undreamed territory and power. The Yahwist explains this as a result of God's fidelity to Abraham. After this we have little indication of theologizing in Judah until quite late. In the north, on the other hand, a new interpretation of Israel's history, influenced by prophetic ideas, the Elohist document (E), took its rise under the later kingdom. Obviously there were fervent Yahwists to study and explain the theological traditions of their people. It is also to the north that in all probability we owe the immensely important book of Deuteronomy which explains how the promise given to Abraham, confirmed through Moses, and apparently fulfilled in the kingdoms could seemingly come to naught with the destruction of the kingdoms.

CHAPTER 4. THE FALL OF THE KINGDOMS

Readings: 2 Kgs 15–17; 22–25

THE EVENTS IN ISRAEL

One could spend a great deal of time on the details of the history of Israel and Judah. They won and lost wars, they had able and feeble kings; in short, they developed as did other kingdoms. However, the important thing for our purposes here is the development of religion under the monarchy. Especially important is the rise of the prophets which began in the northern kingdom, Israel, but continued in Judah. Also important is the gradual rise of the priests in Jerusalem. Originally appointed by the kings and subservient to them, as time went on the priests achieved a hereditary position and consequently a position of independence and even power vis à vis the monarchs. A theological book about the kings, however, cannot avoid a discussion of the historical collapse of kingship, the fall of the kingdoms of Israel and Judah.

First came the destruction of the kingdom of Israel which was completed by the Assyrians under Sargon II in 722 B.C. This people had begun their inroads with attacks which were like raids for plunder, but gradually they worked out techniques of imperial administration. Through a system of provincial governors with occupying troops and of client kings, the first such system known, they absorbed peoples into their empire. When they became successful in this, the era of the small, independent states of Syria and Palestine was over. The reign of Jeroboam II (786–746 B.C.) at the very end of Israel's history was a long era of great prosperity in the kingdom. Actually Jeroboam was lucky.

Assyria, which had long been in a period of eclipse, had begun to renew itself fifty years before his time. A series of able kings developed a warlike people led by a class of nobles convinced that they had a divine mission to spread the honor of their god Ashur by military conquest. However, for a half century before Jeroboam, Assyria fell upon bad times at home, and the western Asian states had a reprieve. Hence Israel was free for a time to develop its own prosperity. This was the easier since Israel's neighbor and hereditary rival, Damascus, had suffered much more from earlier Assyrian invasions, and Israel was able to take over much of the land and resources responsible for the prosperity of Damascus and similar kingdoms.

Thus Jeroboam II had a prosperous if idolatrous reign. But after him, the deluge. The Assyrians restored their power base and renewed their drive to the west. Each summer the campaigning season brought the Assyrian army with it. Israel joined other states to fend off the attack, but the project was hopeless, and Israel along with its allies suffered defeat after defeat. No state can last in these circumstances. Even before its destruction by a conqueror the disorganization and despair brought on by continued defeat lead to internal troubles, and Israel was no exception to this rule. Jeroboam's son was murdered and then one king after another took over in a bewildering succession of revolutions during the last days of the kingdom of Israel. But one king after another persisted in opposing the Assyrians; eventually after an especially important defeat in 733 B.C. most of the kingdom of Israel was taken from the king, who lived at Samaria, and made part of the provincial system of the Assyrian empire. Finally rebellions instigated by the kings of Israel became too much for the Assyrians, or perhaps provided them with the excuse they were already seeking. They attacked the last king of Israel, Hoshea, easily conquered the countryside, and laid siege to Samaria. The capital city managed to hold out for awhile, but it was doomed to defeat and in 722 B.C. it fell. The last king disappeared, and nobles and the educated people, scribes and priests, all who might provide leadership in Israel, were exiled and replaced by foreigners who were the leaders of the new Assyrian province.

It is of some interest to note that this new population, a mixture of the rather ignorant common people who were not exiled and a superior class of foreigners, produced the Samaritans so disliked by later Jews. National differences and ancient regional rivalries no doubt had much to do with this, but more important was the fact that the Samaritans were said to be ready to worship the true God but without abandoning the worship of the pagan gods which the foreign settlers had brought with them (2 Kgs 17:24–34).

THE EVENTS IN JUDAH

The much smaller Hebrew state of Judah managed to survive almost a hundred and forty years after the fall of Israel. Doubtless this was due in part to its insignificance. Judah was not very prosperous, and it stood apart from the major routes of communication. Hence the Assyrians were content to allow it a semi-independent existence as a vassal state.

Judah was put in this position during the time of troubles which destroyed Israel. Desperately trying to form a coalition to stave off the Assyrians, the kings of Syria and Israel joined against Judah to force it into the alliance. They even sought to introduce a usurper, Tabeel, an Aramean, and not even a Hebrew, in place of the legitimate Davidid, Ahaz (Is 7:6).[1] Frightened by this superior alliance, Ahaz turned to Assyria for help despite the prophet Isaiah's stern warnings that he must rely on Yahweh alone (Is 7:1–17). Ahaz lost faith in God's power to preserve his kingdom, sent tribute, and formed an alliance with the Assyrians. This action saved his kingdom, but at a price that required more than material tribute. The king went to Damascus to swear allegiance to his overlord and came back to add to the Temple an altar to the gods of Assyria. In 2 Kings 16:10–18 this is represented as mere interest on his part. Ahaz is supposed to have been so intrigued by the form of altar he saw in the Assyrian camp that he set up a similar altar and the worship that went with it. However, this is simply a rather naïve report of the way of things in ancient times. When one submitted to an overlord he was expected to acknowledge and swear by his gods. Thus, the position of being a vassal-ally demanded that Judah somehow submit to the gods of Assyria. This would have been true of any alliance between a superior

---

[1] See John Bright, *History of Israel*, p. 256 with n. 11.

and an inferior in the ancient Near East, and it was doubtless more so with the Assyrians, who felt that they were called to be imperialists by their god, Ashur.

Hence Ahaz' submission to Assyria saved his kingdom for the time being, but it created a danger because it made it necessary to accept gods other than Yahweh. And Ahaz did not stop with half measures; he introduced this cult into the Temple itself along with its paraphernalia and doubtless its priesthood. The central sanctuary of the Hebrews, the sign of their unity around the unique worship of Yahweh, was profaned.

The son and successor of Ahaz, Hezekiah, rebelled against this knuckling under to the Assyrians. He was assured by Isaiah that Jerusalem would remain inviolate (2 Kgs 19:32–34 = Is 37:33–35). No doubt on the strength of this assurance, though the prophet was against foolhardy alliances, he joined a coalition of Egypt and the Philistine cities against Assyria. The allies were unsuccessful. The Assyrians conquered Philistia, drove off the Egyptian armies, and occupied the whole of the Judean countryside. However, true to the prophetic word, they were unable to take Jerusalem and Hezekiah retained his throne.

Hezekiah's defiance of Assyria was noble but costly. The land outside of Jerusalem was laid desolate, and the renewed demands for tribute were crushing. Surely there were those who longed for the safe and sane ways of Ahaz which had brought reasonable material success. In any event, the next king, Manasseh, grandson of Ahaz, was a thoroughgoing idolator. He was a successful king in terms of political and economic prosperity, but in biblical terms he was a total failure because he was the worst of idolatrous kings. Not only did he imitate his grandfather, Ahaz, in encouraging the worship of the astral deities of Assyria in the Temple (2 Kgs 21:4–5), he also imitated the terrible infant sacrifices of the Canaanites (2 Kgs 21:6).

JOSIAH, REFORM, AND FAILURE

As so often happened, the succeeding king reversed his predecessor's policies. After Manasseh Josiah came to the throne about 640 B.C. Josiah was a reformer, one monarch after David and Hezekiah who receives the full approval of the authors of the books of Kings. He walked in the ways of his father David, he kept and enforced the law, particularly that of worshiping Yahweh alone. He destroyed the shrines which stood "on every high place and under every green tree." These were not all idolatrous; often they were centers of true worship.[2] Nevertheless, the fact is that the multitude of shrines encouraged belief in a multitude of gods among the simple people. They tended to think that each place had its own protective deity.

Undoubtedly Josiah was moved by sincere religious convictions, but he also had political aims. He was aided by the historical situation. After long centuries of dominance Assyria had collapsed. The last great Assyrian campaign against Elam ended in 640 B.C., and after that time there is nothing but decline. The Assyrian empire was unable to enforce its authority over its provinces and such satellite states as Samaria and Judah, and Josiah was using the opportunity provided by this vacuum of power. Hence his move to the north to reunite at last the ancient Davidic kingdom (2 Kgs 23:15–20). He could reassert pure Yahwism at the same time, since he was no longer obliged to perform even lip services to the gods of the erstwhile overlords of the Hebrews.

The most striking incident in all of Josiah's efforts at reform is the discovery of a lawbook in the Temple. As part of his program of restoration Josiah repaired the Temple. The necessary demolitions uncovered an ancient lawbook which impressed priests, king, and people. Scholars commonly hold that this was the core material of the book of Deuteronomy (5)6–28.[3] The ideas of Deuteronomy, total devotion to Yahweh and centralization of cult, were those of the Josiah reform. It should be noted, however, that this reform had begun before the lawbook was discovered. These were ancient traditions of all followers of Yahweh and did not depend on the accidental discovery of rare documents to be known; naturally, of course, a document newly discovered in a holy place and confirming these traditions could only impress the reformers and increase their zeal. The king promulgated the lawbook and instituted its full observance (2 Kgs 23:21–25). However, there was more to the new law than this. It frightened those who read or heard it. Why? Surely because it had the form of Deuteronomy, that is, its laws were followed by a set of blessings or curses whose actualization depended on obedience or disobedience to those laws. The king was so taken back that he sought the word of a prophet to explain the meaning of this. He consulted the

---

[2] Archaeologists have discovered a "house of Yahweh," i.e., a building with the design and name of the Temple, in the south Judean outpost of Arad, indicating that the worship of Yahweh in non-Jerusalem shrines was considered legitimate.

[3] In a reference like Dt (5)6–28 the parentheses indicate doubt about the connection of the chapter or verse so marked with the whole unit; here the question is whether the original Dt contained chap. 5 or not.

prophetess Huldah (2 Kgs 22:11–20) only to learn that the situation was hopeless. The sins of the Hebrews were so great that the threatened curses must be implemented. The only consolation for the young king himself, a true follower of Yahweh, was the meager comfort of a relatively early death which would spare him the sight of this.

Still, Josiah's reform measures and his efforts to restore the Davidic kingdom went on as long as he lived. However, the power vacuum favorable to this did not last long. From 625 to 612 B.C. the powerful nations of the Orient, the Medes and Babylon, were occupied with the final destruction of Assyrian power. As long as these powers were so occupied a minor nation like Judah was able to assert its independence. However, with the end of the ancient Assyrian menace the new powers sought wider influence. Judah was reduced to its ancient position. It was a buffer state between Egypt and the reigning force of Mesopotamia, Babylon. In 609 B.C. the Babylonians moved to destroy the last Assyrian army which had fled west from the conquered homeland. The Egyptian Pharaoh Necho moved north to aid these last Assyrians whom he wished to be a buffer between his nation and Babylon. Josiah elected to oppose this Egyptian movement at the pass of Megiddo on the battle-worn Royal Road. He lost the battle and his life. Thus ended the last flicker of true Hebrew independence. This was quickly demonstrated when the Judeans' choice of a king, Josiah's son Jehoahaz, was deposed and imprisoned by the Pharaoh, who appointed in his place another son of Josiah, Jehoiakim, as his puppet.

This was a return to the bad days of old in more ways than one. The new king turned back to pagan practices and preferred indulging himself in new palaces to dispensing justice (Jer 22:13–17). At any rate, Jehoiakim was a reasonably adroit politician. He owed his throne to Egyptian intervention, but when a Babylonian victory at Carchemish in Syria in 605 B.C. ended all effective Egyptian pretentions in Syria and Palestine, the Judean king managed to make his peace with the new Babylonian overlord.

Still the nationalist party, which was always strong in Judah, began the old, hopeless game of playing off the Egyptian against the Mesopotamian overlord so that Jehoiakim's reign ended with a rebellion against Babylon. As always Egypt was a broken reed, and, unmolested, the Babylonians laid siege to Jerusalem. The only thing the young king, Jehoiachin, who succeeded during these events, could do was surrender and throw himself on the mercy of Nebuchadnezzar. He was spared and imprisoned in Babylon. Along with him the Babylonians took many of the leading citizens of Judah. However, they did not put an end to the vassal kingdom. Rather they appointed Jehoiachin's uncle king in his place, giving him the name of Zedekiah.

He was the last Davidic king of Judah, a good enough man, but weak. For instance, he had considerable sympathy with the prophet Jeremiah and did what he could to protect him against the rabid nationalists. However, he was not strong enough to do more than help him out when he was attacked. He could ask his advice but never follow it. Otherwise, his reign is like many others. According to Ezekiel 8–9 all manner of paganizing practices went on even in the Temple. In politics the old tug-of-war between those who would accept the overlordship of Babylon and the nationalists who sought independence under Egypt's protection continued. The latter were stronger and eventually they led Zedekiah into rebellion against Babylon. For a final time a Babylonian army attacked, drove off the useless force which Egypt sent to demonstrate against them, and laid siege to Jerusalem. After a brave defense of more than a year the situation was hopeless. In July, 587 B.C. Zedekiah attempted to break free but was captured, and the Babylonian forces took the holy city. The king and whatever leaders of Judah who remained after the deportation in 598 were now exiled in Babylon. Jerusalem was leveled, and Judah became an insignificant district in the Babylonian empire. Thus ended the long history of the Davidic monarchy and of the political independence of the Hebrew people.

JUDGMENT ON THE KINGS

For over four hundred years the life of the chosen people was in the hands of kings. There are those who hold that the whole experiment of kingship was simply an error, but the period of the monarchy was not unproductive. Despite the early division of the people into two kingdoms there is no doubt that the institution of the monarchy heightened the consciousness of national unity. It was an extremely important factor in creating a truly united people which was able to preserve itself and its revealed religion in the face of enormous pressures from paganism. Thus the Hebrews did not simply dissolve in the foreign milieu as did all the other people who were taken into exile in those ancient days. They maintained their religious identity. The loosely organized tribes of the premonarchical confederacy could never have managed this.

Moreover the Davidic kings with their Temple in Jerusalem developed the worship of Israel, with its priestly traditions, its psalms, and its ritual. This too was of great theological significance. Finally, the kingship itself was an important factor in the development of the theology of the Old Testament, for the royal ideology, more than anything else, contributed to the development of messianism.

Moreover, it was under the kings that the ancient Hebrew traditions were gathered and their theological richness developed. In large part this was in reaction to the monarchy itself, its success (the Yahwist document [J]), its dangers (Dt), and its failure (the Deuteronomic History [Jos–Kgs]). Prophecy too took a new turn. Always closely linked to the monarchy, it began to look at the institution critically. The older prophets mentioned in the books of Kings have left us no comprehensive collection of their sayings so as to form a prophetic book, and they have, therefore, often been forgotten. However, they were great men who stood up for pure Yahwism in the face of the trend to admit the worship of the Baals. But they did not have to face up to the total destruction of their people, the chosen people of Yahweh in whom was to be fulfilled God's inalienable promise to Abraham. The prophets, like all thinking men during the time of troubles after 750 B.C., had to face this problem. They clearly saw the folly of the kings and of the people. Hence they began to be full of condemnation of the kings for their folly and of the people for their greed and their injustice. They saw that as things were going the kingdom of Israel was coming to an end. A little more than a century later Judah was in the same condition, and the prophetic message is the same. The Hebrew kingdoms had sinned and must pay the penalty. They were indeed God's people, but this privilege depended upon fidelity to Yahweh, and the people had been unfaithful. Hence they must undergo punishment, and this would be very severe: the total destruction of the kingdoms. The condemnation is unwavering, but it is not the last word. There is a ray of hope. Some of the people will be chastised and re-educated and so restored as true and fervent and unwavering followers of Yahweh.

This theology of history is not confined to the prophets of the time. Theologians too arrived at the same teaching, though it is important to note that they did this by a route very different from that of the prophet. The latter, according to his office, was taught directly by God, while the former simply reflected on the history and traditions (among which prophecy was important of course) of the Hebrews and formulated their conclusions. The point is important because it shows how revelation can come in different ways: through direct divine communication or hard thought guided, of course, by God's grace. It also shows the strength of Hebrew tradition. This tradition could develop in the hand of prophet or theologian and become the instrument for understanding new situations.

The clearest expression of all this from the side of the theologian is in the book of Deuteronomy. This magnificent theology seems surely to be connected with the new prophetic movement. It is to be found especially in the essential core of the book, its oldest part, that is, Deuteronomy (5)6–28. The chapters before and after this core were added later to integrate it into the larger history of Israel as told in the Pentateuch and Judges through Kings. The writer of this central portion of Deuteronomy saw his land going under, as kings and people gave themselves to idolatry. He, like the prophets, asked how this could happen to the chosen people, and he arrived at the answer which is formulated in his book. The covenant is solemn but conditional, and the negative conditions have been fulfilled. Rather than fidelity Israel has given infidelity. Put a bit boldly, he teaches that there is a set of laws which the people must keep if it is to prosper in the promised land. If it fails to keep these laws it will lose the land and go into exile.

This Deuteronomic theory is not a mechanical theology. An obedient Israel does not earn the covenant, nor pay for the land by keeping the Law. Rather the covenant is already given, and in the laws God graciously grants its definition. Living according to the laws is living the state of the elect. The Hebrew who failed so to live had already ceased to live in that state. We should not think in terms of reward and punishment; life according to the Law was the life of the elect, the state of reward, so that when it ceased reward ended by that very fact. History merely records the ending of the covenant which has already taken place in the basic disobedience of the people. Moreover the Deuteronomist, that is, the theologian of the central part of Deuteronomy, is much concerned with the attitude of the people and their freedom. He tries over and over to persuade them to keep the covenant. He does not emphasize external coercion. This is especially clear in the introduction to its laws in chapters (5)6–28. The chapters before and after this core were added later to sincere commitment to the service of Yahweh which is defined in the laws he is about to outline. There is nothing here of a mechanical imposition of punishment or prosperity or of an earning of God's grace. Rather he desires and demands a free giving of self to God.

However, men do not live entirely unto themselves. They are part of society and usually they take their cue from their society. Hence the enormous responsibility of the Hebrew kings. According to the theologians who applied the ideas of Deuteronomy to an understanding of Hebrew history in Josiah–Kings the kings had a directly religious task of their own. After David they were the responsible mediators between Yahweh and his people. It was their privilege and duty to support and foster the exclusive worship of the God of Israel. In this they failed. Only three kings, David, Hezekiah, and Josiah, held out for the pure service of Yahweh. Of the others some were true Yahwists but failed to go all the way in the support of Yahwism, while others were simply paganizers and actually fostered the spread of Baalism and other pagan cults. They failed and they led the people to fail to keep the basic law to worship Yahweh exclusively. This failure must eventually destroy the covenant and it did, bringing with it the destruction of the people and their exile.

CHAPTER 5. "A CERTAIN DIVINITY DOTH HEDGE A KING"

Readings: 2 Sam 7; Pss 2; 18; 20; 21; 45; 72; 89; 101; 110; 132; 144: 1–11

This chapter heading quotes a king himself, James I of England. This may seem like a prejudiced source, but he is expressing the attitude of most people most of the time. They see their rulers as something outside the pale of ordinary mortals. Even in this day of democratic leveling we seek something of this mysterious quality in our rulers.[1] Witness the very different charisms of John F. Kennedy and Douglas MacArthur who yet shared this hold over the public imagination. If we seek out this response in our own environment, in ourselves, it is easier to understand the very lofty idea of kingship, its prerogatives, and its responsibilities which the pagans of the ancient Near East, among whom the Hebrews lived, had.

The king was a god or very nearly a god. In Egypt he was literally divine, the physical son of the chief god, Amon-Re. In Mesopotamia he was normally thought of as a kind of an adopted son, especially chosen

---

[1] Walter P. Lippman, *Essays in the Public Philosophy* (Boston: Little, Brown and Co., 1955), has persuasively argued that most men even in a modern democracy need to believe in a mysterious power invested in their leaders.

by the god at the time of his coronation. In the kingdom of Hatti, the great empire of Asia minor in the second millenium before Christ, the king became god after death. This glorious position gave the king vast responsibilities. Upon the proper performance of his functions, both cultic and civil (in the latter sphere the administration of justice was especially emphasized), depended the well-being of the kingdom. If the king preserved the right order in these functions, then right order in nature would be preserved, the crops would grow year by year, and men would prosper. If he failed in his functions, the order of nature as well as society would be destroyed and prosperity ruined. The king, therefore, had important mediatorial functions. Upon him primarily depended right relations with the gods and the consequences of those relations. He was, therefore, a priest, and his presence at certain major acts of the liturgy was indispensable. He even represented the god in the liturgical re-enactment of the basic myths in which the religious ideas of the people were enshrined.[2]

We are, then, generalizing, when we summarize the position of the ancient Near Eastern king as involving a special, responsible closeness to the divinity. It was true in one way or another of almost every king, but not everywhere in the same way. The king need not have been considered a god on earth. Neither can we be sure that he must always take the god's place in the cult, nor do we know what these activities were in every case. It is necessary to note these nuances in the royal ideology, for an important school of Old Testament scholarship sees this ideology as a rigid pattern (hence one of its names for this kind of theory: "patternism") which was followed all over the ancient Near East and was the same in every instance, even among the Hebrews.[3] Briefly, the school holds that the king was truly divine, a god on earth, and that his central function was to play the part of a god in the basic ritual, usually the New Year feast. This feast was a ritual re-enactment of the myth which expressed the basic insight of ancient Near Eastern religion. It was a religion of nature, primarily concerned with fertility, with assuring the annual increase

[2] Such at least is the common idea and it is true of the major ancient ritual text which we possess, that of the Babylonian New Year feast, but this is a relatively late text. There is much evidence that ritual came first, i.e., men acted and then began to explain their actions.

[3] The various proponents of "Patternism" or the "Myth-Ritual School" object correctly that they are not a school, that is, not a single view with a single leader and method. This is admirably brought out in the most recent collection of the "school": S. H. Hooke, ed., *Myth, Ritual, and Kingship* (Oxford: Oxford University Press, 1958), which displays a wide diversity of data and interpretation. The best critical study of the whole set of ideas is still Henri Frankfort, *Kingship and the God.*

of crops, of flocks and herds, and of mankind. Men saw life in terms of the yearly cycle of nature with the birth of the young crops, their growth to maturity, and their destruction at the harvest time followed by the long season during which the lands must lie fallow until the return of favorable climatic conditions for crops. This natural cycle was supposed to be personified in the story of a young god representing the crops in his quick youth, maturity, and death. He disappeared at his death, only to rise again each year with the new crops. However, this return was not automatic. It must be stimulated or forced by the ritual which was essentially the re-enactment of the history of this young god and his struggle against the forces of destruction. In this re-enactment it was the king who was supposed to take the place of the young god. The partially preserved ritual of the Babylonian New Year's feast is supposed to be typical. In it the statue symbolizing the presence of the god was hidden and the king who represented the god was humiliated by being deprived of his royal regalia, thus representing the disappearance of the young god. Then there was a ritual mock battle symbolizing the god's struggle against and final triumph over the forces of chaos. The triumph was made visible in the restoration of the king to his position of honor and glory, a procession restoring the god's statue to its temple, and finally the reuniting of the young god with his consort, the fertility goddess, represented by a priestess.

How much truth is there in this view? We have already seen that it is false to say that all the kings of the ancient Near East were held to be divine. Moreover, we do not have the evidence for the ritual re-enactment of this myth outside of Babylon.[4] It is even doubtful that the religion of Syria, for instance, was based on the yearly nature cycle. In general, a rigid idea of the religion of the ancient Near East and of its ritual is certainly false. There was a great variety of myth, of ideas of the divinity, and of ritual. This is what the evidence has to say, and in the face of the empirical testimony to a great variety, the patternist idea must be judged an abstraction which tries to force varied and often contradictory data into a straitjacket.

However, we must not deny all legitimacy to the position. We have already seen that in a general way the kings were thought to be close to

---

[4] Not even the most complete expression of the rite from Babylon itself (see above, n. 2) contains all the supposed elements since there is no dying and rising god (this used to be supposed on the basis of a misinterpreted text, as Wolfram von Soden has demonstrated).

the gods and did have cultic responsibilities. Moreover, ancient religion like all religions was profoundly concerned with life, and this meant concern with the increase of crops and herds and so with the cycle of nature. Finally, these religions were very conscious of the threat of breakdown in this cycle, this good order, because of drought or flood and other natural disasters, for the ancient economies never had surpluses. One bad year meant famine. Hence men saw life as constantly endangered by the dark forces of chaos, a danger they pictured as some form of struggle by the forces of chaos against the divinities which had imposed order on them. However, such common forms of expression had very different meanings in different months, and the ideas expressed very different contents.

ROYAL IDEOLOGY IN ISRAEL

There being no real pattern of royal ideology throughout the ancient Near East, it is false to argue from it to the elements of the pattern among the Hebrews, as has been done. However, it is equally obtuse to deny all similarity of Old Testament ideas to those of neighboring religions. After all, the Hebrews borrowed the institution of kingship and their way of speaking about it from their pagan neighbors. The sources which reveal something of the theory of kingship in Israel verify this. Apart from Samuel and Kings, these are the psalms, especially the royal psalms (Ps 2; 18; 20; 21; 45; 72; 89; 101; 110; 132; 144:1–11). The psalms are especially significant because they are liturgical poetry, the hymns which were eventually used in the worship in the Temple. The Temple, its sacrificial liturgy, and its poetic styles were borrowed largely from the Canaanites. In such circumstances contact with the ideas of kingship among the Gentiles was inevitable. They came with the very language used. And of course the very fact that a king had so important a place in liturgical poetry is evidence that the kings were closely connected with the cult and the worship of Yahweh at the Temple.

Thus, we find that in fact the *general* characteristics of ancient kingship were indeed verified in the Psalms. The king was indeed especially close to God: in Psalms 2:7 and 89:26–27 he is called the son of God, and in Psalm 45:6 he may even be addressed as "god" (a possible honorific in Hebrew). The terminology is straight out of the ancient exaltation of the kingship. Clearly the king is the adopted son of God, not born of a divine father but son because God gives him a position supreme over the kings of the earth at his coronation.

In addition, the king is especially responsible for the well-being of the people. For instance, in war his success is the success of the people, as in Psalm 18. However, there is much more to it than this. The king has the same sort of responsibility as other ancient kings. If he fulfills his function, making sure that there is justice and good order in society, then there will be good order in nature and man will prosper. The most convincing text on this point is Psalm 72:2–3, which should be read: "May he [the king] judge thy people as he should and thy poor with judgment! May the mountains bear the people prosperity and the hills what they should."[5] Note the parallelism typical of Semitic poetry which links the kings justice ("as he should") with the natural order ("what they should"). The same order of ideas appears in verse 6, where the king is linked to life-giving rain.

Finally, the king does indeed have his position in the cult. Solomon acts as a priest when he is inaugurating the Temple. He offers sacrifices and he leads the prayers (1 Kgs 8; also 3:4). Before him the sons of David were priests (2 Sam 8:18). All this was an embarrassment to the theology of later Judaism which restricted priesthood of any kind to the sons of Levi. Only a very strong tradition starting from facts could have retained these hints at a priestly function of the kings in the face of a theological opposition which would have dearly loved to ignore them. In any event, the kings always were connected with the cult, since its important manifestations were in the Temple of Jerusalem, which, as the Chronicler never tires of pointing out, was a royal work.

The kings of the Hebrews, then, were indeed felt to be very close to God, endowed with responsibilities far beyond the political, and deeply involved in the cult. To that extent, they were like the other kings of their time and place. However, there is nothing to show that they were thought of as God or that they actually acted as God in a ritual such as is posited by the patternists. On the contrary, their position was entirely compatible with Yahwism, and was in fact closely integrated into the Old Testament theory of the government of the people of God.

KING AND COVENANT

The point here is that the king became an integral and most important

---

[5] "As he should" and "what they should" both translate the Hebrew *sdq*, "right order, justice" (reading "right order" in 3b with the Greek text against the Hebrew "in right order") in an attempt to give a meaningful parallelism like the Hebrew.

part in the machinery of the covenant.[6] The Israelite covenant, no matter how it is described (and it is described in many ways), always made an important place for human mediators. The promissory covenant to the patriarchs (e.g., Gen 12:1–3) was a promise to the people through one man who represented the people before God, and to some extent, God before the people. So also Moses at Sinai was a mediator who stood between God and the people both in the act of instituting the covenant (Ex 19:1–24:11) and in its continuation (Ex 34). After Moses Joshua stood between the people and Yahweh as covenant mediator (Dt 31; Jos 1; 24). Much later Samuel stands between the people and God, intercedes for them and restores the broken covenant relationship (1 Sam 12:19–24). In the covenant relationship of Israel with Yahweh, therefore, God did not deal directly with the people as a whole; rather he chose a notable representative who stood between him and the people, and the people wanted it this way. They were far too awed and terrified of the divine to wish to come too close themselves. That was the function of a specially designated "man of God."

Thus there was a place for the king in the covenant relationship as mediator. But did Old Testament theologians actually see the king as the proper mediator of the covenant between Yahweh and his people? Did they so present him? They did indeed, but not by means of a direct assertion, for typically the Old Testament does not discuss theological principles as such. It is rather the story of God's saving intervention in the history of man. It deals with fact, not with ideas, and when we seek an answer to a question about an idea such as this we must usually look behind the facts to their implications. This can be a problem, but in the present case the solution is reasonably clear. For one thing there were certain elements in the royal ideology which fitted very easily into the covenant pattern. Thus the special responsibility of the king for the people is like that of the covenant mediator. Then his closeness to God makes him like Moses and Joshua and Samuel, all "men of God" in a special sense. Hence it was very easy to present the king as being in the same line as these great mediators of the covenant. Small things are very significant here, for instance the title "my servant." In the work of the Deuteronomic Historian this title is reserved for the covenant mediators,

---

[6] This is not always conceded. There are those who find the monarch a fundamental violation of the Mosaic covenant (cf. G. E. Nendenhall, "The Hebrew Conquest of Palestine," *The Biblical Archaeologist* 25 [1962], pp. 66–87), but by invalidating a major institution this view would seem to eliminate all the important contributions which it made to revelation.

especially Moses and David. So it is implied that he had the same office as Moses.

The great promise to David and his line (2 Sam 7) furnishes added evidence. As we have seen in Chapter 1 the complex history of the Hebrews from Joshua through Kings is organized and explained by certain speeches or essays inserted at key points in that history. The promise of Nathan is a kind of program for the monarchy, and 1 Kings 8 and 2 Kings 17:7–17 show how this program was fulfilled. This structure of program and fulfillment is based on the covenant. The program is simply to live the covenant, and the fulfillment is a description of what happened when this was done or not.

Moreover, the very content of this promise to David carries overtones of the basic covenant between Yahweh and his people. The Davidic king succeeds the judges as guardian of the people's prosperity, and this prosperity, of course, depended on fidelity to the covenant (Jg 2:16–18; 2 Sam 7:14). Once more, details are meaningful. In 2 Samuel 7:10–11 the people's security: "dwell in their own place," "be disturbed no more," "no more be afflicted," is directly related to God's "giving rest" to David from his enemies. The king's peace is the people's peace, his security their security. This is obvious enough; the point is the use of the phrase "give rest from." This is a technical term in the Deuteronomic History referring to a life of prosperity in the promised land as the fulfillment of the covenant. The term is now connected with the Davidic promise and so this fulfillment is made directly dependent on the Davidic king.

Finally, the basic duties of the king are described in terms which are taken straight from the description of the covenant language of Deuteronomy. The king must "walk in the ways of the Lord, keeping his statutes, his commandments, his ordinances, and his decrees . . . that [he] may prosper . . ." (1 Kgs 2:3). This language is applied to the king's position as stated in David's prayer, responding to the promise in 1 Samuel 7:18–29. Such Deuteronomic phrases are certainly later than the original promise of Nathan. They are theological interpretations in the standard manner of the historian. This, of course, in no way weakens their claim to fit the king into the covenant structure. In fact, being an historical judgment and not a mere royal claim gives them added weight. The same is true of the Deuteronomic covenant language used in Solomon's prayer in 1 Kings 8.

The Davidic king, then, inherited the office of mediator of the covenant between Yahweh and his people. He was Yahweh's servant who must walk in the way of the Lord in order that he and his people might have rest and prosper in the land promised by the covenant. Thus the king bears a grave responsibility with regard to the covenant relation between the people and Yahweh. This is amply confirmed by the history in Kings. As we have seen, Kings was written to explain the conquest and enslavement of the Hebrew people by Assyria and Babylonia. This is done in terms of the Deuteronomic covenant: since the people have violated the covenant the punishment threatened for such violation has come upon them. However, it is not simply that the people as a whole have done this in some general way by election or popular demand or something of the sort. Rather, the kings who were responsible mediators of the covenant for the people have failed to lead the people in living up to the basic demand of this covenant, the exclusive service of Yahweh. In and with their mediators the people have violated the covenant and hence the covenant conceived in the Deuteronomic manner must have ceased.

MESSIANISM

However, the failure of royalty to perform its proper function in the old covenant relationship is not the whole story. The original Davidic line did indeed fail to fulfill its responsibility to the covenant, but that is not the end of it all. When the Davidic kingdom was overthrown, and with it the last flicker of the independence of the Hebrew people quenched, the promises and hopes and beliefs that clung to the figure of the king were not simply forgotten. Rather they were taken over and gradually turned into the figure of the Messiah, the savior king who was to come. Thus messianism, an extremely complex movement which developed out of many factors throughout Old Testament times and later, depended on the theology of Old Testament kingship as a principal source. If we are to understand the importance of that kingship we must understand this fundamental relation to the idea of the Messiah.

Obviously some elements in the kingship ideology readily explain the figure of the Messiah and the expectations which collected around him. The king was so very close to God, and he had a special responsibility as mediator between the covenanted people and God. These elements loom large in certain of the hopes for the one who was to come. It is even significant that the very name Messiah is derived from the kingship. The king was the anointed one (*messiah* is simply the Hebrew for *anointed*), marked off by a sign as God's chosen one, for in pre-exilic times only he received the ritual anointing. This anointing effectively symbolized the divine choice of the king, that choice so important for the Hebrew king. Furthermore, the rite symbolized that the anointed one was a special vassal and agent of the one who caused the anointing. Typically, the Pharaoh had his subject kings anointed, thereby making them his followers and instruments endowed with some of his power. In like manner anointing in a rite influenced by Egyptian usage symbolized that the Hebrew king shared in a subordinate way the position and the power of Yahweh over his covenanted people.[7]

A further important factor in the development of messianism is the language used about the kings. It is certainly extravagant. In the royal psalms the king is called the son of God, even God (Ps 2:7; 45:6). This is language most uncharacteristic of the Old Testament. It knows that God's people are God's children, but it avoids saying this because of the danger of grave misunderstanding in a largely polytheistic milieu quite ready to take divine sonship as a literal, physical reality, and yet it uses the term boldly of the kings. In addition, the kings of Judah are called the greatest of the kings of the earth who will conquer their enemies to the very limits of the universe and so on (Ps 89:27b; cf. Ps 2; 110). This is an exaggerated way to speak about the king of a minor, backward state. So, it would seem, is the claim that the king's justice determines the proper sequence of seasons so that it is by his decree that the life-giving rains come. The king is Lord of nature as of society. In all this we hear the customary language which the ancient Near East used of its kings. Is it more than this when applied to the Hebrew kings? Many have claimed that this is simply the language of the court flatterers and that it has no significance beyond an illustration of the perennial human aptitude for fawning upon one's superiors.

Such a view fails to understand the religious attitude of the ancients. They sincerely believed that there was a continuity between the king's actions which brought good order to their lives, and their prosperity which depended upon a right order in nature. As for royal power reaching to the ends of the world, they were certainly convinced that "a certain divinity doth hedge a king," so that his power extended beyond customary boundaries, even of kingdoms. The easiest demonstration of this belief among the Hebrews is the very existence of the royal psalms in our day.

---

[7] E. Kutsch, *Salbung als Rechtsakt im Alten Testament und im Alten Orient.* *BZAW* 87 (Berlin: Töpelmann, 1963), has shown that the anointing not only designated the divine choice but communicated a share of divine power. See also Roland de Vaux, O.P., "Le roi d'Israel, vassal de Yahvé," *Mélanges Tisserant I. Studi e testi* (Rome: Vatican Library, 1964), pp. 119–133.

They came down to us because they were incorporated into the official hymn book of the restored Temple. For our psalter is just that, the hymn book used in the Jerusalem Temple after the return of the exiles. This was a Temple which had been built and which functioned without the presence of a king. And still the priests and people respected and used the psalms which lauded the kingship. This could not have been mere flattery because there was no one there to flatter. Neither was it mere antiquarianism. The Bible holds little which stems from a mere interest in the past as such. There is great interest in the past, but only because it shows God's interventions on behalf of his people and so guides the life of that people here and now. In view of this exclusive interest in the past as applicable to the present the royal psalms with their extravagant language must have been preserved because they were felt to be meaningful in the life of the people of God after the days of the monarchy.

The same phenomenon of extravagant language preserved beyond the date of its immediate application occurs in the prophecies of Isaiah. In his magnificent poems about the prince who is to come (Is 9:2–7; 11:1–9) the prophet speaks of him as "a very God of a warrior" who will bring a return to the very conditions of paradise. Undoubtedly all this was originally spoken about a new prince of the Davidic line whom Isaiah knew. But the words have been preserved, written down, and incorporated into the sacred books long after prince and prophet had disappeared from the scene, that is, long after the people had seen that they were not literally fulfilled in their immediate object. Once more this cannot be flattery; rather it is something which was meaningful, because the people preserved and read them long after the time of the prophet. This is not the place for a full discussion of the hope for the future found in the prophets, a subject larger than messianism, but at least these few passages use language borrowed from the royal ideology. Prophets like psalmists learned from these ideas and mediated their influence on future messianic hopes.

Thus the liturgical poet and the prophet preserved great promises and lofty ideas even after the Davidic monarchy had been proven a failure by the destruction of Jerusalem and the exile of the people. This was possible only because the men who included these extravagant sayings in their holy books had come to believe that they had some application beyond the mere human dynasty which had failed. This is not to say that they had clearly seen the promise of a divine savior or anything of the sort, but they were on the road to realizing that God's promises offered something more than mere human kingship.

This is demonstrated in another way by the problem of the return from the Babylonian exile which began in 538 B.C. and the restoration of the Jewish commonwealth which followed. The restoration is a theological problem if one takes seriously the Deuteronomic analysis of Hebrew history. According to it the covenant between Yahweh and his people was strictly conditional. If the people were faithful to the covenant, they would prosper; if not, the covenant was ended and they would suffer. But under the kings they had failed and the covenant had ended. How, then, could the people of God persist? How could there still be a Jewish commonwealth? By very definition this was the people of the covenant and the covenant had come to a close. How, then, could the people still persist as a people? The men of the return wrestled with this problem and managed to find solutions. The covenant in the Deuteronomic form had indeed ended and with it the privileges it brought. But this was not the total expression of the covenant between Yahweh and his people. There were also the purely promissory covenants with Abraham and with David. These covenants were based on God's simple word that he would stand by his mediator and his people. There were no conditions, and hence the covenant persisted despite human infidelity.

One school of post-exilic theologians explained the return in terms of the promise to Abraham: "When you are in tribulation, and all these things come upon you in the latter days, you will return to the Lord your God and obey his voice, for the Lord your God is a merciful God; he will not fail you or destroy you or forget the covenant with your fathers which he swore to them" (Dt 4:30–31). Others based their explanation on the formally similar covenant with David in 2 Samuel 7. This also was a simple promise, and as it was developed it became explicit that the promise would continue even though the recipients of the promise were disobedient (2 Sam 7:13). The prophets of the return, Haggai and Zechariah, turned to this promise made to David. They were confident that the ultimate restoration of Israel would be led by a prince of the line of David (Hag 2:20–23; Zech 4:6–7: the Zerubbabel who is the object of these oracles was a Davidid).

This line was also followed by the historian of Chronicles. To him the covenant with David was all-important, so much so that he almost entirely ignores the covenant made on Sinai through Moses. This has ended with the destruction of Jerusalem. The covenant with David occasioned by David's concern for the Temple counts because it continues. Once again the promissory covenant explains the restoration and continuity of the

Hebrew people. Moreover, this connection between cult, Davidic king, and covenant is much older than the Chronicler. In the ancient royal psalm 132 it is clear that Yahweh's covenant with Israel is centered around the worship of the Temple of Jerusalem. Yahweh has "chosen Zion as his resting place," and choice means covenant in the Old Testament. Here the choice is parallel with God's choice of the Davidic kings who are responsible for the cult centered on Zion. It must be admitted that neither the Psalmist nor the Chronicler explicitly draws the conclusion that as the cult continues so must the Davidic line somehow continue, but this was implied. It certainly fostered the hope for the coming of a Messianic prince of the line of David as long as the cult persisted.[8]

With the return from exile enthusiastic hopes for a restored Davidic kingship (see Haggai and Zechariah, to whom we have already referred) flared up, but the restoration was impossible. The community of the return settled down as a tiny unit of the Persian and later empires. It was a religious state governed by its high priests (in internal affairs) according to its own law now codified in the Pentateuch. If the adage is right, this was a happy nation for it has almost no history, but it was not perfect from the Jewish viewpoint.

With regard to our topic, messianism, it represented another education in disappointment. The hopes for a new kingdom of Judah on the old model had been dashed. It was beginning to look as though messianism might not be political at all, not, at least, in the sense of a politic managed by men. Hopes were turned in other directions to some extent.

The other development was more positive and also symptomatic of the future. Up to now messianic ideas had grown largely in terms of new insights into the meaning of the Hebrew version of the royal ideology. Now, while such development of the kingship concept continued, new factors began to broaden messianic ideas. The idea of the priesthood was introduced. This was natural, for the priests had assumed the role of the former kings. They assumed some of their prerogatives too. Specifically, they were anointed now where before only the king had been. They were, in Hebrew, *messiahs*. This continued a development in the later prophets. Zechariah 4:1–14 had associated the high priest closely with the Davidic

---

[8] For the Chronicler see R. G. North, S.J., "The Theology of the Chronicler," *Journal of Biblical Literature* 82 (1963), pp. 376–380. The Priestly Document in the Pentateuch is more radical still; it excises the Mosaic covenant from its story of Sinai even though the Priestly tradition had included such a covenant (cf. Ex 6:2–13; 31:17; and Lev 17–26, all P and all implying the Sinai covenant), as Walter Zimmerli, "Sinaibund und Abrahambund." *Gottes Offenbarung* (Munich: Kaiser, 1960), pp. 212–216 shows.

line, and before him the priesthood had been given a great role in the ideal Jerusalem Ezekiel had envisioned (Ezek 40–48). Thus a new element was added to messianic speculation, the Priest-Messiah. This could lead to ideas of a plurality of messiahs as at Qumrân with its separate royal and priestly messiahs. But it could also lead to a deeper insight into the Messiah and his work.

One should note that there is a dialectic of disappointment in this development of messianism. At the first stage, the pre-exilic monarchy, there is no real messianism in the sense of a long-term future hope. Rather, the claims and hopes of the royal psalms and the prophets are centered upon the continuity and purification of the present kingship of the sons of David. In accord with their times they use lofty language about this, and they certainly mean that this kingship is religious, near to God. However, they are essentially concerned with "rest," the continuity of the life of the Hebrews in their homeland. After the destruction of Jerusalem and the exile all these hopes were destroyed. And yet they are preserved with all their extravagant expression. Under the blows of the fall of Jerusalem and the exile this language is seen to mean something beyond a mere poetic description of the life in the land given by Yahweh. Perhaps this significance could not be specified more exactly, but it must have been, or otherwise the language would not have been preserved when the land and life it described had been lost. Thus adversity led to reflection upon the idea of kingship and there came a perception, vague at first, that this kingship had a meaning beyond a mere Hebrew dynasty in its homeland.

It is impossible to go further into the details of the development of messianic hopes in the so-called intertestamental period, the time which elapsed between the last books of our Old Testament and the New Testament. These hopes were manifold and complex. Nor was there total consistency throughout Judaism. There was no central doctrinal authority, of course, and the many schools held separate doctrines and opinions. In this atmosphere many ideas of the time to come and the Messiah who might lead that time developed. In all of this the effect of adversity on this development continued to be important. After the earlier years of the return from the exile the Jerusalem Temple state seems to have enjoyed a fairly long period of peace and quiet, but in the second century B.C. the Jews suffered persecution for their religious beliefs, and this persecution stimulated anew the hope of the coming of the final intervention of God which would restore the people of God to their proper position and even raise the martyred faithful to enjoy their reward — again a new idea developed by the pressure of opposition. Each new idea produced further ideas as minds and imaginations were stimulated by a rich theological and poetic heritage and the pressure of adversity.

For a long time the future hopes of the Jews had centered on the coming of a leader, the Lord's anointed, who would lead them into a new era, God's final dispensation. As time went on and the welter of ideas increased, this no longer remained true. It was realized that God could bring on the new era without using a leader other than himself. Thus we must distinguish messianism from eschatology, that is, from the hopes which looked to the final end of time ("eschatology" comes from the Greek, meaning simply "end"). All messianism was eschatology since it looked for a final intervention of God on behalf of his people through the instrument of a Messiah, but not all eschatology was messianic since many expected the new era without any leader but God.

Besides all this, matters continued to develop and to be complicated by the addition of ideas to the eschatological and the messianic hopes. It seems that a major source for these ideas was contact with Iranian (Persian) dualism and certain of its ideas about mediators between the divine and the human. The religion of Iran had looked forward to a time when the world would be purified by fire. This no doubt fostered the Jewish ideas and especially imagery about a total change when God would intervene to bring about the new times. And the other Iranian idea of some sort of a mediator higher than man but lower than God, a quasi-divine figure, also influenced the development of the idea of the Messiah in certain circles, while in others it encouraged speculation about angels.

Thus ideas proliferated and multiplied. It is simply false to say that one picture of the new era, that is, one eschatology, dominated Judaism at the end of the old era, just as within the larger area of eschatology it is false to say that a single picture of the Messiah dominated among those who believed in a Messiah. Just about everyone believed that some new and final intervention of God was on the way, but their ideas about how this was to come about were confused and obscure. Literally hundreds of silhouettes of the new era were drawn. When the new era with its Messiah actually came, he could be seen to fit the main outlines which had been drawn. However, we can hardly say that those who saw the outlines beforehand should have known exactly what was to come.

PART II: PROPHETS

CHAPTER 6. THE NATURE OF PROPHECY

Readings: Is 6; Jer 1; Ezek 2–3; Am 3:3–8; 1 Kgs 17–19, 21; 2 Kgs 1:2–17; 2–10, 13:10–21

The primary meaning of the word prophecy in English is prediction, so that we think of the prophet as one who predicts the future. This is misleading when applied to the Old Testament. It is an exaggeration to say that there was no concern about the future in the Old Testament prophets, since they often speak of what is to come to be, but concern with the future was not their major interest. Essentially the prophet was the man who spoke for Yahweh. He passed on to the people a message which he had received from God. Thus he could speak for Yahweh in the first person. There is even a technical phrase for introducing such words: "thus says Yahweh."

This phrase comes from the diplomatic language of the ancient world. It was the formula which the ambassador of an ancient king used to validate his message. He came to speak not in his own name but to deliver the message confided to him by his lord. Thus the prophets used a formula made vivid by the experience of their time to show that they spoke as ambassadors from Yahweh and not in their own right.[1]

---

[1] Note that later prophets also favor the formula *ne'um yhwh*, "murmur of Yahweh," which, though of a different origin from the messenger formula, expresses exactly the same thing.

How could the prophet make this tremendous claim? To do so validly he must have been specially called by God. This means that typically the prophet's career began with an extraordinary experience. We have information concerning these experiences from four great prophets in Isaiah 6, Jeremiah 1, Ezekiel 1–3, and Amos 3:7–8; 7, where we learn that the call had three essential steps. (1) The prophet had a vision of or audition from Yahweh, wherein (2) Yahweh communicated his word to the prophet, and (3) the prophet was officially commissioned to pass this word to the people. A fourth characteristic may be noted: the commission made the prophet Yahweh's representative even though he was reluctant, as was, for example, Jeremiah. This may seem to invade man's freedom, but Amos 3:7–8 shows that the compulsion involved was not contrary to human nature. It was rather the instinctive reaction of the whole man to a striking experience. In essence, therefore, the prophet claimed to have listened to Yahweh just as an ambassador did to his human king so that he could speak for him. Moreover, these experiences did not end with the initial call which constituted a prophet. They continued throughout the prophet's career, so much so that it is worthy of note when the prophet had to wait for them (e.g., Is 8:16–17; Jer 42:1–7).

Recently there has been a reaction against interest in the psychology of the prophet and more concern for the objective, the verbal forms of the prophetic message itself. This is the result of a certain skepticism about the extraordinary experience of the prophets, skepticism aroused by much of the material from comparative religion used in the effort to understand the prophetic phenomenon and the ecstatic phenomena which accompany prophetism in its primitive forms. The frenzies of the medicine man are an example of this. This is a type of prophetic experience because the frenzied person does claim to speak for the divinity. However, often it is the product of a disturbed personality or of undesirable techniques of psychic manipulation. It does seem somehow demeaning to compare the great prophets of the Old Testament to disturbed personalities. Hence the tendency to deny any sort of extraordinary phenomena connected with biblical prophetism. However, this negative conclusion leaves us no means of understanding the prophetic phenomenon unless we reduce it to a purely natural level, the effect of an extraordinary religious genius or the like. We should rather seek the proper category of experience to which the prophetic phenomena may be compared. This is not the form of ecstasy characteristic of the whirling dervish, but rather higher mystical phenomena which demonstrate that men can have a more direct experience of the divine, an experience indeed unusual but not abnormal. The proper understanding of prophetic phenomena will be reached through a comparison with the great mystics, but theologians must still provide satisfactory analyses of mystical experiences before we can use them to elaborate our understanding of prophetism. So far only a beginning has been made. At least we know that man can have high converse with God.[2]

There is one limitation to the comparison between prophet and mystic. Ordinarily the mystics have great difficulty in verbalizing their experiences so as to communicate them to others. Hence there is always the danger that the communication will not be adequate. It may even be misleading. On the other hand, though the prophets like the mystics received direct communication from God, and though the prophets maintained a remarkable individuality and diversity in the expression of what they learned, in the case of the prophets God guarantees the expression of the experience as well as the experience itself. This had to be, since the message communicated to the prophet was not for himself but officially for the people of God. It was not the prophet's own interpretation of his experience; it was God's own word in the prophet's mouth.

TRUE AND FALSE PROPHETS

We do not understand the full vitality of the prophetic phenomenon if we look at it merely from the point of view imposed on us by the fact that there are sixteen "official" prophetic books in our English Bibles. We know that these books communicate true prophecy because they have been received into the canon of inspired Scripture. Confining ourselves to the listing of books in our Bible gives the impression that this was all the prophecy there was among the Hebrews. Quite apart from the prophets mentioned in the historical rather than the prophetic books, this was not the case at all. In fact, prophets seem to have been at least as common as political speakers in a campaign year. They came in bands of hundreds, and they came as individuals who claimed to speak for Yahweh just as much as the prophets whose names are attached to biblical books. Although they had a very different message.

The problem is a classic one. It is easy enough to claim to speak for God, and it is not hard to work oneself up into a state of exaltation that seems quite extraordinary. In such circumstances, how was one to tell the word of the Lord from mere human words? The men of Old Testa-

---

[2] Johannes Lindblom, *Prophecy in Israel,* has done much to restore proper perspective in this matter.

ment times, confronted by these rival claims, felt the problem acutely. They sought signs that would discern the false prophet from the true. One indication that they noted was the independence of the prophet. Prophets who were too directly dependent upon the kings, for instance, might well lack undivided devotion to God's word (1 Kgs 22:5–38), and a prophet who spoke of good when he was paid and evil when he was not was properly suspect (Mic 3:5). Jeremiah warned against prophets too dependent upon dreams (Jer 23:25–28) as well as those whose message was salvation and only salvation since authentic prophetic tradition was primarily threatening in character (Jer 28:5–9). These touchstones helped eliminate some of the grosser forms of false prophecy, but they are limited. Yahweh's word could come in dreams. (For example, in 1 Sam 3:1–8 Yahweh speaks to Samuel in a dream.) Again, not every true prophecy was an oracle of doom, as in Isaiah 9:2–7 and Jeremiah himself (Jer 30–21). Finally, fanatics can often be very disinterested, at least about payment and the like. They will put up with a great deal for the program upon which they have a fixation.

Hence it was necessary to try to establish more universal norms for judging a prophet's claims. There is Jeremiah's appeal to a basic tradition. Most of the prophets had some words of hope, but it is certainly true that the central element in the preaching of the prophets devoted to Yahwism was the threat of judgment. This is, then, a kind of general norm. Deuteronomy too sets out to establish criteria of wider application. Its first is orthodoxy; a prophet whose words led the people from strict Yahwism could not be true (13:1–5). And, in fact, we shall find that the central character of prophetism is total devotion to Yahweh. And then, of course, the fulfillment of a prediction is a good sign that the prophet speaks truth (18:22). These are useful criteria but they do not solve all the problems. As a matter of fact in the heat of the moment it was almost impossible to pick out the true prophet. Here again the comparison with later mysticism is enlightening. It is extremely difficult to decide where genuine contact with God occurs and where illusion begins, and we know that the Church is very hesitant to decide on the validity of claims to a special revelation. In any event later experience agrees with the Old Testament: orthodoxy is the first test. Paul found it necessary to say: "But even if . . . an angel from heaven should preach to you a gospel contrary to that which we preached to you, let him be accursed" (Col 1:8). This must be so in any community committed to a tradition. Beyond this, it is well to note that the mere fact that a message seems inspiring or timely is not enough to guarantee that it comes from God. In fact, the words of the true prophet were commonly the opposite of inspiring; they were depressing, even defeatist. They often seemed to work against the immediate good of the people of God. Ultimately it was the working out of history that showed what prophet had spoken the truth. The prophets whose vision was verified in history were truly the men of Yahweh, and it was their words, harsh though they often seemed, that worked to build up the people of God. Ultimately prophecy, compelling though it was for the one who experienced God's word, demands faith from the people of God just as does all revelation.

HOW THE PROPHETS TAUGHT

So far all we have said has referred to the word heard by the prophet and relayed to the people. This should alert us to the real nature of the prophetic message. We find it in books, but it began as preaching. The prophet was essentially an orator. He did not hand out notes, he preached God's word, just as the ambassador of a king did not come simply to pass on a letter; that was the job for the postman. Rather he came to speak directly in the king's name. The prophet, therefore, was moved to speak a message in God's name to the people of his time. This implies many things about his manner of speaking and about the way his words turned into the books in which we now find them.

For us, it is the word in writing, the inspired collections we know as the prophetic books, which is the word of God given to us. However, if we are to understand these inspired collections of prophetic sayings for the purposes of theology, it is a great help to understand the original shape of the prophetic messages. This is true in either of the forms in which the word has reached us: (1) The message has been somehow altered by the later writers to meet their special purposes. For example, in Jeremiah 30–31 what were originally oracles of hope about the eventual return of the exiled tribes of the old northern kingdom of Israel have been extended by the editor(s) by the insertion of the name of Judah into the appropriate places. (2) The original saying has been kept unaltered but it has been lumped with others in a collection of sayings. In this case it is often difficult to separate the different units. If we can determine how the saying was put together in the first place it is easier to note the changes which it may have undergone, and this helps to understand its final inspired form in the Bible. When the saying has remained unaltered, a knowledge of the prophet's manner of speaking helps to sort out the

various sayings. As things stand, they are not marked off in our manu-
scripts; yet it is obviously important to the understanding of a discourse
to know where it begins and ends.

How, then, can we work back as near as possible to the originals?
The chief instrument of the modern student for this is a knowledge of
the forms of discourse characteristic of the prophets. A characteristic
form will usually have been an originally separate and unified whole.
Hence the importance of knowing something about these characteristic
forms.

The fundamental form seems to be one derived from the prophet's
basic office. He was Yahweh's ambassador, and he used the formal style
in which the ambassadors of his time delivered their official dispatch:
the reference to their principal, "Thus says King N.," followed by his
message in direct quotation. The prophet simply announced: "Thus says
Yahweh" and went on to relay the divine decree. This is generally called
the *messenger* form.

However, this form was quickly expanded for obvious reasons. Men
wanted to know why Yahweh announced what he did. Hence the prophets
soon began adding an explanation. Typically this came before the quotation from Yahweh. Thus the structure was: explanation, the formal statement "thus says Yahweh," and then the words of the Lord. Since Yahweh's words are almost always a *sentence* passed on his people's conduct,
the whole structure is called the *judgment oracle*. Furthermore, since the
judgment was usually a condemnation, the explanation generally had the
character of an *indictment*. In the classic form of the judgment oracle the
indictment is not attributed expressly to Yahweh. The prophet himself
explains the sentence which is Yahweh's word. However, in calling these
forms "typical" and "classic" we do not mean that all the speeches of
the prophets are in these forms nor that all the prophets used them. A
most significant variation is the presentation of the indictment as well as
the sentence as Yahweh's word.

However, the prophets by and large were anything but formalists. They
burned to communicate the message Yahweh had entrusted to them. They
aimed at effectiveness, not conformity to canons of preaching or the like.
They were ready to use any form familiar to their listeners to move them
and to explain the prophetic message to them, for instance, the love song
(cf. Is 5:1–5) or the funeral dirge (cf. Is 14:4–21). They used these
forms to express the indictments or the sentences which were their message. "Indictment" and "sentence" are, of course, the language of courts

of law. Since Yahweh was judging his people through the prophets, the language is appropriate, but examples like these show how ready the prophets were to use other language in the courtroom atmosphere. Neither were they afraid to emphasize the latter. So they imitated the forms of the law court itself and particularly the covenant lawsuit which invokes creation to witness the reproaches of Yahweh against the Hebrews for breaking the covenant (Mic 6:1-6).

Still, prophetic thought and language did not always center on the courtroom. One example is the oracle of doom which is borrowed from the liturgy. Apparently in times of national danger there were liturgies in which prophets connected with a shrine spoke against those who threatened the nation. The oracle of doom was taken over by the prophets and turned against the nation itself (cf. Am 3:1-2:16). The prophets used other liturgical forms, hymns and songs of thanksgiving (Nah, Hab 3). Another form which the prophets often used has yet another source. This is the admonition or prohibition modeled on the teaching passed on in the schools of the scribes, the Wisdom tradition.

In addition, note that the prophets were not confined to using words. They could express the "word" of Yahweh most forcefully by symbolic acts. When a prophet did something meaningful his action effected what it expressed. Perhaps it was felt to be more effective even than the word which, because it was Yahweh's, was itself efficacious. But a symbolic act such as Ahijah's dividing his cloak to show the division of the kingdom (1 Kgs 11:29-37) was so graphic and so startling that it was far more forceful an expression than mere words. The symbolic acts of the prophets were a solid part of the tradition too. They were never given up. Hosea married a faithless wife, symbol of faithless Israel (Hos 1-3). Isaiah gave his son a portentous name (Is 8:1). Jeremiah's yoke was a vivid sign of coming enslavement (Jer 27-28), and Ezekiel's whole life was full of symbolic actions.

WHAT THE PROPHETS TAUGHT

No one can synthesize adequately the doctrine of the prophets. Had there been an easily definable prophetic doctrine, the whole problem of distinguishing the false prophet from the true would not have arisen. But of course it did. The problem stems in large part from the fact that the prophets were inspired messengers from God and poets in the bargain, each dealing with special situations largely in images and symbols. This is not the stuff of a systematic theology. However, the true prophets shared certain basic attitudes in the face of what was basically a similar situation, and it will help to understand what a prophet was if we note the situation, the attitudes, and the resultant reactions before turning to the details of the doctrines of the various prophets.

The situation was simply one form or another of what is technically called syncretism. This was the effort to include the worship of other gods, the Baals and the rest, with the worship of Yahweh. As we have seen, the conditions of agricultural life in Canaan made this a constant temptation, and many of the kings of Israel and Judah lent their influence to the foreign cults. The prophetic reaction to this was always the same: total rejection. The true prophet was Yahweh's man, and his alone. He fought anything that did not fit with exclusive Yahwism, even when he was an official court prophet and yet had to condemn an erring king (e.g., Nathan in 2 Sam 12:1–15), or when he stood against a crowd of Baalist prophets supported by the political power (e.g., Elijah on Carmel, 1 Kgs 18). In every case the prophet stood for absolute, exclusive devotion to Yahwism.

The way this dedication was exercised might vary a good deal. The earlier prophets resorted to political means to further Yahwism, and this could mean considerable violence (Elijah on Carmel; Elisha and the revolution of Jehu, 2 Kgs 9). Later prophets seem almost to have reversed the process. With Isaiah the renunciation of the political route to a pure Yahwism is complete. He demands perfect trust in the Lord alone (7:1–9; 28:14–22), and Jeremiah actually advocates submission to the pagan enemy (Jer 27:4–8). But all these are simply means to the single overriding object: total fidelity to Yahweh.

Because of the ever-recurring demand of the prophetic books for the worship of Yahweh alone, it is easy to lose sight of another aspect of the central concern of the prophets. This is a deep interest in justice in the broad sense of proper treatment of one's neighbor. The prophets were the angry defenders of the poor and the oppressed. This is not merely an addition to their preoccupation with the commandment: "Thou shalt not have false gods before me." It flowed from this basic principle, for Yahweh was a God of justice, concerned with his people. Hence it was infidelity to him to violate justice (Hos 4:1–2). An unjust man cannot be a true devotee of a supremely just God.

The things which the prophets condemned were closely connected with institutions. The shrines (e.g., "the sin of Jeroboam" at Dan and Bethel) were the places where one put other gods before Yahweh, that is, accumulated idols and pagan symbols and performed devotions to them.

The palace often fostered syncretism, and it was a prime example of injustice: Ahab and Jezebel stole a commoner's vineyard by engineering his judicial murder (1 Kgs 21:1–16), and Jehoiakim preferred embellishing his palace through dishonest gain to administering justice (Jer 22:13–17). Amos even links the two institutions together as objects of condemnation (3:13–15). It might have seemed the logical step to condemn the institutions as such, but the prophets themselves do not indulge in the classic confrontation: the prophetic against the institutional. No one was readier to condemn the abuse of institutions than the prophets, but they lived by a tradition which they knew survived only in its institutions. Hence they condemn false worship and empty worship, but they fiercely demand a Temple with true worship (Ezek 40–48; Haggai; Mal 1:6–14). Equally, the monarchy is part of their theology. As we shall see, not every prophet is an enthusiast for the Davidids, but after Isaiah Davidic messianism was a *locus classicus* in prophetic theology, and every prophet has his promise about him who is to come.

The doctrinal unity of the prophets, then, is very simple: basically they call for commitment to Yahweh no matter what this demands. One had to forgo the attractions of the sensuous fertility cults. One must never use another, especially the poor and defenseless, for his own enrichment. One had to trust Yahweh when all human prudence cried out that he should seek the strong battalions. A simple doctrine, but not an easy one.

Not so many years ago it would have been necessary to explain and defend the pre-exilic prophets' attitude toward cult. The older critical school held that they proposed an ethical monotheism, an individualist religion devoid of liturgical practices. It is, in fact, easy to find prophetic condemnation of a false view that cult was a kind of magic ritual which automatically appeased God. The God of the prophets did indeed demand obedience before sacrifices: "though you multiply your prayers, I will not listen; your hands are full of blood. Wash yourselves; make yourselves clean . . . cease to do evil . . ." (Is 1:15–16). However, texts like these are attacks on a false view, not a condemnation of cult as such, and scholars now recognize this.

The bases for this new, correct idea of the relation of prophet to cult are many. For one thing, there is the fact that the bands of prophets of earlier times had their centers at the great shrines, and they were not men to associate themselves with abominations. Then there is good evidence that certain of our prophetic books (Nahum, Joel, perhaps Habakkuk) are actually the products of official liturgical ceremonies. Once more, this is hardly compatible with a total opposition between prophecy and cult. Also many of the great prophets, among them Jeremiah, Ezekiel, perhaps Hosea, were from the priestly class, and Ezekiel especially thought in priestly or cultic terms. Finally, the very Isaiah who could speak so strongly against a corrupt cult saw his inaugural vision and received his commission as a prophet in terms borrowed from the concepts of the Temple and its liturgy. This is but an outline of the massive evidence now available to show that the prophet had no disagreement with the cult as such but only with its abuses. In fact, no prophet imagines a religion without a cult.[3]

THE BACKGROUND OF HEBREW PROPHECY

The prophetic phenomenon is not confined to the revealed religion of the Bible. Even the most primitive religions manifest some form of prophetism which claims to speak for the divinity in virtue of some direct revelation. Often enough the prophet is less one called by the divinity than one who can call upon the divinity as need be. Prophecy is more or less a seeking of oracles, a process of divination. Even this is not foreign to the Old Testament. (Cf. 2 Kgs 3:15: Elisha works himself up to receiving a message by means of music.)

In the ancient Near East itself Israel made no exclusive claim to prophecy: 1 Samuel 6:2–9 and Numbers 22–24 accept non-Israelite prophets without question. As early as the eighteenth century B.C. there were prophets among the Amurrites at Mari (remote collateral antecedents of the Hebrews) called *maḫḫu,* a name which emphasizes the idea of frenzy. However, these prophets could speak like the noblest of Hebrew prophets: "Thus says Adad: am I not Adad . . . who put [the king] on the throne? . . . just as I put him on the throne, I can take the city . . . out of his hands. If he does not make the [required] offering . . . I can take what I gave, but if he does what I wish, throne upon throne I will give him." Then we find frenzied prophets in Phoenician Byblos about 1100 B.C., and the frenzied behavior of the Baalist prophets at Carmel (1 Kgs 18) is solid evidence for the continuation of this type of prophecy among Israel's neighbors. Assyrian records show a Philistine prophet advising his king at the same time that Isaiah was doing this in Judah. Thus Hebrew prophecy fits into the cultural patterns of the ancient Near East. It is significant that all these references to prophecy are related to

---

[3] On the prophets and the cult see A. R. Johnson, *The Cult Prophet in Ancient Israel* (2nd ed. Cardiff: University of Wales, 1962).

the activity of kings. So also among the Hebrews prophets began to appear close to the beginning of the monarchy, and though there were a few prophets in the time after the Israelite monarchy, prophecy as a vital element in the life of the people practically disappeared with the monarchy. In this as in so many things the Hebrew people lived fully in the cultural context of their time. Characteristically God made use of the human means most easily understandable to them as a vehicle for his revelation, and when prophecy was no longer a readily understood and no longer an acceptable institution in the Mediterranean world — roughly, that is, when Hellenism began to dominate that world — he ceased using it among his people.[4]

PROPHECY IN HEBREW HISTORY

Understood in this way, the place of prophecy in Old Testament revelation is an excellent illustration of the close connection between the progress of history and revelation. It should make obvious the need for some historical background if we wish to understand the prophets of Israel. To take the Bible at face value men like Abraham and Moses were prophets (cf. Gen 20:7; Dt 34:10), for they were close to God, and they received revelation for all the people. These were the functions of later prophets, and it was entirely natural that later writers give them this title. Actually prophetism proper begins only late in the period of the Judges. 1 Samuel presents it as an established institution, settled enough to be recognized as legitimate but so new that it had not as yet its own proper name. In those days a prophet could be called "man of God" (1 Sam 9:6), or a seer (ro'eh or hozeh, literally "see-er," one who sees; ibid., 9:9). Only later was the descriptive word, "prophet," (Hebrew nabî', "one spoken to [by God]," or "one who communicates [for God]," 1 Sam 10:10) adopted as a fixed term for the prophet. "Man of God" is obviously a more general name. It was applied to anyone who had a special relationship to God. "Seer" also was not entirely appropriate. A man like Samuel received revelations from God (1 Sam 9:50). He anointed kings (1 Sam 9:15–17; 10:1; 16:1–13), and he told the king that God has rejected him (13:11–14). These are functions befitting the noblest of prophets. However, the seer was also consulted about trivial matters such as finding lost donkeys,

---

[4] See chap. 1, n. 1, and John Gray, "The Period and Office of Isaiah in the Light of a New Assyrian Tablet," Expository Times 63 (1951–1952), pp. 263–265, on prophecy outside the Bible.

thus joining a more numerous and humbler class, the readers of signs and casters of horoscopes and the rest.

However, the prophet quickly assumed his own distinctive character. What first struck men was his exotic behavior. This was the frenzy when it was said that the spirit or the hand of God had seized the prophet (1 Sam 10:6, 10; 9:18–24) or even overpowered him (2 Kgs 2:16). When the spirit did not move, the prophets had means of inducing ecstasy: music (2 Kgs 3:15), dancing ("going down" to the music of harps in 1 Sam 10:5), concentrated meditation (1 Kgs 18:42), perhaps even blows or cutting oneself (1 Kgs 20:25, 38–41, provided it is a scar which identifies the prophet). A further important characteristic of the early prophets was that they acted in groups, the so-called prophetic schools. This is how they first appear in Samuel, and the stories of Elijah especially and of Elisha from the ninth century B.C. indicate that the bands of prophets flourished. They seem to have had their fixed customs. They gathered around cult centers like Gilgal and Bethel. They addressed their leaders as "Lord" or "Father" (2 Kgs 2:3; 6:21). They had a special costume (2 Kgs 1:8). They received the necessities of life, in rather short supply it appears, because they were members of these bands (2 Kgs 4).

When we characterize the early prophets as being ecstatics and members of well-defined bands, we must not mistake this for an exclusive definition. Nathan, David's constant advisor, is always called a prophet, but he is not a member of a group nor does he show any signs of frenzied activity. Other prophets like Micah ben Jimla work alone.

However, the great thing about the prophet was always that he was the bearer of God's word, and this is indicated by the very name, *nabî'*, which quickly became the standard designation of the prophet, as we have just seen. The prophet was an important figure because he brought Yahweh's own word to the people. This prophetic word, precisely because it stemmed from God, was felt to be more than mere forecast or admonition or direction. It was in itself efficacious. It brought about what it said. This belief is indicated by 1 Kings 22:8, where the prophet is attacked because his prophecy warns of ill success. Advice against a trap is reason for gratitude, not hatred, unless it is somehow the advice itself which causes the trouble. Even more striking is 1 Kings 17:1: Elijah's word alone will undo the drought, as though the prophet had control of the weather.[5]

---

[5] On the efficacious word of the Prophet see Gerhard von Rad, *Old Testament Theology* II (New York: Harper and Row, 1965), pp. 89–94, and C. Stuhlmueller, C.P., *The Prophets and the Word of God* (Notre Dame, Fides, 1966), pp. 19–62.

It is characteristic that the first important prophet, Nathan, was a court prophet. As a matter of fact the Old Testament prophets are always closely connected with the Hebrew kings. This is partly due to the fact that the author of the Deuteronomic History saw a recurring rhythm of prophecy and fulfillment as the articulating factor in the history of the monarchy. Hence he had a special interest in the words of the prophets. However, prophets from Nathan through Jeremiah are closely concerned with the royal policies. Prophecy and monarchy were bound tightly together. This is understandable enough.

First of all, the Hebrew kings normally had the approval of a prophet, whether this was because the king was the legitimate successor of David to whom Nathan's promise had been given, or because another prophet had proclaimed him or his family God's new choice to be king in the northern kingdom of Israel.

Besides, as in all kingdoms of the era, prophets were a normal source of counsel for the Hebrew kings, members, as it were, of the cabinet. Not all prophets, however, were officials of this sort. Elijah, for example, certainly was not. Neither were the men who have left prophetic books. Even so, the kings had plenty of prophets who were their own men. In 1 Kings 22:6 the king of Israel assembled as many as four hundred (a round number, to be sure, but surely indicative of a crowd). Moreover, the Hebrew kings turned for advice to men outside their regular retinue, men like Micah ben Jimla and Elisha earlier, and later to Isaiah and Jeremiah.

Another interesting thing about Hebrew prophecy is the connection between it and the time of troubles. The first prophets flourished when the Philistine attacks forced the foundation of a Hebrew monarchy. So also a century and more after the foundation of the monarchy. The kingdom founded by David had split in two, and the larger of the Hebrew kingdoms, Israel, seemed to flourish. It was most prosperous and powerful. However, the prosperity was paid for by foreign entanglements which carried with them a grave threat to the Yahwist religion. Furthermore, it was a time of constant war. It is against this background of war and idolatry that the time of Elijah and Elisha must be seen as a time of troubles.

There is the same intriguing connection between the times of troubles and the prophets in the case of those men who have left collections of sayings as prophetic books. Thus the earliest of them, Amos and Hosea, appear about 750 B.C. when the aggressive Assyrians threatened a corrupt land. Amos the Judean shepherd appeared in Israel to warn that the seemingly prosperous society of Israel was rotten and in danger. So too his younger contemporary, Hosea, an Israelite and perhaps a professional *nabî'* connected with a cult center,[6] actually lived through the turmoil which threatened, though he did not, it seems, experience the final destruction of Samaria by the Assyrians in 722 B.C. He did see one ephemeral king succeed another in Israel as its society cracked under its own corruption and Assyrian pressure. There was even fratricidal war with Judah which led to the first intervention of the Assyrian and the loss of the ancient Hebrew lands of Galilee and Gilead in 733 B.C. All this Hosea saw and interpreted as a punishment upon the people because they had been faithless and had worshiped the Baals along with Yahweh.

At the time when the Assyrians were destroying Israel they made Judah a vassal of their empire. Then for years they were on the march in Palestine, even laying siege to Jerusalem in 701 B.C. It was in these violent times that the first great prophet preached in Judah. This was Isaiah. Certain aspects of style and his concern for social justice demonstrate the influence of Amos. Thus we learn that the great prophets, marked individuals though they were, did not stand alone. They stood in a prophetic tradition. Contemporary with Isaiah the Judean Micah also prophesied. He was concerned to defend the common people against the injustice of their lords.

After the turmoil at the end of the eighth century the surviving kingdom of Judah enjoyed more than a half century of quiet under Manasseh because he was utterly subservient to Assyria. Moreover he flouted the central command of Yahwism by the worst idolatry (2 Kgs 21:4–6). Nevertheless, it was a time of quiet and no prophets are mentioned.

In the last quarter of the seventh century things changed. The once invincible Assyrians were on the decline. As new powers struggled to replace them Judah was free to engage in a national revival, as we have seen. King Josiah (c. 640–609 B.C.) attempted to reconstitute the kingdom of David and to establish a pure Yahwism in all the expanded kingdom. Strangely, this attempt to return to the past corresponded to a wave of antiquarian interest all over the ancient world, as is illustrated by the archaizing art of the period. It was a time when men sought the authentic ways of old. Doubtless this urge contributed to the political and religious reform of Judah.

If the decline of Assyria was a time of opportunity, it was also a new time of troubles. The empire which had maintained peace had been

---

[6] On Hosea's connection with the cult see Henri Cazelles, "The Problem of the Kings in Os. viii, 4," *CBQ* 11 (1949), pp. 14–25.

broken up and the would-be successors fought for the spoils. The great powers imposed their will and their puppet kings on Judah. There were revolts and sieges until finally in 587 B.C. the Babylonians, who had come to be the dominant power in western Asia, ran out of patience and put an end to Judah as a kingdom.

Once again, during all this upheaval there was a great resurgence of prophetism among the Hebrews. The prophecy of Zephaniah may refer to the invasion of the ancient Near East by Scythians about 630–625 B.C. which unsettled the whole area. The book of Nahum seems to be a prophetic liturgy celebrating the fall of the Assyrian capital of Nineveh in 612 B.C., and the book of Habakkuk may be a similar text relating to the same occasion, although this is less sure. Most important of all was Jeremiah. He lived through all this tumultuous time, and his prophecies refer to all the great events which affected Judah. He seems to have taken part in Josiah's reform. Like Isaiah he was a conscious follower of the prophetic tradition, he used the language of Hosea in his condemnation of deserting Yahweh for the Baals, and he excoriated the kings for their injustice and folly. He was a part of the violent political scene in the last years of Judah. He realized that Yahweh had given the land over to the Babylonians as instruments of divine punishment. Hence he called fearlessly for submission to this divine will even when the anti-Babylonian party threatened his life.

After the final fall of Jerusalem the prophets faced a new situation. No longer were they the advisors of Hebrew kings There was no longer a nation in the political sense. The elite, the nobility, the learned, and the priests, the artisans, had all gone into exile in Babylon, and it was to them that the great exilic prophets Ezekiel and Deutero-Isaiah (the prophet whose sayings are recorded in Isaiah 40–55) actually worked in Babylon. This mere fact was revolutionary. The ancients tended to conceive of a divinity as tied to a particular place (2 Kgs 17:15–29 is a good illustration of this). It was already a great breakthrough to realize that Yahwism was alive in Babylon as in Jerusalem. It was the task of the religious leaders to keep this truth before the people, to maintain their religious identity while scattered among strangers.

The older of the exilic prophets, Ezekiel, actually was a deportee. He was a member of an important priestly family and as a youth had been taken to Babylon in the first exile in 597 B.C. Like his predecessors he teaches that the fall of Jerusalem is divinely ordained punishment. Nevertheless, God is still with his people, and in elaborate visions the prophet sees the divine presence symbolically leaving Jerusalem and coming to the people in exile in Babylon. On the other hand, Deutero-Isaiah stands at the end of the exilic period. He was stimulated by knowledge that the Persian Cyrus was destined to conquer Babylon. This he did in 539 B.C., breaking up the Babylonian empire, and allowing the Hebrews to return to Jerusalem. Once again a time of violent change is a time for prophecy which explains this change as a new exile and a new exodus, a new saving of Yahweh's people.

After the return to Judah the great problem was to form anew a national life around the cult of Yahweh in Jerusalem. The proponents of restoration had to struggle against the opposition of the Samarians from outside as well as face apathy on the part of the people in Judah. The prophets Haggai and Zechariah addressed themselves to this situation. They proclaimed Yahweh's wish for the restored Temple and cult. Significantly they also proclaimed that a full restoration must involve a king of the Davidic line.

When the Judeans had finally managed to rebuild the Temple and the city of Jerusalem, they established themselves as a self-governing province in the Persian empire, and there came a kind of pause in the long and varied history of the Old Testament people. Judah was a backwater. The people survived and worshiped Yahweh in tranquility. And in this tranquility prophecy ceased.

STORIES ABOUT PROPHETS

We have already made mention of many prophets who appear as figures in the history of the monarchy, not as men who have left books bearing their names. Often we know little about them, but this does not mean they were unimportant. Samuel and Nathan, Ahijah and Elisha were makers of kings. Others were advisors to kings, others led important bands of prophets who were vigorous defenders of pure Yahwism.

We cannot learn a great deal about these men in detail, but neither should we ignore them. They help us understand what prophecy was, and properly studied the stories about them reveal a great deal concerning the handing down of revelation. By far the most important are the stories of Elijah and Elisha. The former is called a "man of God." Except in 1 Kings 18:36 he is a solitary figure, unlike the prophets of his time, who were members of groups. In contrast, Elisha is the very model of the father of the prophetic band, concerned for the welfare of his followers and for the prophetic state in general. But different as the men were, their stories have much in common.

Our source of information about Elijah is a cycle of popular stories in 1 Kings 17–19; 21 and 2 Kings 1:2–17. The stories do not give us a complete biography of the prophet, but as far as they go they are largely a consistent and unified picture. Certain elements are easy enough to separate out: 1 Kings 21:21–26 seems to be a commentary added to the earlier texts. The story of the resurrection of the woman's son in 17:17–24 is similar to a story belonging to the cycle of Elisha (2 Kgs 4:18–37). Finally 2 Kings 1:9–16 does not advance the story and is just the sort of wonder tale which the popular imagination loves to attach to notable figures.

It is worthwhile to note this analysis with some care, for it is a good sample of the way we can distinguish secondary material in our sources, and we have time only for one sample. I Kings 21:21–26 looks like a commentary on 21:19 because it develops the verse without adding anything new, and it concludes with the sort of generality clear to commentators. The resurrection story in 1 Kings 17:17–24 is not closely attached to its content, for it has nothing to do with the drought which is the central feature of 1 Kings 17–18. The influence from the Elisha story appears in the title "mistress of the house," which fits the "rich woman" of 2 Kings 4:8, not the wretched peasant of 1 Kings 17. Such are the marks of additions to basic material: sudden, unnecessary changes of style and inconsistency with a context and/or unlikely similarity with comparable material. By noting these we can separate mixed materials not just here but in the prophetic books and, indeed, the rest of the Bible.

If we use these techniques as indicated on the Elijah cycle we can separate out the additions. Then we have a consistent story of a great prophet who appears to warn Israel and to condemn the attack upon the Yahwist religion and its prophets led by Ahab of Israel's queen Jezebel. He begins this courageous attack upon the powers by predicting a three-year drought because Yahweh is offended. During this time the prophet must retire to Phoenicia, but then he returns to challenge the prophets of Baal in the episode on Mount Carmel where 450 Baalist prophets cannot move their god, while Elijah alone brings about the intervention of Yahweh. This success makes the prophet even more hateful to Jezebel. He must flee. Now under divine direction he appears as the new Moses who goes to the desert, to the holy mountain of Horeb to receive the revelation of Yahweh and comes back to lead the people, making kings and religious leaders (1 Kgs 19:15–16). In the two separate episodes in 1 Kings 21 and 2 Kings 1 Elijah remains in character: he bravely reproves the royal couple's judicial murder of the innocent Naboth and he condemns Ahaziah, Ahab's successor, for his idolatry.

This cycle of stories has certainly been stylized. Elijah is the lonely hero who by himself opposes the mighty power of the kings. He is a new Moses. However, this is not the whole story. The essence of Elijah's story is consistent and believable. Then other sources report the revolution of Jehu (2 Kgs 9), Ahab's building a temple to the Baal of Tyre (2 Kgs 10:18–19) and the murder of Naboth (2 Kgs 9:25–26). The description of the activities of the prophets of the Baals on Carmel fits what we know of that cult. We have, then, a basis of history filled out and explained according to the norms of popular oral literature. Hence the stylization (hero) and the symbolism (new Moses). That was how one explained things to ordinary people.

And what can we learn from it? First, there is the basic prophetic idea: total dedication to God. The prophet is ready to proclaim this message despite the gravest dangers. There is even theological subtlety. God is not present in the hurricane nor the earthquake nor the fire. These were traditional signs of the divine presence in ancient Hebrew religion. However, they are natural phenomena and therefore too easily associated with the nature worship of Baalism. Therefore, they are rejected to preserve the purity of Yahwism.

Then there is that other aspect of biblical religion. Commitment to Yahweh means a commitment to all that is his, and that means to one's neighbors. Hence the unwavering demands of justice: the rights of a man to his family land should be proof even against the desires of a king. It is interesting in all this to note the utter singleness of purpose of the prophet. From the purely material point of view Ahab was one of the most successful of Hebrew kings. For the Elijah cycle this is entirely beside the point. A king of the chosen people was a true king if he was true to Yahweh. No matter what else he did, if he failed in that central duty, he failed entirely.

From the strictly literary point of view the stories in 2 Kings 2–10; 13:10–21 about the chosen successor of Elijah, Elisha (1 Kgs 19:16), are rather different in style from the Elijah cycle. There are, for one thing, many more stories about the prophet's miracles (2 Kgs 2:19–25; 4:1–7; 4:38–44; 6:1–7). These obviously reflect delight in the strange and marvelous. Of a somewhat different type — longer and serious —

Elisha restores a young man to life (2 Kgs 4:8–37 and 8:1–7; the separation is the work of an editor) and cures a Syrian general of leprosy (2 Kgs 5). A different sort of tale shows Elisha deeply immersed in political life, unlike Elijah. These are the sober tales about Elisha's activities during the siege of Samaria (6:24–27) and in Jehu's overthrow of the dynasty of Omri (2 Kgs 9). There is nonetheless a difference between these two narratives. The account of the siege in Samaria is circumstantial, but the political aspects are there simply in order to illustrate the prophet's greatness. The story of Jehu's revolution is something else again. The central interest is on the royal history, and the prophet appears simply in function of his important role in this history.

Thus we have several quite different major types of story in the Elisha cycle, not a basic cycle with additions as with Elijah, and the picture is not quite so clear and consistent in the case of the earlier prophet. The numerous short miracle stories betray the common interest in the marvelous. The two longer stories illustrating Elisha's special powers show an interest in composing a good narrative more or less for its own sake. A third sort of story is actually more concerned with the history of the kingdom in which the prophet appeared as one actor among many.

Still, the doctrinal content of the Elisha cycle is to a great extent like that of the Elijah story. Elisha is truly Elijah's successor in the struggle against the paganizing tendency fostered by Ahab and his successors. If Elisha is less obviously concerned with social justice than Elijah in the Naboth incident, we do find him concerned about the welfare of his prophets and others. It must be admitted that there is less grandeur in Elisha. He upholds pure Yahwism but at less personal cost. Inevitably this fact, combined with his involvement in politics, makes his Yahwism seem somewhat more narrow and particularist. However, we must not judge this devotion to the national religion of Israel as something narrow and ungenerous according to our modern standards. In the circumstances of the times it is hard to see how a preoccupation with pure Yahwism could be anything but exclusive and nationalist. Religion was so mixed into all aspects of ancient life, even the political and commercial, that it seemed impossible to avoid contamination by false religious ideas except by avoiding many of the contacts with the foreign, contacts which seem normal to us.

THE "WRITING" PROPHETS

Elijah and Elisha are but the most notable of the prophets whom we know only through the historical books of the Old Testament. There were many more like them, valiant fighters for true religion, advisors and admonitors of kings, defenders of the people. Men of this type worked as long as there was a monarchy among the Hebrews. But we must turn to the so-called classic or writing prophets. These are simply those men who have given their names to prophetic books of the Old Testament. These books are divided into the four major prophets, Isaiah through Daniel, and the twelve minor prophets, Hosea through Malachi in our Bible. Major and minor have nothing to do with importance or greatness. They simply refer to the relative size of the books. Even the number of these prophets is really a matter of convention. Among the major prophets the book of Isaiah actually contains the words of two or more significant prophetic figures: Isaiah 1–39 belong to the original Isaiah; 40–55 are the work of a great, unnamed prophet (customarily called Deutero-Isaiah) who worked during the Babylonian exile almost two centuries later; and the last chapters of Isaiah stem from a post-exilic source. It is unlikely that these last sayings come from a single prophet. Rather, we have a kind of anthology of prophetic sayings from the post-exilic period.

Besides all this, Daniel is not really prophecy at all. It comes from an age much later than the period of the prophets, the second century before Christ, and it is a form of the apocalyptic literature characteristic of that era. Apocalyptic differs from prophecy in its style. Typically, prophecy was delivered and recorded in short, usually poetic speeches. On the other hand, apocalyptic uses much longer literary forms, and while it is highly imaginative it is usually prose, not poetry, in form. More important, its conceptual world is not that of prophecy. It is concerned with the marvelous and with the remote, indefinite future. It usually is a message of consolation to a suffering folk in the form of a prediction of a future intervention in which God will bring to an end the course of history and himself set up the perfect age to come. This easily leads to determinism. The good can only suffer patiently. Men are not looked upon as instruments through whom God guides the course of history. Rather, superhuman forces necessarily govern the world until a force on their level, God, comes to put them down. All this is quite unlike prophecy but a little study will show it is typical of the book of Daniel.

Among the minor prophets the book of Jonah is quite special. It does not record the sayings of a prophet; it tells the tale of a man called to speak for Yahweh who refused because the message was one of salvation for non-Jews. The tale teaches a moral, namely, that Yahweh is concerned for all men and not simply for the Jews. Thus it emphasizes an important doctrine and we shall look to it, even though it is not prophetic in the strict sense, because it is short enough to allow consideration of it here. However, in a book concerned with prophetism we cannot deal with anything so extensive and important as Daniel and apocalyptic.

Furthermore, we shall deal with the prophets in their historical order, and not in the conventional literary order.

The "Writing" Prophets

Amos Hosea	c. 760–730 B.C.
Isaiah Micah	c. 740–700 B.C.
Jeremiah Zephaniah Nahum Habakkuk	c. 630–585 B.C.
Ezekiel	c. 593 B.C.
Deutero-Isaiah (Is 40–55)	c. 539 B.C.
Haggai Zechariah 1–8 Trito-Isaiah (Is 56–66)	c. 520–500 B.C.
Malachi	c. 515–450 B.C.
[Jonah]	c. 440–400 B.C.
Joel Obadiah	After 400 B.C.
[Isaiah 34–35 (Lesser Apocalypse)] [Isaiah 24–27 (Greater Apocalypse)] [Daniel]	Late 3rd–2nd century B.C.

Furthermore, it must be emphasized that the difference between these prophets and the older prophets of whom we have record in the historical books is largely the accidental fact that we have more or less extensive collections of their words in place of mere stories about their lives. All true prophets were essentially the messengers of God, and it is, strictly speaking, accidental to this central function that in some instances their words have been preserved in the Bible and in others only their names and their activities.

Therefore, there is a certain superficial accuracy in the name, "writing prophets," in that it calls attention to the relative importance of the record of their words. However, it is an unfortunate misnomer. Even long after Amos the prophets were not and did not profess to be writers. They were preachers who proclaimed God's word aloud to their contemporaries. They did not produce prophetic books, and many true prophets in these later times (e.g., Huldah, 2 Kgs 22:14–20) never gave rise to prophetic books. What we have in the books of the prophets are really collections of the short sermons of these preachers.

The prophets did not themselves ordinarily write down their words, nor did they indulge in long discourses. Their sayings were rather short, pithy, and poetic so that they were easily remembered. Thus they were first preserved in the memories of the devoted hearers, the so-called "disciples," of the prophet, although this, of course, does not rule out the noting down of this or that speech. In fact Isaiah and Jeremiah arranged to have some of their oracles noted down for more or less immediate purposes. Gradually and only much later these fugitive notes and memories of the prophet's words were collected.

Usually this process began with the collection of the sayings of a prophet which concerned a single topic, for example the condemnations of idolatry in Jeremiah 2. Often, however, such collections did not share so much a common topic as certain merely verbal similarities, key words and the like, which served as aids toward remembering the sayings, for example, the repeated occurrence of "in that day" in Isaiah 7:18–24 or "Woe" in Isaiah 5:8–12, 18–23. Evidently the governing factor in such collections was ease in memorizing. The same factor kept them short. Often we can actually discern small collections which have been incorporated into our larger prophetic books. These are marked, for instance, by headings within the book, for instance, Isaiah 2:1 and Jeremiah 23:9. Then many prophetic sayings were passed on by themselves and not as parts of the larger collection.

Besides the actual words of the prophets, men preserved the stories about the prophets themselves. These are usually classified as *first person narratives,* that is, stories by the prophet about himself, and *third person narratives,* reports about the prophet. Gradually all these various materials, collections of oracles, fugitive sayings, stories about the prophet, which the tradition attributed to a certain one of the prophets were gathered together until our present prophetic books were formed. Generally this was done in a quite haphazard manner. Certain of the prophetic books such as Isaiah, Ezekiel, and Jeremiah in the LXX show a kind of order according to a large scheme: first come threats against Israel, then threats against the Gentiles, and finally oracles of consolation for Israel. Even here, however, this scheme is very loosely followed, and in most of the other books there is little evidence of a general plan. Thus we cannot interpret the prophetic books as though they were originally intended to be read as large literary wholes even though they appear to be such because of the way many of our modern Bibles are printed. In fact, to interpret prophecy correctly we have seen that we must isolate the basic units of discourse which have been gathered into our present books. Then these units must be interpreted for themselves or by the light of any internal links that they show to a given literary or historical context. Once again, this fact about the history and interpretation of the prophetic books must not obscure the basic facts about inspiration and therefore about the books as theological sources. It is the prophetic word as edited, arranged, and even added to by these writers which is the inspired word of the prophets for us, since this word reaches us only as writing. We must, therefore, keep clear in our minds that there are two levels of prophetic inspiration. First of all the prophet is inspired to speak for Yahweh; only later was someone inspired to gather together and write down his words for us. This latter is a scriptural inspiration. In fact, so gradual was the growth of most of the prophetic books that several persons must have participated in the inspiration, that is, the divinely directed production of books which it took centuries to complete.[7]

_____

[7] For a study of the complicated process by which the prophetic (and other) books were produced see D. J. McCarthy, S.J., "Society, Personality, and Inspiration," *Theological Studies* 24 (1963), pp. 553–576, (= *Theology Digest* 13[1965], pp. 177–184). Also in *Modern Biblical Studies* (Milwaukee: The Bruce Publishing Co., 1967).

CHAPTER 7. AMOS AND HOSEA

Readings: Am; Hos

Before going on to particulars, there are a few general matters one must keep in mind all through this discussion. One is the problem of the text. Do we have the true text of a prophet? Is it in its proper place? Does it come from the prophet in question at all? In discussing the doctrine of a prophet one must answer such questions. The doctrine may be inspired, as it is in a truly biblical text, no matter what its origins, but if it is not this prophet's it does not enlighten us on *his* doctrine. Obviously, we cannot discuss all the niceties of textual criticism in a book like this. In almost every case the basic texts used here in discussing a prophet are those that scholars generally accept as his. Where this is not the case we will argue briefly the reasons for using the disputed text.

Second, we have noted that the prophetic doctrine cannot be synthesized. It is too varied, too intuitive, too much bound up with symbols, for this. However, it does not help to say this and then wander off into trackless thickets of data. We ask the same basic questions of each prophet: (1) What particular circumstances in his life and times affected his message? (2) What was the special point of view from which he saw the divine? (3) What demands did he make, usually as a result of his special perception of God? (4) What kind of future hope did he offer his people? (5) What was his attitude toward the Gentiles? It will help if the reader keeps this organization in mind as we approach each prophet.

AMOS

Amos was a country man from Tekoa, a small place in the hills some twelve miles south of Jerusalem. He is sometimes said to have been one of the dispossessed who hired themselves out for a day's work if and when they could get it. However, his command of the Hebrew language implies an education which was beyond that of the lowest classes. He must rather have been a substantial peasant holding family land. However, he was not of the ruling classes, nor was he wealthy. This background contributed to his shock at seeing the luxury of Samaria, where powerful men built themselves ornate palaces with money gained by the oppression of the poor (Am 3:15–4:1).

Despite his Judean background Amos was led to preach in Israel and almost all that he says has to do with its affairs. He knows of Israel's wars with Damascus and of the threat of Assyria (6:2 refers to an Assyrian conquest opening the way into Syria); still his doctrine is Judean. He accepts the primacy of the Temple on Zion (1:2) and the tradition of the Davidic promise (9:11–12). Why then the exclusive concern with Israel? Probably because it had gone the farthest astray and therefore had the greater need of God's word.

In any event Amos is remarkably single-minded. He preaches Yahweh's condemnation of Israel because of the social injustice flourishing in the prosperous kingdom. This is not to say that he is monotonous. His preaching is powerful and vivid. For instance, he involves his audience immediately in his preaching through questions. Only when their interest has thus been aroused does he supply them with answers (cf. 3:3–8; 5:25–27; etc.). His masterpiece is surely 1:3–2:3 plus 2:6–16 — the oracle against Judah in 2:4–5 is an interpolation — which is a series of oracles against nations. One after another he ticks off the crimes of Israel's principal enemies. Six have been covered, and the seventh has the climactic place of dishonor. One can hear the audience's expectant murmur: Which enemy will suffer the supreme condemnation? A pause — and the answer is Israel herself. The prophet has taken a favorite oracular form and turned it against the chosen people who, especially favored, are especially guilty! Amos likes this shock technique; he repeats it in 5:18

with the warning that the day of the Lord "meant judgment, not vindication." His language too is vivid, if not gentle: the guilty women of Samaria are "cows," and their coming enslavement is brutally pictured (4:1–3).

Amos was a visionary. He himself describes what was revealed to him (". . . the Lord God showed me . . .") in 7:1–9; 8:1–3; 9:1–4. These may be his inaugural visions, his call. At any rate they illustrate an important prophetic function, intercession, which can delay (8:3; 6) but not set aside the judgment of a faithless people. Finally, a third-person account of Amos' difficulties at the royal shrine of Bethel finishes the biographical content of the book and shows admirably the prophet's courage (7:10–17).[1]

THE GOD OF JUSTICE

We have, then, a poet of vivid but rather harsh power, a man of courage, a fanatic for justice. What can we learn from all of this? What does Amos tell us about God and man's relation to God? For one thing Amos gives us some information about the nature of prophecy and so about how God works his revelation. Emphatically, God's word will be proclaimed; the prophet can hardly refuse his vocation. Yet God respects his prophet's personality, as appears in the highly personal style in a prophet like Amos. God does not destroy what he was; he remains the peasant with his vigorous and sometimes earthy style.

With this God who makes irrevocable demands and yet respects man Amos opens a new aspect of the divine for us. However, beyond any doubt the point of emphasis in Amos is that of God's justice. His words spoken through the mouth of Amos are almost entirely concerned with those sins which disrupt the proper relationship between men. It is because men have failed in this basic requirement that they stand under divine judgment. Thus in the great series of oracles against nations the prophet is largely concerned with crimes against society. Most often he condemns unjust war (1:3b; 1:11b; 1:13b; 2:3), but other injustices are noted: driving a people into exile (1:6b), enslaving men, and violation of contract (1:9b). These are crimes committed by a whole nation. They show that God expects the same morality from a people as he does from an individual. However, he concerns himself not only with crimes on a

---

[1] This is a very difficult text. Generally 7:14 is taken to mean "I am no prophet," i.e., Amos dissociates himself from the regular *nabî'*-type of prophet. However, the very word taken to mean "no" has been shown in recent years to stand also for a strong *affirmation;* probably we should translate: "I am indeed a prophet," or the like! See H. N. Richardson, "A Critical Note on Amos 7:14," *Journal of Biblical Literature* 85 (1966), p. 89.

grand scale but also with the fate of the individual. In the climax of the oracles against the nation he condemns his own people, Israel, because they deprive the poor and helpless of their rights (2:6–7).

This climax must have shocked, angered, and frightened Amos' listeners. Remember that the prophet spoke for God so that his word had more than human value. It produced what it said. Israel was used to hearing the nations condemned. Now it learns to its terror that God is indeed the guardian of the whole moral order. He is concerned with the sins of the nations who harm Israel, but he is more concerned with his chosen people, Israel, who failed to live according to his directions.

How could this be? By judging nations for crimes which had nothing to do with Israel, Yahweh was claiming a dominion which extended far beyond his own chosen people. The typical Israelite, like all men of his time, would have said that Yahweh chose the Hebrews and that therefore he was concerned with outsiders only to smite them when they made things hard for his people. Now the prophet says that he is concerned with all men:

"Are you not like the Ethiopians to me,
   O people of Israel?" says the Lord.
"Did I not bring up Israel from the land of Egypt,
   And the Philistines from Caphtor and the Syrians from Kir?" (9:7.)

God's providence extends as much to the hated traditional enemies and to the far away Ethiopians as to his own people. Moreover, since the Hebrews had indeed been especially singled out, this means special obligation and liability to judgment: "You only have I known of all the families of the earth: *Therefore* I will punish you for all your iniquities" (3:2). A terrible truth! Of those to whom much has been given much will be demanded. This is very much a matter of morality, obedience, and justice. There is a special religious aspect too. The divine is something immensely attractive but equally something strange and terrifying. Those who are especially close to it are in special danger.

As we have said, God's care extends to every man, and the more especially to the poor man (2:6b). Who is the poor man? Of course, he is one who has no property, but there is more to it than this. Because he is poor he lacks a following, friends to aid him. Thus he must depend entirely upon God. This is the significant characteristic of the poor. They are under Yahweh's special care, and those to whom he has given power are obliged to take care of them. If they fail they will pay terrible penalties (cf. 4:1–3; 8:4–8 and many more texts). The poor must, of course, be in the right. This is understood: in 2:7 the poor is equated with the just man. An unjust policy, be it favorable to the poor, is itself an injustice.

We can understand some of Amos' passion for justice and its expression only if we know something of the peculiar system of his time. To "sell the righteous for silver, the needy for a pair of shoes" means that the creditor could sell his debtor into slavery to pay his debt. In ancient society one's very person could be security for a loan. A really poor man would have no other security, so that any difficulty in repayment put his person in jeopardy. This was the commercial law of the time, but such treatment of a member of the people called by God was abhorrent to true Yahwism, so that Deuteronomic law (15:12–18) attempts to put an end to slavery, making any personal service by a Hebrew temporary.

But there is more. The wealthy and powerful ". . . have turned the decision of the judge to poison" (6:12).[2] The background of this problem is the peculiar character of the ancient administration of justice. There was no full legal system established and supported by the state. Judges were simply the "solid citizens" of a community naturally favorable to other "solid citizens." In addition, one could pay a fee or influence the judge in other ways. The system was such that the poor became poorer and the rich richer precisely because in the law courts they had an instrument for oppressing the poor. So the unscrupulous and powerful "stored up . . . robbery in their stronghold" (3:10). Amos' word, "robbery," of course stands for the goods stolen from the poor, and it is a very strong word indeed. It emphasizes violence in the act of taking possession (the related verb means "to devastate"), what we might call "armed robbery" in our legal terminology. No matter how legal-seeming the means, then, Amos saw such riches simply as the results of viciousness. Furthermore, Amos saw more here than the activity of individuals; it was characteristic of the class of national leaders. Even the wives of the rich and the noble participated in the activity because of their selfishness (4:1). So avid were the rich that the prophet can say that "they pant after the very dust on the head of the poor."[3]

Thus a system existed that enabled, even encouraged, the worst offenses against the rights of the person. Through the prophet Yahweh reacts violently. Such sins are condemned in the strongest terms, and, because this is God and not man speaking, it is sure that the crimes will find their

---

[2] Note the proper translation, "judicial decision," which is rendered "justice" or the like in most English versions of the Bible.

[3] "Pant after" may possibly be translated "trample," but this is the less likely meaning.

authors out. Punishment will be severe and very appropriate. The fancy houses built with money wrung out of the poor will be destroyed (3:15). Those who grew at the expense of the poor know hunger: "I left your teeth clean in all your towns, left you without bread in all your villages" (4:6). This reveals a compassionate God. It is almost as though the sufferings of the poor and oppressed were his own. However, most of all he is the God of justice. Men violate right order and attack the person. He will right the one and defend the other. This is how Amos sees God primarily, and this is the vision he reveals to us.

However, Amos was no monomaniac concerned with justice to the exclusion of all else. In accord with the basic prophetic stance, absolute devotion to Yahweh, he is concerned with idolatry. Still Amos' doctrine is remarkably unified. For him idolatry is connected with justice. In the great oracle against the nations he parallels sins of idolatry with sins of injustice. Among those who sell the righteous are the

> ... man and his father (who) go in to the same maiden
>   so that my holy name is profaned;
> they lay themselves down beside every altar
>   upon garments taken in pledge;
> and in the house of their god
>   they drink the wine of those who have been fined (2:7b–8).

These activities are characteristic imitations of the cult of the Baals, fertility cults characterized by sacred prostitution and orgiastic rites. Such practices were abhorrent to Yahwism. Here they are doubly evil because blasphemous men presume to devote their stolen goods to worship.

Probably, however, the prophet's major concern is the utterly false concept of worship which lies in back of their doing this. This was a concept of God as one unconcerned with morality. What counted was the splendor of his cult. The more magnificent such a liturgy was materially, the more it was thought to please God. Hence, the malignancy of the evil. It was bad enough that men used in the cult goods unjustly acquired at the cost of suffering or even death (cf. 1 Kgs 21) to the poor and the powerless. It was worse when such use came not from thoughtlessness or indifference but from an idea that one could purchase God's favor in this way. Men thought they could cover their crimes with a sumptuous liturgy. It would be hard to go further into blasphemy than so to think of God as eager for bribes and flattery.

Amos knew that Yahweh was no such God. The prophet spoke for one who had a special concern for the poor and helpless, not for the splendor of his cult. This is his ironic reply to the false hopes placed in the cult:

Come to Bethel and transgress;
    to Gilgal, and multiply transgression;
bring your sacrifices every morning,
    your tithes every three days;
. . . proclaim your voluntary offerings,
    yes, advertise them;
for so you love to do,
    O people of Israel! (4:4–5.)
. . .
But thus says the Lord to the house of Israel:
"Seek me and live;
    but do not seek Bethel,
and do not enter into Gilgal
    or cross over to Beersheba;
for Gilgal shall surely go into exile;
    and Bethel shall come to naught" (5:4–5).

The blasphemous worship at these famous shrines will fail. Far from gaining the favor of the Lord for the men who use the shrines, the shrines themselves will be destroyed. They are even unable to earn the favor of God for themselves.

This, then, is God as Amos presents him. His demands are absolute, and they are demands for social justice. This is God's primary concern, and through the prophet he sneers at the hope that he can be bought off from his demands by an elaborate cult. Cult he will have, but one offered by those free from injustice. For the unjust the divine guardian of rights has only condemnation.

"SEEK GOOD THAT YOU MAY LIVE"

All that we have been saying gives the impression that Amos is a prophet of almost unrelieved doom. He is overwhelmed by the evil he sees around him, and his message is overwhelmingly one of condemnation. To emphasize this he even takes one of the great sources of hope in Israel and turns it into a threat. The people hoped for the time when Yahweh himself would intervene to give them "their place in the sun." In the popular mind this "day of Yahweh" meant that he would come as war leader of Israel to smash forever the enemies who threatened her.[4] Not

---

[4] "Day of the Lord (Yahweh)" became a favorite phrase in later Jewish eschatology, but in the time of Amos it simply referred to a divine intervention in case of need, for instance, to help in war or with the crops. This is not the meaning in eschatology where it refers not to such temporary or natural helps but to a total change, a new creation; hence one should not speak of "eschatology" in Amos or other early texts on the basis of the phrase.

so, Amos warns: the day of Yahweh will be a day of woe to Israel. "It is darkness and not light," that is, not a day of victory for Israel but a day of judgment without escape (Am 5:18). Here as in the oracles against the nations Amos has taken a way of speaking familiar to Israel, one which led them to expect a comforting tirade against their enemies, and turned it around so that it shocked them with its condemnation of themselves.

Still Amos is not entirely negative. He offers the hope of a conversion which will change things and allow Israel to survive. Repentance is never excluded in the divine scheme. So Amos says "seek good and not evil, that you may live" (5:14a). Compared to the whole extent of the book of Amos such sayings are rare (only 5:6–7, 14–15). Nonetheless, they are there, and they allow a measure of hope. We need not ask what the "good" is which Amos wants. It is, of course, justice. What else could the just God's spokesman wish?

Amos also uses the theme of the remnant which allows for a certain sort of hope. The concept of the remnant is a metaphor drawn from the ancient experience of war. Often a conqueror attempted to destroy his enemy entirely. The defeated people were slaughtered down to the last woman and child, or at least taken into remote exile without hope of return. However, it is difficult to carry out such measures fully. A nucleus of the defeated people might escape, and if the situation were favorable this remnant could restore itself and rebuild the nation. Such is the origin of the remnant idea which appears already in prophets like Elijah. Thus Amos uses a theme linking him to the ancient prophetic tradition even though he may have dissociated himself from the professional prophets dependent upon king or cult (Am 7:14).

This remnant idea at best held out hope of only a partial salvation. The larger part of the people perishes, only a small group escapes to carry on the national life. In one mood Amos does not even allow this minimal hope. In 3:13 he refers metaphorically to the Israel that will escape ruin as the torn bits of a lamb which a shepherd manages to snatch from a lion, two legs or a piece of an ear. This obviously holds out no hope for the restoration of the lamb. Or the remnant is like a fragment of broken furniture. Such survival is the survival of ruins without hope of future growth. This use of the remnant concept emphasizes the deadly seriousness of the judgment that has been passed upon the people.

There appears to be another use of the concept in Amos 5:3, where the prophet says that a thousand men left the city and only a hundred remained. Then these hundred ventured forth and but ten survived. The tone of the saying is gloomy. The metaphor is military. The men who venture forth from the city are an army who go out to meet the enemy, are defeated and practically destroyed. There are only ten survivors, an insignificant number in terms of armies. Still there is a remnant; things are not so absolute as in the earlier passage.

We have then in Amos the elements which can be used to build some sort of hope for the future in spite of the punishment to which Israel is condemned. There is the prospect that repentance will lead to justice and so to a mitigation of punishment. There is the hope that despite the destruction wrought by that punishment a remnant of the people will survive. So far this is vague enough. There is some hope for survival, but there is no picture of it. This void is filled by 9:11:

" . . . I will raise up the booth of David that has fallen
    and repair its breaches,
and raise up its ruins,
    and rebuild it as in the days of old;
that they may possess the remains of Edom
    and all the nations who are called by my name," . . .

Here is a clear promise of restoration and reunion under the leadership of the son of David. This is clear enough, but many authors refuse to believe that Amos said this. They object that the Davidids otherwise play no part at all in the theology of Amos. Moreover, they point out that elsewhere Amos is concerned only with Israel, yet this is a typically Judean saying. Then the critics find the reference to the fallen booth of David an anachronism since they believe that such an expression can refer only to the fall of David's city, Jerusalem. This happened some one hundred and fifty years after Amos' time so that he could hardly be expected to speak of it. Finally, the element of hope is very small in Amos and never as specific as we find it here.

These arguments have weight, but we prefer to hold this oracle as an authentic saying of Amos. He does not otherwise speak of David, but he was a Judean and therefore likely to respect the Davidic tradition. Moreover, Amos held Jerusalem and its Temple to be the proper Hebrew holy place (1:2), and in the era of the monarchy the Temple was inextricably bound up with the Davidic idea. These same arguments dispose of the objection that Amos could not speak of things Judean. As for the charge of anachronism, the "fallen booth" probably refers not to the fall of Jerusalem but to the split of the old Davidic kingdom. This interpretation is the more likely because the oracle is concerned with the unity of "all the nations who are called by my (Yahweh's) name," that is, it seems to refer to the hope for a reunited kingdom. Finally, though hope is not a prominent element in Amos, it is there. In fact, the whole book is so short that arguments based on the frequency of an idea are not strong.

These seeming inconsistencies in the prophetic books are not really as great a problem as is sometimes thought. Since these books are collections of oracles spoken in many different places and at many different times, it would be strange if they did not contain many different ideas. What was appropriate to one place was not appropriate to another. Hence the prophetic oracles contain many disparate ideas which seem in their *written* form ill-connected and ill-organized. In their actual situation they were vitally connected with their context. To demand an iron consistency is to deny the prophet the chance to adapt and grow.

We may, then, take 9:11–12 as an authentic saying of Amos. It adds to our knowledge of the hope which he offers the people of God. He has taught that, if they must be punished so that only a remnant will survive, at least repentance will keep the judgment from being absolute. Now he adds something about the things to be hoped for. The cities are to be rebuilt as they were before. This refers to more than the cities themselves; it is a symbol of a return to prosperity for the whole people united under the leadership of a Davidic king, that is, of the proper leader of the Hebrews, the one whom God had chosen and through whom his promises to Israel would be fulfilled.

We should not be disturbed by the apparent limitation of this hope to material horizons. This is not peculiar to Amos. The early hope of Israel was in the fulfillment of the promise that Yahweh had made to the Fathers, and this meant simply the prosperous possession of the Promised Land. Thus through Amos Yahweh is simply renewing the promise of the great grace of the Old Testament.[5]

HOSEA

Hosea, Amos' younger contemporary, is the only one of the "writing" prophets native to the kingdom of Israel. He was a poet of great power.

---

[5] Chap. 9:13–15 is not from Amos himself. The verses are a later addition developing the concrete details of the promised life in the land. This is a good example of the way prophetic books grew: an editor added a bit of poetry which seemed pertinent to the prophet's theme, or perhaps he was moved to compose the development himself. Thus one idea led to another so that the resulting books are inspired anthologies, not single compositions.

In his personal life he suffered greatly because of a faithless wife. This is about all we know about this great prophet, though it has been plausibly suggested also that he was a Levite and a professional prophet.[6] As we know, Hosea's lifetime was a time of trial for his homeland. Israel was going to pieces, and cruel Assyria was knocking at the gate. Like the other prophets, Hosea was not a man of the ivory tower. He saw the dissolution of his country and he knew that worse threatened. Indeed, the prophet was surely moved to preach by a desire to interpret these terrible times for himself and the people. However, beyond this human motivation he had the essential motivation of his office: the call and revelation given him by God.

We have called Hosea a great poet. His language is powerful, his imagery striking, and his message deeply felt. Yet he attains this striking individuality while clinging to the standard prophetic forms. There is biography and autobiography, and there are speeches in poetic form. Like Amos he may begin with the call "Hear!" addressed to his special audience (e.g., 4:1; 5:1). He favors the standard judgment oracle except that he does not use the phrase "thus says Yahweh." In his judgment oracles the condemnation follows immediately upon the indictment without the phrase asserting that the judgment comes from Yahweh.

The book of Hosea is an accumulation, as are most of the prophetic books. As is usually the case this process has produced no particular order in the book, though there are certain large, rough divisions. The first three chapters are biographical. The second large division extends from 4:1 to 9:9, a collection of sayings concerned largely with the sin of idolatry and its consequences. To a lesser extent it notes the criminal violence of political life. These sayings are usually directed against the leaders of the people, who are doubly guilty. They sin themselves, though they are the ones who have the opportunity to know better, and by their sinning they lead the simple people astray. The last portion of the book, 9:10 to 14:9, also collects sayings against Israel's sins, but it is characterized by the fact that it connects Israel's present sinfulness with episodes of infidelity from its past history.

How much of this comes from Hosea himself? Practically speaking, all of it except a few glosses such as the proverb-like conclusion. It used to be held that the oracles of hope at the end of the book could not have come from the prophet himself. However, this idea was simply based on the assumption that the earlier prophets never spoke of hope. The as-

---

[6] See above, chap. 6, n. 6, page 82.

sumption is unproved, and the oracles are in the style of Hosea so that there is no reason to consider them unauthentic. The book of Hosea, then, is truly from Hosea, which is not to say that every word in it is his. The Hebrew text is one of the most corrupt in the Old Testament. Evidently its poetry confused the scribes and they made more than the usual quota of errors in copying.

Now we must consider what this book tells us about God and man's relationship to God. As we have seen, Hosea is intensely aware of the political corruption of Israel. However, it was not political folly which chiefly concerned Hosea. This was but a symptom of the fundamental disorder: Israel had forsaken its true lord, Yahweh, and taken up the cult of Canaanite fertility gods. They attributed their prosperity not to Yahweh, but to the Baals, that is, to the many local gods to whom fertility was attributed. These gods had proper names, but so impersonal was their function that they tended to be known by the title Baal ("lord"), not by name. The Baalism which Hosea reproaches is complex. There was out-and-out devotion to pagan gods (9:10–14) but commonly the very cult of Yahweh was contaminated. Yahweh was thought of as a god like the others, bound to the land and worshiped in the Canaanite manner. There were prostitutes "devoted" to the cult (4:11–14). Furthermore, men felt that the ritual forced Yahweh to grant what was desired. Or the false cult simply added the worship of other gods to the worship of Yahweh. In any case, this was the ultimate sin, the betrayal of the one God to whom alone Israel was pledged. Hosea is unsparing in his condemnation of this sin and sure of the punishment which it will bring upon Israel.

But all this tells us is what Hosea is against. What is he for? Basically, total devotion to a God of love. Central to his vocabulary is the Hebrew word *hesed*, "faithful love," which denotes the disposition which should characterize the faithful party of a covenant agreement. This may sound legalistic, but true *hesed* has little to do with courts and justice. It is a matter of mind and heart, real devotion to the covenant partner. Yahweh has this devotion to Israel, and Israel should return it. A truly devoted Israel would be ready to follow his wishes. It is ever so with a true lover who pleases the beloved by seeking out and doing his will. However, this point of view, emphasizing a proper human devotion to God, is not central to Hosea. Rather he is concerned with God's attitude toward men, his faithful love for his people. Another typically Hosean word, *rechem,* which is usually translated by English "pity," brings this out. The translation is inadequate and even misleading. The Hebrew word does not refer to sorrowful compassion with its frequent overtone of condescension as does the English "pity." It means love which is eager to help and protect, for the root of the word refers to the womb. Hence it connotes the attitude of mother to child.

However, the richest element in Hosea's idea of God's love for his chosen people is that image which is especially his, the figure of Yahweh and Israel as husband and wife. When he uses this image Hosea is speaking from his own experience, for he loved faithfully and well a wife who was faithless (cf. 1–3). Such was the love Yahweh revealed for his people, a love that remained even in the face of their repeated failures. The prophet asks us to understand his experience so that from his human understanding we may glimpse the character of divine love. This is always the case; we do not know God directly but only by analogy from our own experience. Understanding of Hosea's experience is not, it must be admitted, easy. Not everything in chapters 1–3 is crystal clear.

Is this really just allegorical function, a story invented to illustrate a point? This was once a popular view, but it hardly does justice to the realism of the symbolic actions of the prophet, a realism which is not confined to Hosea (cf. Is 20:2–6; Jer 19; Ezek 5). Neither would we expect in an allegory the intense feeling which we find in Hosea's story. Moreover in true allegory we expect all significant details to have a meaning. However, here important details like the name of the wife, Gomer, and the sexes of the children do not refer to something beyond themselves as they should in true allegorical style. Actually, the origin of the allegorical view was probably a certain prudishness which felt that it was unworthy of a great prophet to have had an adulterous wife. This is to fit the prophet and the God who reveals himself through the prophet to our standards rather than to try to understand and measure ourselves by their standards. Only the latter is the proper procedure. In view of all this we may safely abandon the allegorical view of Hosea's marriage.

Another question is: Do chapters 1–3 recount a continuous story? If they do, we have here a tale in which a woman is taken to wife by the prophet, bears his children, and then deserts him. After this the husband redeems the woman from some scrape into which she has gotten herself, and after he does so, subjects her to some form of discipline, and eventually takes her back to his bosom. A variant of this interpretation of these chapters holds that in chapter 3 we do not have an account of a remarriage with the erring Gomer but the story of an entirely new marriage.

However, to get a good sequence one must rearrange Hosea's text, since chapter 3 should precede much in chapter 2. Even so the story is incomplete and filled with problems. The account of the marriage in chapter 3 does not really fit with that in chapter 1 (e.g., chap. 1 uses "harlot," chap. 3 "adulteress") and it is scarcely credible that a continuous story would not explicitly fit its conclusion to its beginning. However, the most important point is that the text as it stands presents three well-defined literary units, 1:2–11; 2:1–25; and 3:1–5. In each of these we have the same movement from accusation through chastisement to reconciliation. This must surely be a conscious arrangement of the text which emphasizes the theological meaning of the marriage symbol.[7]

Thus it is most likely that chapters 1–3 contain different accounts and comments about the prophet's single experience. In chapter 3 we have a parallel to the story of Hosea's marriage in the prophet's own words. The same story is recounted from the point of view of a third person in chapter 1. Thus in 1:2–11 we have a biographical account of the prophet's marriage with its meaning explained through the names given to the children. Chapter 2 extends and deepens this meaning by introducing a series of the prophet's oracles which show that Yahweh's dealings with Israel are like dealings with a faithless wife. Chapter 3 returns to narration, but now the form is autobiographical — it uses "I" rather than "he" as in chapter 1. This new narrative goes beyond chapter 1 in showing the prophet taking back his chastened wife, but the prophet's action corresponds to God's as described in chapter 2.

It pays to look closely at some of the details of the story of Hosea's marriage. He is told by God to take a "harlot wife" (1:2). This may be the figure of prolepsis, that is, the woman may be called a harlot in view of her future unchaste conduct. Still, if this is the case, why is the word "harlot" used and not adulteress as in 3:1? It seems more likely that Gomer was a woman who had taken part in the orgiastic rites which were a major part of the worship of the Baals. If this cult was as widespread as our sources indicate, this must have been a common enough situation. The emphasis put upon the virginity of the bride in the roughly contemporary Deuteronomic law (Dt 22:13–21) is evidence pointing in this direction. Men make laws to protect what is seriously threatened. Moreover, if Gomer were a devotee of such unchaste rites, the deeper

---

[7] This is not to say that the 3 chapters were *composed* as a unit; they are a collection of sayings etc. *constructed* into a unity as is evidenced by the structure outlined and by details, e.g., the use of the connective "therefore" (on these latter see von Rad, *Old Testament Theology* II, p. 139).

meaning of Hosea's marriage is clearer. His wife was unchaste, but her very unchastity was idolatry. The faithless wife would be an exact symbol of a faithless Israel. This is clear in chapter 2 where the woman who represents Israel plays the harlot by being a devotee of the Baals (2:5, 8). She attributes the good things which come from the Promised Land not to Yahweh but to the Baals (2:12). Thus the great gift, the object of Yahweh's promise, is the occasion for deserting him. Furthermore, rather than being a holy land, it is the place for bloody deeds (1:4).[8]

Ordinarily such conduct would surely destroy the lover's affection, but Yahweh's love does not waver. We learn this from the conduct of Hosea. He, a mere man, can have compassion for the wife who has betrayed him, save her from the results of her folly, and restore her to her place (chapter 3). If a man can do this, much more God. So we read that the symbolic names of the children are changed. "Not my people" becomes "Sons of God," and the memory of this joyful change wipes out the ancient bloody deeds (1:10–11; cf. 2:23). The process and the parallel with the prophet's conduct are shown in detail in the fate of the faithless woman (Israel) in chapter 2. She has deserted Yahweh and given herself to the Baals because she believes that they will give her all the good things of the earth. This idolatrous folly brings its own punishment. The sinner must leave the land of promise for the wilderness (2:14), but this is not merely a penalty imposed for its own sake. The desert is harsh, but just as in the old days Israel met its God in the wilderness so now in this deprivation and return to the desert will Israel learn anew to respond to Yahweh's love (2:15–17). So the nation learns again that Yahweh alone is the living God and the giver of life.

Thus Yahweh treats Israel as Hosea did his faithless wife, and the prophet's tragic marriage helps reveal the meaning of the love which God has for his people. This is indeed a faithful love; it is not blind. Infidelity cannot be ignored. It must be punished, not for the sake of the punishment but because this is the way which shows the sinner where true life lies. This is the way that he will learn to respond to God's *ḥesed*, the love he gives because of his covenant. Notice how the marriage analogy also helps to see how this can be a matter of the heart and not merely a legal *quid pro quo*. In itself marriage is a contract, a legal agreement binding the partners together. It is therefore a covenant by which the partners guarantee their exclusive love to one another. Yet we hardly

---

[8] Jezreel refers to the murder of the kings of Israel and Judah in that Galilean town by Jehu (2 Kgs 9:14–28).

think of married love as a merely juridical relationship. Just as the marriage contract should imply depth and tenderness so also should the covenant between Yahweh and his people.

Marriage is not the only analogy Hosea uses to explain the divine love. He appeals also to the devoted love of a parent for his child in one of the most beautiful passages of the Bible:

> When Israel was a child, I loved him,
>   and out of Egypt I called my son.
> ... it was I who taught Ephraim to walk,
>   I took them up in my arms;
>   but they did not know that I healed them.
> ... My people are bent on turning away from me;
>   so they are appointed to the yoke,
>   and none shall remove it.
> How can I give thee up, O Ephraim!
>   How can I hand you over, O Israel!
> ... My heart recoils within me,
>   my compassion grows warm and tender.
> I will not execute my fierce anger,
>   I will not again destroy Ephraim;
> for I am God and not man,
>   the Holy One in your midst,
>   and I will not come to destroy.[9]

God is a god of justice. He must punish transgression and yet here we see in him the passion of his love. So strong is it that it must burst forth with redeeming force in the face of God's own justice and the punishment it entails.

WHAT LOVE ENTAILS

For Hosea, then, God is essentially a God of love. He has loved his people, he has brought them out of Egypt — Hosea knows the ancient traditions and speaks of Moses (12:13), the Exodus (11:1; 12:10; 13:4), and Jacob (12:3) among other things — and his love will stand in the face of Israel's stubborn refusal to accept that love as it should, for an aspect of this love is the demand it makes. All love does this. If the lover wishes to please, he does what the beloved wants, he accedes to the will of the beloved.

Hosea is very clear on what Yahweh's will is for Israel. First and most basic is the demand that Yahweh alone be worshiped. It is Yahweh who has chosen the people and given them a prosperous life on the land, and

---

[9] Hos 11:1–9. The text is in a bad state and the meaning of many details is conjectural, but the general sense seems clear.

this must not be attributed to any other. But there is more to it than this. Israel is bound to certain norms in relation to other men. Thus a war between the Hebrew kingdoms, Israel and Judah, is really fratricide (5:8–11). But most interesting is the allusion in 4:1–3. Israel is reproached because it is without fidelity. It is failing to live up to its covenant with Yahweh because "there is swearing, lying, killing, stealing, and adultery . . . and murder on murder." Here is a little scheme which sums up the basic duties of men toward one another. We have here, in fact, equivalently the commandments, and this is one of the oldest allusions to something like these famous precepts.

Like most prophets Hosea is concerned with preaching which is pertinent to his own time. He warns of the judgment which hangs over a faithless nation. However, this is not the sum of his message for men. He holds out hope for the future. Israel must undergo a terrible punishment. Because it has abused God's gifts it will be deprived of these various gifts, it will go into exile (10:5–6), it will be deprived of the fruits of the earth (2:11), and its kings and priests will be rejected. But for Hosea this is not the end of the story. As we have already seen, the basic experience of the broken marriage included the idea of chastisement which was a disciplining to bring a renewal. This concept is basic to the prophet's theology. Israel must be punished precisely in the very areas in which it has sinned. However, this will also be a sort of training period in which the people will be purged of their old sins and so restored to the old, true relationship to Yahweh.

Neither does the prophet leave us in total ignorance of what the restoration will be like. In 14:4–9 he describes it. It will be a personal intervention by God. He will heal his people and restore them gloriously to their place. The restoration, in fact, is a return to the conditions of paradise, peace, plenty, and beauty. This image is a common way of expressing the belief that God will indeed intervene and restore things to the glorious condition they had when he first brought order out of chaos in creation and his fresh and beautiful world had not yet been disturbed by sin.

What is unusual here is the absence of any reference to a fulfillment of the promise to David. We have seen that Amos' brief oracle of hope is based upon the expectation of a Davidic restoration. We can find similar things in the major prophets down to Ezekiel. Only Isaiah, perhaps, is an enthusiastic follower of the Davidids and so devotes much attention to the hope based upon them, but the Davidic hope was too important an element in Israelite theology for any prophet to ignore. Hence men like

Jeremiah and Ezekiel, though they do not develop the idea very much, do present a future hope which emphatically includes a Davidic king. Not so Hosea, since the single reference to David in 3:5 is universally accepted as a gloss. This is the more striking because we know that Hosea was eager for a reunion of the separated Hebrew peoples. Israel and Judah are to be reunited under a single head (1:11). Thus it is clear that he knew the traditions of a reuniting of the people under a divinely appointed head, but he is careful to speak of a head and not a king. Commonly it is assumed from this that Hosea is antimonarchical. As a matter of fact he is very hard on kings in all of his references to them. However, it is not clear that this is a rejection of kingship as such. All his reproaches are directed to particular situations, not necessarily to the institution itself. If this interpretation of his attitude is problematic, there is no doubt that the theology of the Davidic promise was something which belonged particularly to Judah where the Davidids reigned. It is entirely natural that a northern prophet like Hosea does not take account of this specifically southern development.

In Hosea we can touch very briefly on the final point we have said we shall consider in each prophet: his attitude toward the Gentiles. Hosea has almost nothing to say about them. It may be that his condemnations of Baal worship implied condemnation of the Canaanites from whom it came, but he never says so. Otherwise, the nations appear simply as instruments of God's chastisement (8:13; 9:6; 10:6; 11:5). This may reflect little interest in them, but it shows the unquestioned belief that Yahweh's power and so his providence extended over them. This may seem jejune to us, but in the eighth century B.C. it was an implication of a startling universalism.

We may sum up the chapter with a review of our five points. Both Amos and Hosea prophesied during the deterioration of the kingdom of Israel. Amos teaches that this is the result of neglecting the justice which a just God demands, Hosea of infidelity to Israel's loving God. Hence a varying emphasis in their demands. Amos calls for social justice as a prelude to true worship (5:6), Hosea for a devotion to the Lord which will bring about social justice (4:1–3). Amos hardly notices a future hope, Hosea is sure that chastisement will bring restoration. On the other hand, Hosea almost ignores the Gentiles, while Amos emphasizes that they are Yahweh's charges too and that Israel's favored position means heavier obligations (9:7; 3:1–2).

CHAPTER 8.   ISAIAH AND MICAH

Readings: Is 6:1–5; 7:1–9:7, 11:1–9; 14:24–32; 28–32; Mic

Isaiah, commonly considered the greatest of the prophets, is a poet of extraordinary power with a message outstanding for the breadth and richness of its theological insights. These things we learn easily from the book of Isaiah, but it has less to offer about the person of the prophet himself. He was married and had children, and like Hosea he weaves his family into his prophecy. They are "signs and portents in Israel" (8:18), perhaps, that is, a sign of fidelity and a reproach to a faithless Jerusalem. Moreover, he gives his sons symbolic names. This is similar in some respects to the symbolic marriage of Hosea. However, it obviously goes less deep. It is not a profound personal experience of Isaiah in his own marriage which is revealing here. It is only the attitude of the family and the names given the children which are meaningful. This is in line with the tradition of symbolic actions by the prophets, who preach not only by word but by activity.

Apart from this we assume that Isaiah prophesied in Jerusalem because of his preoccupation with Zion and its Temple. It has also been conjectured that he was a man of noble, even royal blood. He deals with the king with remarkable freedom, and he is able to summon men of highest rank to act as witnesses to his activities (8:2). This may indicate a prophet who was of high rank, but, as we have seen, prophets were important and respected functionaries in the governments of the time. Perhaps Isaiah commanded such respect as a prophet that he enjoyed this entrée to the highest circles. Whatever may have been Isaiah's position, he was deeply involved in the life of his nation. He worked from about 745 to 700 B.C., that time of turmoil and great changes in Palestine. His prophecy is commonly concerned with the great events of the time, which, as we have seen, revolved around Assyrian invasions. Isaiah touches them all from the so-called Syro-Ephraimite war in 734–733 B.C., when Damascus and Israel banded together to attack Judah, down to the uprising in 704 which led the Assyrian king Sennacherib to invade Judah, conquer the countryside, and in 701 lay siege to the capital city itself.

How did he go about speaking of all this? Isaiah commanded a great variety of forms of expression. He used the standard prophetic judgment oracle which we have seen so often, but he was ready to apply any literary technique which was useful to his purpose; the love song (e.g., 5:1–5), coronation hymn (9:1–6), and a host of others. His language is pure and uncluttered, and his imagery is striking.

As for the book of Isaiah, it is a complex affair. First of all, chapters 40 to 66 stem from later prophets, not from Isaiah. We shall consider these chapters later on in their proper place. In the first part of the book, chapters 1 to 39, there is little evidence of an overall structure. In general, it is possible to see an order which collects oracles against the Israelites, then a section of oracles against the nations, and finally a collection of oracles offering hope to the Israelites, but there are many exceptions to this ordering. Within these larger sections there is evidence of smaller divisions. Thus there is the famous "book of Emmanuel" (7–11) with its collection of sayings about the coming of a prince of the royal line. Then the headings of chapters 6 and 7 are introductions to collections of prophetic sayings comparable to the present beginnings of several prophetic books. Observing these details increases our understanding of the processes of composition of books like this, but thorough discussion of these must be left for more specialized books.

For us it is more important to see what is generally considered to be genuine Isaian material. The most important passages which are clearly not Isaian are chapters 24 to 27 and 34 to 35. The first set of chapters is apocalyptic in tone. This is a style of literature which did not develop until much later than the time of Isaiah. Chapters 34 to 35 reflect the style and ideas of chapters 40 to 55, that is, of an exilic prophet who lived almost two hundred years after Isaiah. Some authors believe that these chapters in fact come from the prophet of chapters 40 to 55, the so called Deutero-Isaiah, but it is more commonly held that they are religious poems influenced by the style and ideas of that prophet. There is also a good deal of unauthentic material in the oracles against the nations which begin in chapter 13. Chapters 13 and 14 contain two splendid poems condemning Babylon, but Babylon was insignificant in Isaiah's day. Hence it is extremely unlikely that Isaiah composed these pieces. Rather an inspired writer added them to a collection of Isaiah's oracles against the nations, connecting them with the genuine Isaian oracle against the Assyrian in 14:24–32. After all, in the later days of Judah it was Babylon that replaced Assyria as a threat to God's people. Someone felt, not without reason, that a kind of anthology of materials concerning the Mesopotamian threat was in place. Other oracles against the nations which are not considered Isaian are the ones against Moab in chapters 15 and 16, against Egypt in chapter 19, and against Babylon in 21:1–10. Many doubt that the oracle against Tyre in chapter 23 is authentic. Finally, among the oracles of hope most think that chapter 33 is unauthentic. It has been classed as a "prophetic liturgy." It does in fact display something of the style of the psalms, while the emphasis on the future downfall of the ruler of the world and the exaltation of Jerusalem is characteristic of post-exilic Judaism. The historical materials in Isaiah 36–39 repeat 2 Kings 18:13–20:19. They do not, of course, stem from the mouth of the prophet Isaiah. So much for separating out these portions of the Book of Isaiah which are not authentically Isaian. These sections are still the inspired word of God, and we may have occasion to refer to them as such. It will help to see what is Isaiah's and what is not if we summarize what we have been doing in a single scheme. Brackets indicate non-Isaian sections:

> Oracles against Judah and Jerusalem (1–12)
> [Oracles against Babylon (13–14)]
> [Oracles against Moab (15–16)]
> Oracles against the Nations (17–22[23])
> [The larger apocalypse of Isaiah (24–27)]
> Sin and Restoration (28–32[33])
> [The smaller apocalypse of Isaiah (34–35)]
> [The historical appendix (36–39)]

THE HOLY ONE OF ISRAEL

The individuality of the prophet Isaiah stands out in many ways, not least in his doctrine. He is the only one of the prophets of the pre-exilic and exilic period who does not concern himself at all with the Exodus as the sign of God's choice of his people. His theology centers around the holy city. It is concerned with the Temple and its cult, with the Davidic dynasty, and it views God from this perspective.

The essential point in his perception of the divine is that God is holy. Characteristically he speaks of the Holy One of Israel. The idea is essentially religious in the narrower technical sense of that word. That is, it refers to God under the aspect in which he is seen in the Temple cult. The divine is the totally other, who may be approached only by certain people and under certain conditions. It is a fact of experience, amply demonstrated in historical and anthropological science, that man never approaches God without some feeling of awe. If he thinks he does so, he is not really approaching God. Hence all religions have surrounded some aspect of life with a barrier which separates it from common things. This makes it cultic, part of the divine, or a point at which men can approach the divine. Here and now we are not concerned with the exact meaning of this, but rather with the fact of its separateness. To be holy is to be cut off from everyday life and everyday things.[1]

These may seem exceedingly primitive ideas, hardly religious at all. However, this is not really the case. Perhaps a given expression of the attitude is alien to us, but the attitude is essential to any religion. Man cannot approach God on any basis of equality. He can never really be familiar with God. However much he strives for divine wisdom and moral perfection he remains infinitely inferior and very different from God, and the more he progresses in these directions the more he will realize this fact. Hence awe is an indelible part of the religious experience. God is ever a mystery, and it is simply impossible for a normal man to approach this ultimately powerful mystery without trepidation. This, of course, is not the whole of the story. God is the totally other precisely because he is perfect, utterly beyond us and all created things. Hence he is not only awesome. He is also the ultimate desire of the human heart.

[1] The basic idea of holiness as "otherness, unapproachability" is reflected in language. The Semitic root used to mean holy goes back to the idea of being cut off, separate, and the Greek *temenos*, "temple district," means originally an area cut off from profane use. Even the primitive idea of taboo use based on this feeling of the otherness of the divine, for what belongs to the gods is forbidden (taboo) to ordinary men.

All true human activity is directed toward reaching him, whether this be consciously known or not. Thus the concept of holiness combines in itself two seemingly contrary concepts, or better, reflects the complex attitude of man in the face of the divine. God is a mystery at once awesome and yet fascinating.[2]

All of this is admirably illustrated from the text of Isaiah himself. The connection with the liturgy, the aspect of life where a man comes closest to the divine, appears in the vision where Isaiah receives his prophetic call (Is 6). This takes place in the Temple and the vision is shaped by the Temple and its services. Isaiah sees the Lord sitting upon a throne with his train filling the Temple, reflecting the concept of the Ark of the Covenant in the holy of holies as God's symbolic throne. The paraphernalia of the cult are there: incense, smoke, and an altar with burning coals (6:6–7). Finally the famous "Holy, holy, holy, Lord God of Hosts" in verse 3 is a liturgical chant placed on the lips of the court of the divine king. This little chant, by the way, shows that while Isaiah developed the idea of holiness he did not invent it, as is evident in any case. The triple repetition of the word "holy" is a very ancient form of the superlative in Hebrew, a way of saying the holiest, and this ancient linguistic phenomenon proves the chant much older than Isaiah, who uses a far more developed form of the language. The connection of holiness with the cult is demonstrated by another aspect of Isaiah's thought. He is much concerned with Zion, the place where God is specially present, and he knows that such a holy place cannot be defiled by profane hands. Hence he can confidently predict that the Assyrians will not capture Jerusalem (37:35).

Besides its cultic connections the vision of Isaiah in chapter 6 exemplifies other aspects of the concept of holiness. The immediate reaction of the prophet to this vision which brings him so close to the divine is fear. As a man he is not fit to approach God (6:5). Here we see the awe aspect of the divine experience. At the same time, however, the divine is not so utterly alien as to repel the man entirely. Having undergone a ritual purification by fire — some such rite which marks off the priest or other man who is about to approach the divine from the everyday world is a universal religious phenomenon — the prophet is quite ready to answer the Lord's call and come close enough to him to be his spokesman. Here we have the aspect of the attractive and fascinating.

---

[2] The basic study of the concept is Rudolph Otto, *The Idea of the Holy* (Oxford: Oxford University Press, 1924).

It is sometimes thought that this concentration on holiness, on God as the all-powerful precludes connection with any moral norms. Thus in Isaiah 29:22–24 the prophet proclaims that his people will recognize his holiness in his mighty works which are the destruction of the enemies of Israel, and the defense of Jerusalem against the Assyrians, the most powerful nation of the day. This indeed might seem like power and nothing but power. However, this would be a total misinterpretation of Isaiah. In the first place, despite the opinions of certain earlier students of comparative religion, the religious and the holy is never entirely separate from a concern with the rightness of human action. To be qualified to approach the divine, to be pure in this sense, means not only that one must have undergone a ritual purification, but also that one must have lived according to the rules which the divinity enforces. This is evident in Hebrew religion from texts like Psalms 15 and 24, the so-called entrance liturgies where the man who wishes to take part in a liturgical service asks the priest the conditions under which he may thus approach the divine. The priest replies with a list of moral precepts. Only one who has lived according to these lofty principles may "dwell on the holy mountain" (Ps 15:1).

This was certainly true of Isaiah's concept of God as the Holy One of Israel. He knew God as an awesome being hard to approach. But he also knew that holiness is connected with morality. Indeed, he identifies holiness and righteousness:

But the Lord of hosts is exalted in justice,
and the holy God shows himself holy in righteousness (Is 5:16).

The word here translated "righteousness" has none of the vaguely pejorative connotations of the English word, which so often connotes a legalistic and "holier than thou" attitude. The Hebrew word covers the whole range of moral conduct. Isaiah 28:16–17 confirms this union of holiness and justice in a strikingly concrete image:

... "Behold, I am laying in Zion for a foundation, a stone, a tested stone,
a precious cornerstone of a sure foundation. ...
And I will make justice the line,
and righteousness the plummet. ..."

The prophet is speaking of the holiest of places, the mountain of the Temple, but what is it that makes it holy? Not merely its religious, i.e., liturgical character. The basis in its solid construction — "line" and "plummet" are builder's tools — is the upright life of the people.

"CEASE FROM EVIL, SEEK JUSTICE"

Hence it is entirely natural that a main consequence which Isaiah draws from his knowledge of the holy God is the demand for justice. Holiness in God is justice and to be near to God one must be like him, just. He reproves the oppression of the weaker by the stronger, and he confidently proclaims that those who fail to live by this rule will eventually be punished for it. In this he shows an acquaintance with the prophecy of Amos, since he has not only the common idea of the oppression of the poor by the rich but also much of Amos' way of expressing it. Hence we conclude to some sort of connection. To give but one example, one may compare Isaiah 3:16–17, 24–26, and Amos 4:1–3. For further details on the connections between Amos and Isaiah the reader should consult various introductions. It is worth the time to study the connections among the prophets, to see the continuity in their ideas, images, and language. Only so do we see revelation properly as the organic, developing thing, which it was, rather than as a series of unconnected lightning flashes of divinely given knowledge, which it largely was not.

But to return to Isaiah: so closely is righteousness identified with the Holy One of Israel, and so deep is his concern for righteousness among his people that it seems to bridge the gap which separates the totally other, the holy, from all that is not divine. Thus the prophet sings a love song for his people in the name of Yahweh. Chapter 5 begins: "Let me sing for my beloved a love song concerning his vineyard." The beloved is Yahweh and the vineyard is his people Israel, represented in one of the great traditional images.[3] The prophet continues to describe the tender care with which the lover, Yahweh, treated his beloved vineyard. But so intense is the emotion, so deeply is God concerned with his people, that the prophet cannot maintain the pretense. He manages two verses in which he speaks of Yahweh in the third person, but 5:3 breaks this down into direct address from Yahweh to his beloved: "Judge, I pray you, between me and my vineyard. What more was there to do for my vineyard that I have not done?" (5:3b–4a.) The lover is disappointed in his beloved. And why is he disappointed? Because his vineyard, his people, was where he looked for righteousness and mercy but found injustice and bloodshed. Here in Isaiah we have language and imagery utterly different from that of Hosea, and yet they tell of the same basic thing, of a divine love

---

[3] See Hos 10:1; Ezek 19:10; Ps 80:7–13; Jn 15:1–11 for other examples of the use of the vine as an image of the people of God.

tenderly concerned with the people of God and especially compassionate toward the humble members of that nation.

Isaiah, then, knows Yahweh not only as the awesome holy one, but also as the one who comes close to his people through love and demands righteousness of them. This concern is realistic too. It recognizes that the rich and powerful have special duties in this regard. They must guide the nation in the paths of justice. Thus it is all the more criminal for them to use their power to deprive the poor and increase their own holdings (Is 5:8–10). The prophet makes sure that they will realize that their special opportunities are special responsibilities.

These responsibilities are not confined merely to the economic sphere. Righteousness demands that the powerful, the rich, the priests, and the rulers, direct the nation in the ways which lead to its true good. This is the way things should be, but in fact they are far otherwise. Those who should direct the people in the knowledge of Yahweh, priests and prophets, do not simply neglect their role; they are drunk, drunk with power and drunk in reality. They stagger and fall, and when the natural leaders of the nation are in such a state, what hope is there for the rest? (Is 28:5–10.) Notice that the complaint is not primarily that the religious leaders bring in false worship, as in Hosea 4:4–14, for instance, though Isaiah like all the prophets is sometimes concerned with the problem of idolatry, the constant temptation to turn to false gods (cf. 2:18), but this is hardly a central concern with him. In this too he resembles Amos. Perhaps this reflects their common Judean background. The out-of-the-way kingdom of Judah had less contact with contaminating foreign influences. Moreover, it had the Ark of the Covenant, from time out of mind the center of true Yahwist worship. Without doubt this contact with the central cultic tradition of the Hebrew people also helped to preserve Judah from idolatry.

However, this protection given by the Ark was by no means all to the good. If the central shrine of Yahwism kept peoples' attention on Yahwist religion it also encouraged them to consider the elaborate liturgy of the Temple as the whole of that religion. It is a common prophetic theme that God would have obedience and not sacrifices, but nowhere is this idea expressed more forcefully than in Isaiah:

> . . . who requires of you
>   this trampling of my courts?
> Bring no more vain offerings;
>   incense is an abomination to me.

Feasts of new moon and sabbath and assemblies —
    I cannot endure iniquity and solemn assembly.
. . . remove the evil of your doings
    from before my eyes;
cease to do evil,
    learn to do good;
seek justice,
    correct oppression;
defend the fatherless,
    plead for the widow (Is 1:12b–13; 16b–17).

What Isaiah reproves here is not the liturgy as such but the false interpretation and the misuse of the liturgy. Men were tempted to believe that the ritual was enough in itself to propitiate God. It did not matter what one did, just so long as one worshiped according to the rubrics. This is gravely false, but it is not idolatry.

TRUST IN THE LORD

It is not only in the religious sphere that the leaders are found wanting. The political rulers of the nation are equally foolish. As we have noticed already, Isaiah time and again tried to give advice to the kings and to warn against a mad foreign policy. However, he was never listened to. The leaders preferred to make "a covenant with death" so as to "make lies their refuge" (Is 28:14–15; see also 30:1–14). The rulers of Jerusalem are fools and worse because they have to rely on a treaty, probably with Egypt. They do this when they already have a covenant, that is, a treaty, with the one true God. To turn from him to a human ally is sinful folly, for he is the God of Armies. The problem here is not that the rulers rejected sensible political advice, although it was good advice in the military situation of the time, since Egypt could not stand against Assyria. The prophet condemns because these people put their trust in created things, not in God alone. Neither may they excuse themselves by saying that they did not know what Yahweh demanded. The prophet was there, and when he would not be heard he has his admonitions written down as permanent testimony that Yahweh did warn of the ruin that they were bringing upon themselves, and soon (Is 30:8–14). More striking still are Isaiah's efforts to direct King Ahaz in the ways of the Lord. The prophet is sent to give the king a sign to strengthen his confidence during the crisis of the Syro-Ephraemite war. However, the king will not follow Yahweh, and a hopeful sign becomes an ambiguous one. A child will indeed be born and bear the name Emmanuel, "God is with us."

Surely this is a hopeful sign, yet it concludes with a threatening note. God is with the king, and his immediate enemies will not harm him. So far so good, but the end result of his lack of faith in Yahweh is that things do not stop there. The king has refused to rely upon Yahweh alone and preferred to seek an Assyrian alliance to protect his nation (2 Kgs 16:7–9). But Assyria was a dangerous ally and the prophet assures the king that it will eventually cause devastation in Judah such as it has not seen for three hundred years (Is 7:10–17). Here we see the special responsibilities of the powerful and the terrible effects of their failure to live up to these responsibilities. They destroy not only themselves but their whole people. Hence Isaiah's concern that these leaders be righteous.

The discussion of the responsibilities of the leaders of the Hebrews, then, emphasizes a further characteristically Isaian demand. The leaders sin through greed and irresponsibility, but most of all they sin because they do not trust in the Lord. The problem of confidence in God stands out in the conduct of the leaders simply because they are more conspicuous and the results of their actions more widespread. However, it is not only the leaders who must put their entire faith in the Lord. All the people must do so; and with reason, for even the poorest and weakest are under the hand of the Lord (Is 14:32).

Hence we find the prophet calling upon the women of Jerusalem to stop being complacent. Rather they should bewail the troubles coming on the city because it has been self-satisfied, trusting in itself, not in God (32:9–14).

TEMPLE AND HOLY WAR

Isaiah does not state his doctrine of complete trust in God merely negatively. He affirms that a quiet trust will be the strength and salvation of Israel (Is 30:15). This is the proper way even though the holy city is surrounded by mighty armies, for in an instant a mighty stroke of its God will save it. This oracle is obviously talking about something real, armies and a siege. Isaiah's paradoxical demand that the people be quiet and trustful in a time of great turmoil applies to a brutally real world and does not refer merely to a state of soul. Isaiah 29:1–8 speaks of the holy city, for Ariel (29:1) is a symbolic name of Jerusalem. Isaiah is the prophet of Jerusalem and its Temple, the special place of God who will try not to destroy his city. How can the Holy One of Israel allow the city where he is enthroned (Is 6:1), whose very stones are precious (Is 28:16), the chosen city of his favorite servant, David (Is 37:35), to come to harm? In this confident theology of Zion Isaiah was following an ancient and popular tradition among the Hebrews documented in the psalms of Zion (Ps 46; 48; 76; 84; 87; 122; 132). These psalms sing of the glory of the Temple. They assert its foundation upon the everlasting stone. They hymn Yahweh who protects his dwelling upon Zion and destroys the enemies of the city.

Partly this is the theology of the Temple found in other ancient religions. For instance, the hymn to the Temple is typical of Mesopotamian literature. However, Psalm 76 and Isaiah add something. They sing of the glories of the holy place, but they attach the tradition of Yahweh the Warrior, one of the oldest titles of God. In some ways this is so obviously justified that it needs no explanation. The very nation came into existence because Yahweh imposed his will upon Pharaoh and his army in freeing the Hebrews from Egypt. Quite simply, he won a military victory. So a very ancient hymn celebrating the deliverance from Egypt calls God a warrior and describes in detail how he defeated his enemies and the enemies of the Hebrews (Ex 15:2–18). This is no mere figure of speech. Ancient Israel believed in the holy war. When the people of God went into battle God fought for them. This was taken very literally: it was not the Hebrew warriors who won battles, it was Yahweh himself. He acted directly and not through human instruments.

The clearest indication of this is not the use of the title "God the Warrior" and especially "God of Armies," although these are important. Rather it is in the great pains taken to show that it was Yahweh who won the victory and not the Hebrews, as in the story of Gideon's battle against the Midianites (Jg 7). The Israelite leader musters an army of 10,000 men, but against all good military sense God demands that this number be cut down drastically. This illustrates a fundamental point of the holy war: it must be clear that Yahweh alone attains the victory, and this is so when a number totally disproportionate to the task gains the victory. The surprise night attack by which Gideon achieves his victory illustrates another element of the holy war. Yahweh fought and conquered his enemies by causing them to panic. To understand this, remember that to more primitive peoples the phenomenon of panic is a mystery, and they associate the mysterious with the divine. Our own word "panic" comes from the name of the Greek god Pan, who was thought to produce this odd phenomenon. The theology of the holy war is developed in the laws of Deuteronomy 20:1–9, and the sacred character of such a war is shown in the instructions in Deuteronomy 23:9–14. These laws simply guarantee that the army is ritually pure and therefore may engage in a sacred activity.

Thus Isaiah's theology combines his own insight into the holiness and power of God with several strands of the tradition, the ideas about God the warrior and the inviolability of his Temple.[4] This theology of Mount Zion and of the holy war, even though complemented by Isaiah's brilliant insight into the nature of God, was not without its dangers. It could give people an unreasonable confidence. They could and did come to believe that they were safe because they lived in Yahweh's city even though they failed to obey his commandments or hear the voices of his prophets. This is a natural enough interpretation of a text like Isaiah 37:35: "I will defend the city for my own sake and for the sake of my servant David," and this interpretation was made according to Jeremiah 7:1–15. There the prophet warns not to trust in the Temple (Jer 7:4), as though this would protect them against all dangers. They must do justice to their neighbor and serve Yahweh alone (Jer 7:5–10). Unless these conditions are fulfilled, it is useless to take part in the Temple worship (Jer 7:10–11), and the point is driven home by the example of Shiloh, once the place where the Ark was kept, but now in ruins (Jer 7:12–15).

It would be completely unfair to impute this gross misunderstanding of the theology of Zion to Isaiah. The false confidence resulting from a wrong understanding of the meaning of the Temple is the same error which Isaiah condemned with regard to sacrifices (Is 1). Indeed this same chapter warns that those who rely upon the Temple to cover their sins will pay for this error, as indeed did the people of Jerusalem in Jeremiah's time.

A PRINCE OF DAVID'S LINE

If Isaiah's theology of Zion demanded that one trust in a holy and powerful God, another major element in his preaching bolstered all this by offering tremendous hopes for the future. This was his devotion to the Davidic monarchy. Despite the fact that his message had been rejected by one king, Ahaz, and that he often condemned the officials of the kingdom for whose actions the king was ultimately responsible, Isaiah never wavered in his confidence in David's line.

We shall not call this messianism because, as explained earlier in the section devoted to the topic, this term is misleading when used of pre-

---

[4] On the theology of the holy war in Isaiah see von Rad, *Old Testament Theology* II, pp. 157–195.

exilic texts. Still, Isaiah is the prophet of the Davidic king, the anointed leader of God's people.

His essential teaching on the subject is contained in Isaiah 7:1–9:7 plus the poem about the peace to come in 11:1–9. There has been a tremendous amount of discussion of these passages and serious doubt has been cast on the authenticity of everything that is important in them. Many would deny that the magnificent poems in 9:2–7 and 11:1–9 come from Isaiah. There are those who believe that the Emmanuel prophecy in chapter 7 has nothing positive to say about kingship, and so forth.[5] Nevertheless, we can reasonably accept this material as being from the prophet himself. This is not to claim that the present arrangement comes from him but only that the arrangement has been made out of genuine Isaian material. We have already seen something of the Emmanuel prophecy. Originally an offer of a favorable sign to the king, it has become ambiguous or ironical because of his lack of faith. Hence the Emmanuel saying has its dark side, but it is not simply a judgment against the kingship, and we may include it in a study of Isaian doctrine on that institution. As for the poem in Isaiah 9, there is really no solid reason for denying it to Isaiah. If it is different from much else that he says, this is entirely appropriate because it is about different subject matter. The major objection to the passage was that it reflects ideas which were applied to kingship only in very late Judaism. This is untenable. The royal ideology reflected in this poem was known in Israel from the beginning of its settlement in Canaan. In fact, it has been argued convincingly that this poem reflects the ritual which surrounded the king of Judah so that it would be entirely natural from a prophet close to the Judean court like Isaiah.[6]

The poem in 11:1–9, picturing the peace which the Davidic prince is to bring, was also commonly thought to be much later than Isaiah because of its concepts and images. To some extent they are unusual, especially in the idyllic picture of peace in the last verses, but the occasion once again is special and calls for something special. Once again the major objection came because it was believed that ideas like this came to the Hebrews only very late. This is simply not the fact. To repeat, these

---

[5] For reference to interpretations of the Emmanuel prophecy as adverse to the kings see von Rad, *Old Testament Theology* II, pp. 170–172.

[6] Albrecht Alt, "Jesaja 8, 23–9, 6. Befreiungsnacht und Krönungstag," *Kleine Schriften* II (Munich: Beck, 1953), pp. 206–225, and Gerhard von Rad, "The Royal Ritual of Judah," *The Problem of the Hexateuch and Other Essays* (New York: McGraw-Hill, 1966), pp. 222–231, have shown the influence of ancient coronation rites, especially Egyptian, on texts like these.

are the common ideas and images surrounding kingship in the ancient Near East. The king was the bringer of prosperity. A man of Isaiah's culture and intelligence could hardly be unaware of these things, and it is quite unreasonable to use this argument any longer. Our increased knowledge of the ancient milieu has simply rendered invalid the argument from the falsely supposed late date of such ideas.

We may turn, then, to what Isaiah has to say about the Davidic king. First of all, as we have seen, the failure in trust of the reigning monarch, Ahaz, has changed the force of the Emmanuel prophecy. Offered as a sign of pure hope, it has become ironical. It is not totally negative. The name Emmanuel, "God with us," is enough to show that. Furthermore, the reference to curds and honey in verse 25 is obscure, but it can hardly picture hardship. Such food would have been considered a delicacy, not the food of poverty. Moreover, the king is assured that he will survive the war which frightens him, though his survival will be paid for by the fearful cost of Assyrian overlordship. Therein lies the irony; it might have been so prosperous a time and just enough remains to remind one constantly of what might have been. At the end of the Emmanuel prophecy beginning with 7:18 we have four short prophetc sayings, each beginning with "On that day" and probably stemming from a later time, namely, from the actual Assyrian invasion of Judah at the very end of the eighth century B.C. They have been added here to point up the threat which the reference to the king of Assyria in verse 17 contains.

Isaiah 8 does not seem to continue this subject, nor even to have anything to do with the problem of the Davidic kingship. The connection is not as easy to see as we might wish. In fact the situation is that of the Emmanuel prophecies. Chapter 8:4–6 refers to Damascus and Samaria, and in 8:8 the recurrence of the name Emmanuel is a sure link to chapter 7. In chapter 8 the prophet is inspired to add to the sign given in chapter 7. Now the prophet and his son take the place of royalty. This substitution of the lesser for the greater and especially the boy's ominous name (8:1), "The spoiling speeds, the preying hastens," indicate that troubles will come, and Isaiah insists that what he is doing be properly recorded and witnessed to as a sign justifying the truth of Yahweh's words which he repeated. Thus the prophet certainly sees his family as signs (8:18) to a faithless nation which must be punished. Though obscure, the whole of the chapter, then, carries on the idea of a sign and of coming devastation begun in chapter 7.

This dark picture changes dramatically with the brilliant poem in 9:2–7.

The people, who have wandered in a darkness of fear and oppression, suddenly are flooded with a great light. The enemy is put down utterly, and this by the hand of Yahweh. No human instrument is mentioned in 9:4–5. Furthermore, the new victory is compared with the victory of the judge Gideon over Midian, the very model of the holy war, that is, of God's direct intervention on behalf of his people. But the climax comes in the next verse in the Davidic prince, the wonder figure who will reign over a restored and purified people of God. He will do work even beyond that of the great David, restoring the kingdom of God's people to its true confines and upholding it firmly. Thus it will endure as David's kingdom had not except for the pitiful fragment of Judah, for the bases of this renewed kingdom are justice and righteousness, the justice and righteousness of the king who represents on earth the God whose justice and righteousness are as unshakable as the holiness from which they come.

The splendid titles in 9:6b are worth special attention. The attributes of this new king are very close to the attributes of God himself. Normally, the Hebrews were shy of such language, because it was dangerous in a culture totally polytheistic except for the tiny island of Judah. It was all too easy to divinize the king literally; yet the prophet dares to speak like this as the psalmists sometimes do: Psalms 2:7; 45:6; 89:26–27, for this new king is to be so close to God as to deserve godlike titles. He will be "a very god of a warrior" (the literal version of the second title in 9:6b). Such a title is especially striking in Isaiah, for it clearly refers to the idea which he emphasizes: God is the chief Warrior of Israel. Of course, this does not mean that the ideal king, eager for battle, will lead his country into war after war. The enemy must be put down, but once that is done he brings peace and prosperity to his people and in this sense is their true father.

After 9:7 the editors of the book of Isaiah have inserted several oracles which have no special reference to the Davidic kings. We return to them only once more, in 11:1–9. Once again, there is a prince, newborn or newly crowned, of the Davidic line (11:1). The new scion of David's house has all the endowments which will make a great king: wisdom, power, and especially devotion to the Lord (11:2; cf. 9:6). He will be the special protector of the humble and the oppressed just as in 9:2–3 the advent of the prince brought the people from the dark rule of foreign oppression into the light of God's kingdom. Again, in chapter 9 the enemies of the people were destroyed by God without the intervention of any commensurate human power. So here through the power of Yahweh the prince's mere word will destroy the wicked (11:4). The ideal Davidic prince will be ideally successful because his work is based on the proper foundation, a righteousness like that of Yahweh (11:5).

Evidently, then, the first five verses of Isaiah 11 come from the same thought world as the poem in 8:2–7, with one significant advance over what is revealed in chapter 9. There the people are saved without any explanation at all of how this is done. It is not evident that the simple will of Yahweh does it directly, but we must infer this. Chapter 11:4 specifies this more precisely and indicates the role of the true prince. He is the instrument through whom Yahweh's will works. Some of God's power has been delegated to him so that his word alone is enough to shake the earth and destroy the wicked (11:4b).

Chapter 11:5–9 describes the perfect peace which will be brought about by Yahweh through the Davidic prince. The images of paradise used to describe this peace are not common in Isaiah, but then the conditions under which he lived and worked hardly gave him much occasion to talk of peace like unto paradise. When he has occasion, he does so. This is to be taken literally. The images which are used to describe the perfect peace are drawn from stories about the golden age at the beginning before man sinned when the whole world was at peace with itself. It extends even to the animal kingdom. Species which seem natural enemies will be at peace with one another. This recalls Genesis 1:29–30 and 2:19–20. But the most striking indication of the return to the times of peace at the beginning of creation is in 11:9 where the snake is no longer the enemy of man.

Before going further in interpreting Isaiah's great poems about the Davidic prince, we must note that many see significance in the fact that he does not use the word "king," Hebrew *melek,* but instead prince, Hebrew *shar.* Is this a deliberate avoidance of the word "king," because it rejected *in toto* the monarchy as it had developed from David? Hardly. It is inconceivable that Isaiah, the enthusiastic poet of Jerusalem, the city of David, was expressing reservations about the whole idea of the Davidic monarchy in the midst of glorious hymns about the new prince of that line. The use of the word "prince" for "king" proves nothing. This substitution was a commonplace in ancient literature and as such it cannot be pressed. But to what prince do these magnificent prophetic poems look? Is it simply a question of a new prince born to the line of David? A reference to a particular new prince or newly crowned king seems very likely in view of the reflection of the coronation ritual in Isaiah

9:6 and of concrete historical circumstances of Isaiah's period in 9:1, namely, the Assyrian conquest of Hebrew Galilee. However it seems impossible to stop here. Isaiah knew what was to be expected of the ordinary princes of David's line. He had a long history of their inadequacies as well as experience of their malice to teach him. If he wrote such magnificent descriptions of a Davidic prince after such history and such experience and then meant to speak of another prince like others of his line, this can be interpreted only as flattery of the basest sort. But whatever Isaiah may have been he was no flatterer. Isaiah 7 shows him standing up to the king in a way no flattering courtier ever did. Such magnificent language must have another explanation. It is very like the language of the royal psalms, and we may apply to it the words of John L. McKenzie, S.J. on the psalms: "The accession of the king is a pledge of the covenant and a step toward the realization of Israel's destiny; and the king is addressed in terms which anticipate the realization of the destiny. Therefore they speak of complete victory over the enemies of the king and of the marvelous prosperity which his reign will bring."[7] Thus it is in view of the promise to David (2 Sam 7; Ps 132) that the prophets see these things. They are well aware that the here and now which they experience is not the full realization of God's magnificent promises. But they know that God will keep his word and so they can speak of the present very partial fulfillment of the promise in terms which imply the complete fulfillment which is to come.

Furthermore, this is a concrete example of the problem of future applications of prophecy, a problem already discussed. It will be remembered that it is significant that these oracles were collected and preserved for us by the successors of the prophets. There is no doubt that the collection of sayings in Isaiah 7:1–9:7; 11:1–9 is the product of a later hand organizing the prophetic oracles which seemed relevant. That is, the actual inspired writing of our book was done after the time of Isaiah and therefore by someone who knew that Isaiah's splendid words had not been fulfilled even in the reign of the virtuous King Hezekiah or any other king of Judah. Why did this inspired compiler preserve these sayings of the prophet? Surely because he knew that they had not yet been completely fulfilled and still had utility for God's people.

Precisely because our sacred books were not the product of the activity of a single person or a small group but essentially the work of the people

<hr>

[7] John L. McKenzie, S.J., *Dictionary of the Bible* (Milwaukee: The Bruce Publishing Co., 1965), p. 570.

of God in time, we can be sure that things like Isaiah's great word about the prince to come were preserved with a view to their future utility and their present encouragement to the community. Such future reference is not a kind of prophetic broad jump which skips seven hundred years to land on Christ. It is rather a growing realization whose meaning is constantly increased and deepened until it is fully revealed in him who is to come.

THE REMNANT

Isaiah, then, definitely holds out a future hope to his people. However, it is a future which demands that basic Isaian virtue of total trust in Yahweh, because the future will be attained only by passing through tribulation. It is a remnant of Israel which will be saved. We have already seen the military origins of this metaphor, and in Isaiah the term is very close to those origins. The people must undergo the terrors of war and defeat. In the symbolic name of one of Isaiah's sons we are told that the takers of spoil are rushing upon the people (Is 8:1), and his other son has an equally ominous name: "A remnant shall return" (Is 7:3). Only a small number will survive the cataclysm and even they must suffer through the time of troubles. The clearest text here is the very end of Isaiah's inaugural vision. We are told in 6:11–13 that this people must be punished and this land destroyed. If but a tenth part of it should remain, it would be cut down still further. This process of trial will result in a nation which will truly make holy the name of Yahweh (Is 29:23), for only those who are able to put their faith in Yahweh alone (10:20) will form the remnant in whom the promise will be fulfilled and for whom Yahweh will be the very crown (28:5).

Once more, in his steady use of the remnant idea Isaiah introduced an important element into the growth of revelation. In his own use the term is ambiguous. It seems largely to be threatening. It certainly has its original nonmetaphorical sense of the miserable survivors of a terrible war. However, the idea grew as the Hebrew people lived on and learned to understand their position in God's plan through their experience of history. Though the remnant will be scattered, they shall return (Jer 23:3; Mic 2:12; etc.). It is not surprising, then, that the prophets of the post-exilic community saw the people of the return as the remnant of Israel (Hag 1:12; 2:2). However, this did not end the development of the idea of the remnant. The tiny community formed around Jerusalem after the return from the exile scarcely fulfilled all of the great hopes and promises of the past. If they found refuge with Yahweh (Zeph 3:12–13), that protection was very modest, and they hardly enjoyed the paradisiacal prosperity offered the remnant (Zech 8:10–12). Hence the concept of the remnant took on an ever more eschatological aspect. The remnant were to be the true followers of Yahweh who would be purified and saved in the end of days (Zech 13:8–9). Only then will the true chosen people be relieved of all purifying afflictions (Mic 4:6–7) and hold sway over the nations, who will be saved only if they cease to oppose the people (Mic 5:7–9).[8] Once again the historical experience of the people of God taught them the meaning of revelation. They had to undergo the actual experience of being a remnant, a defeated and deported population. Only then could they realize that redemption involved a return of a purified people to a better union with God. It is this full realization of the theological meaning of the remnant which Paul applies to the Church as the true remnant, God's people (Rom 11:5).

The final question we have for Isaiah concerns his attitude toward the Gentiles. Much of the genuinely Isaian material dealing with the nations is contained in the traditional oracles against enemies of God's people. Thus, while Isaiah is quite sure that the Assyrians are God's chosen instrument for the punishment of his faithless people, the Assyrians themselves stand under judgment, and there are many oracles directed against them (10:5–15, 24–34; 14:24–32). Despite the fact that the Assyrians were the nation which actually attacked Judah and laid siege to Jerusalem, it is not the Assyrians but the Egyptians who are Isaiah's prime concern. In Isaiah 18–19 and 28–31 Egypt is condemned over and over again.

The prophet directs all this indignation against the Egyptians because it is their plotting which has been leading the people of God astray. They persuaded the kings of Judah not to submit to the Assyrian attack in perfect trust in Yahweh but rather to make alliances in the hope that human power could save them. Isaiah knows that Egypt is a broken reed which will cut the hand of the man who leans upon it. But even if it were a nation of immense power, it would still be worthy of condemnation because it led Judah to lean upon it: "Woe to those who go down to Egypt for help . . . who trust in chariots because they are many and on horsemen because they are strong . . . the Egyptians are men and not God and their horses are flesh and not spirit" (Is 31:1–3).

---

[8] Both Micah and Zephaniah are pre-exilic prophets, but the passages used here from the books under their names are later insertions and so valid illustrations of later ideas.

It would seem that in all this we have a very negative attitude toward the Gentiles. They are merely objects of condemnation. This seems even to be a decline from the attitude of Amos, who saw that the Philistines and Arameans were God's people like Israel itself. Still, Isaiah is not entirely negative. The non-Hebrew people can be the instrument of God's work in history. Sometimes this is put quite contemptuously as when he says that "the Lord will whistle for the fly that is at the source of the stream of Egypt and for the bee which is in the land of Assyria" (7:18). This likens the nations to animals, dogs which must come at call. In 5:26–30 their role is described somewhat more nobly. The power of the Assyrian armies is recognized as a fitting image and instrument of God's wrath. Thus it would be false simply to assume that Isaiah was an exclusivist who merely ignored or condemned the outsiders. Even in his time followers of Yahweh like Amos realized that Yahweh was God over all men, and that his promises were to all mankind. The promise to Abraham in Genesis 12:1–3 makes the patriarch a source of blessing for all nations. This text derives from the Yahwist document and is older than Isaiah. However, we need not look so far for an expression of interest in the Gentiles. The very text of the book of Isaiah as it has come down to us shows an attitude which was current and even official in the very time of Isaiah. In Isaiah 2:2–4 we have a bit of liturgical poetry, a hymn taken from the Temple services. We see this in the very nature of the piece; it conforms to the hymnic style characteristic of the Temple. More importantly, this same bit of poetry appears in Micah 4:1–4. It seems really to belong to neither prophet. It is a liturgical piece speaking of all men coming to Yahweh and is incorporated in appropriate places in the prophetic books. Thus it is evidence of Isaiah's background of belief against which we must read his statements about the Gentiles. In other words, the Judah of his time and presumably her prophets were interested in the fate of the nations, and realized that Yahweh sought the salvation of all.

MICAH

Another prophet was active in Judah in the time of Isaiah. This is Micah of Moresheth-gath, a town in southwestern Judah on the border of Philistia. He began preaching before 721 B.C., because he threatened Samaria with conquest (1:6), which makes sense only before the fall of the city in 722–721 B.C. It has often been the custom to contrast Micah, the country man, with Isaiah, the city dweller, since Isaiah is confident that Jerusalem will not be destroyed while Micah can accept to the loss of the capital of Judah (3:12). Nonetheless the message of the two prophets is very similar. Each has heard Amos and cries for justice. There was, in other words, already something of a prophetic tradition at work in Judah. So Micah, like other prophets, is concerned with false worship. Samaria is doomed because of her idolatry (1:7), and Judah itself is not innocent (1:9). It too must suffer the horror and humiliation of conquest.

However, Micah saw God as concerned less with the cult and more with the basic attitude of the people, an attitude which could only be true justice toward all the people of God. Thus 2:1–11 is a diatribe against the powerful who oppress the poor. Like Isaiah, this country man condemns the large estates which the rich have built from the small holdings of the peasantry (compare 2:2 and Is 5:7–10). These holdings were acquired through unjust dealings, and the fact that such actions deprived individual families of their share of the land which God had promised to *all* people made them even worse.

Thus the prophet specifies the guilty, the leaders of the people, the rich and powerful. Chapter 3:1–4, 9–12 explicitly condemns the rulers of Judah. They were the chosen guardians of God's people, and therefore had to know what true justice is (3:1). And yet how did they act? They used their position for their own aggrandizement and so destroyed the simple people. They "built Zion with blood and Jerusalem with wrong" (3:10). They were truly those "who eat the flesh of my people and flay their skin from off them . . . and chop them up like meat in a kettle" (3:3).

This violent language, denouncing a people who have forgotten justice, is in the direct tradition of Amos and Isaiah. Micah, however, has something of his own to add to the picture. Yahweh is not only an observer who sends prophets to denounce injustice, he is a judge and he calls his unrighteous people to account. This is magnificently expressed in the formal courtroom scene in Micah 6:1–8 in which Yahweh summons the guilty people to trial. There are the witnesses (6:2), there is the indictment (6:3–5), and an effort at a defense (6:6–7) based on a claim of ignorance and good intention. However, this feeble defense is swept aside and the prophet proclaims that the guilty really did know the true wishes of Yahweh: "To do justice, to be devoted with a faithful love, and to walk humbly with God" (6:8b). Yahweh is appealing precisely to his election of his people and saying that because of this they knew what they should do. He had made his will clear in his commandments when he chose the people. Thus election is a responsibility, not simply a privilege, just as in Amos 3:1–2. The God of justice must and will call his delinquent partners to account.

So far all is condemnation. Moreover Micah, unlike Isaiah, could face the total destruction of Jerusalem (3:12). This cuts off one of the major themes of hope which appeared in Isaiah. Zion and its Temple are no assurance of protection. Earlier critics believed that Micah stopped here. All the oracles of hope beginning in chapter 4 were declared unauthentic. Once more, the reason was the presupposition that the older prophets never spoke of hope. This *a priori* method forces us to throw out of these prophets an embarrassingly large amount of material which is, in style and vocabulary, similar to their other sayings. This is reason enough to question the method, but in addition we now know that very lively hopes as well as fears were associated with institutions like monarchy and Temple in ancient Near Eastern culture. Furthermore, the Psalms and the Deuteronomic school of theology prove that the Hebrews shared in this association, as they did in this culture in general. It would be odd if prophecy, itself a phenomenon shared with this culture, alone failed to take up this aspect of the Hebrew cultural heritage. Hence the modern attitude is to accept the authenticity of such passages.[9] We except only Micah 2:12–13 and Micah 4 which are in the apocalyptic manner of late Judaism, not in the prophetic style. Some other material has suffered editing or glossing (e.g., 7:11–14), but there is no reason to doubt that the basic material of Micah 5–7 came from the prophet himself.

So Micah is not entirely negative. He offers a splendid hope to his people. In 5:2–4 there is the famous passage about the new Davidid who will come forth from Bethlehem and lead the restoration of his people. In many ways this short oracle sums up the message of Micah. The people must pay for their sins by a chastisement which is apparently a purification necessary to prepare for the coming glory (5:3 — the threatened devastation of Judah will take place but it is not the end). The leader of the restoration will be the true David who will reverse the evil practices of those who used their high position, not to build, but to destroy. He will be a true shepherd who will give his flock security (5:4).

It is entirely natural that a peasant could have a confidence in the Davidids which he did not feel toward the big city, Jerusalem. We know that the country folk of Judah were devoted to David's line (cf. 2 Kgs

---

[9] The basic study of the noneschatological character of Hebrew hopes in the monarchical era is Sigmund Mowinckel, *He That Cometh.*

11:18, where they take part in restoring the Davidid Joash after Athaliah's attempted usurpation), and by mentioning Bethlehem (5:2) the prophet emphasizes that David himself was one of these folk. Thus he would base the future hope on the promise to David and not upon the privileged position of Zion. This explains why the prophet can reject one of the themes from which Isaiah drew hope and retain the other. A man of Judah in the time of Micah would normally be faithful to the Davidids and hence quite capable of a burst of enthusiasm based upon the promise made to David. This was part of his Judean religious heritage. The claim that the "rest of his brethren" (5:3) refers to the Judean exiles in the sixth century B.C., which would deny the oracle to Micah, has no real force. The prophet speaks of the hope for a restored kingdom uniting the whole Hebrew nation once again. This dream of a reunion of all Hebrews, Israel and Judah, under a Davidic king had never been lost in Judah. Hosea 1:11 and 3:5 are admitted to be glosses on the original prophecy, but they therefore attest the vitality of this dream since they are the work of Judean scribes. In view of all this there is little doubt that the "rest of the brethren" in Micah 5:3 refers to the hope of the return of the people of the northern kingdom, Israel, not merely from exile, which they had already suffered, but to union with Judah.

This interpretation indicates that Micah's prophecy looked to fulfillment in the more or less immediate future. The prophet foresees a terrible punishment for Jerusalem, but he does not look to an exile which would include the people of Judah. Thus he does not even look to the exile of the people of Judah into Babylonia in 587. And yet this is a messianic text in the New Testament (Mt 2:6; Jn 7:42). How can this be? We have here the same situation as that we have seen for messianic prophecy in general. Their careful preservation after their modest first fulfillment or even apparent failure to be fulfilled indicates that the prophets and the people of God realized that God's word reached out beyond its immediate and sometimes rather unimpressive immediate application. In fact, Matthew 2:6 gives us a concrete picture of the way the process worked. The teachers of the people of God remember and apply an ancient prophecy to a new situation. They knew it must have some further validity. Exactly how they knew this is a difficult question to answer, but surely one cause was the education which history forced upon the people of God. They had looked for perfect salvation, now in a king like Josiah, now in the return from exile, now in the Maccabean revolt, only to be disappointed each time. Such a history forced them not to abandon but to reconsider the meaning of the promises and find in them an ever deeper significance.

Micah has very little to tell us about the Gentiles. While he threatened the Hebrew people with a punishing destruction, unlike Isaiah he does call the armies which will perform this an instrument of Yahweh's judgment. In fact, the nations appear only in the prophetic liturgy in Micah 7:8–20. After God restores his people, the Gentiles will be ashamed of the mockery they had visited upon them (7:10), and they will bow down before God's people in abject subservience (7:16–17). This hardly shows much concern for the Gentiles, but there is something in it for them. They come to recognize the true God, and they learn to fear him (7:17), and, as the whole Old Testament knows, the fear of the Lord is the beginning of wisdom. This is not yet a true universalism, a real insight into God's concern for all of his creatures. Nevertheless there are elements here which can and will lead to a deeper recognition of the meaning for all men of the promises God has made to and through his people.

The contemporary Judean prophets, Isaiah and Micah, have, not surprisingly, much in common, as we see when we try to sum up their doctrine. Both emphasize the justice and righteousness of God, although Isaiah alone connects this with his holiness. This insight is a major step in religious history, for it is one of the earliest realizations that the divine mystery, awesome and so strange as almost to be alien, has a moral will, a concern for man. This emphasis on holiness is related to Isaiah's other interest which is not shared by Micah, Zion and its cult, the very realm of the holy on earth. However, both prophets again share a zeal for justice among men, the basic response to the just (and holy) God. Furthermore, they hold out hope for a purified remnant of the people, and they connect this with the dynasty of David, though once more Isaiah adds the holiness of Zion as a reassuring element. Finally, the text of these prophetic books, if not the prophets themselves, evidences a belief in a salvation offered to all men (Is 2:2–4; Mic 4:1–3). At least, the prophets teach that foreign nations are as much under Yahweh's control as their own, for these nations have a role as punishers of his people's sins in the history he guides.

CHAPTER 9. NAHUM, HABAKKUK, ZEPHANIAH AND JEREMIAH

Readings: Nah; Hab; Zeph; Jer 1; 11:18–12:6, 15:10–21, 17:12–18, 18:18–23, 20:7–18; 2–6; 21:1–23:8; 7, 26; 30–31; 36

Isaiah and Micah must have ended their work about the end of the eighth century B.C. After them evidence of prophetic activity ceases for almost three-quarters of a century. It is only after the quiet and thoroughly paganizing reign of Manasseh that prophecy reappears. In fact, the violent upheavals of the ancient Near Eastern world at the end of the seventh century B.C. were just the kind of circumstances in which prophecy flourished. Before taking up the great prophet of the period we shall look at three lesser figures.

NAHUM

The first of these is Nahum. We really know nothing about the man, although at present it is fashionable to think of him as a cult prophet, that is, a prophet in the service of the Temple. Hence the book of Nahum would represent an official "prophetic liturgy." Although popular now, this view is by no means certain. There is no doubt that the prophecy

134

has been influenced by liturgical language. However, this merely shows acquaintance with the cult, not necessarily official participation in it.

Therefore we really know nothing of the prophet himself, but there is little doubt as to the circumstances in which he prophesied. His book may reflect the time immediately before or after the fall of Niniveh in 612 B.C., but in either case it is concerned with the destruction of the Assyrian empire in the last quarter of the seventh century B.C. It opens with a hymn which describes in traditional terms the appearance, technically the theophany, of Yahweh coming for judgment (1:2–10). Apart from a few lines offering hope to Judah (1:12–13; 15; 2:2) the rest of the book is given over to rejoicing at the fall of the Assyrian oppressor. The poetry which depicts the fall of the hated enemy is great literature. However, many question whether it deserves the name of prophecy for Nahum does little but rejoice at the destruction of the enemies of his people. Unlike the great prophets who so often condemned the conduct of the people of God, his rejoicing at the enemy's fall seems to be the work of an uncritical nationalist.

It is true enough that the message of Nahum is limited. His short poem does not achieve the stature of an Isaiah or a Jeremiah or a Micah. However, we cannot set our own standard for what a prophet must be and then refuse the title arbitrarily to one who does not conform to our arbitrary standard. Nahum at least affirms the important doctrine that Yahweh controls all that goes on in the world. To the secular eye Assyria fell before the onslaught of the Medes and the Babylonians; to the eye that could see deeper this destruction of a sinful nation (3:1, 4) was the direct work of Yahweh, the Lord of all armies and guide to all history (2:13; 3:5). Nor was Yahweh merely asserting his control over everything in all this. He also fulfilled his promise and saved his people (1:13; 2:2).

HABAKKUK

Habakkuk offers more difficulty to the interpreter. Once again we know nothing of the life and circumstances of the prophet. Beyond this there are difficulties in Habakkuk that do not occur in Nahum. The structure of the book is less clear, the dating and exact reference of its oracles less certain, and the authenticity of parts of it less sure.

Despite the difficulties, however, there is a certain structure to the whole book. The opening verses (1:1–4) are a complaint of the prophet against oppressors. There follows the prediction of the coming of the

Chaldeans (Babylonians) as conquerors (1:5–11). Chapter 1:12–17 resumes the complaint against oppression. There follows in 2:1–5 the proclamation that ultimately the righteous man shall live because of his fidelity, and that the evil man shall perish. The rest of chapter 2 is given over to a series of five woes called down upon oppressors. The last chapter of Habakkuk is in psalm style and describes the theophany when Yahweh comes to save the faithful people. This poem is full of mythological motifs, and it was once the practice to declare such materials unauthentic without further consideration, but there is no real reason why the psalm could not come from the prophet.[1]

A great amount of ink has been spilled over the identification of the oppressors in Habakkuk. They are said to be the Assyrians, the Babylonians, even the Greeks. Full discussion of such problems is matter for the specialist. Here we adopt a reasonable and widely held modern position which provides a satisfying interpretation of the book. This position asserts the unity of authorship of the book and ascribes it to the last part of the seventh century B.C. This allows the book a rational, even climactic structure. If we allow that the oppressors mentioned in the initial verses are the Assyrians, then the following announcement of the Chaldeans teaches that God makes use of human instruments to punish evil. In this instance one imperial power is put down by another. But this is no final solution and the prophet's complaints continue. Chapter 2 gives a new and deeper answer: amidst the clash of nations, personal righteousness brings true life (2:4). This is all very well, but it is evident that it is not always the good man who prospers and the evil man who suffers, and the renewed bewailing of oppression in 2:6 ff. calls attention to this constant problem. Only chapter 3 gives anything like a complete solution. We learn that Yahweh will ultimately deliver those faithful to him. Man cannot count upon human help or even upon his own righteousness. His only sure salvation lies with God. Thus we have an educational dialectic: human oppression offset by human means which themselves become oppressive, then a turn to reliance on personal fidelity which fails so that man is forced back on God alone.

---

[1] The idea that allusions to Canaanite myth are conscious archaism possible only in an era much later than Habakkuk when Canaanite religion was dead and so no longer dangerous to the Hebrews is popular among French scholars; an example of the argumentation is Lucien Legrand, "Creation as Cosmic Victory of Yahweh," *Theology Digest* 11 (1963), pp. 154–158 (= *Nouvelle revue théologique* 83 [1961], pp. 449–470). The basic study of Hab 3, its use of myth, and its pre-exilic date is W. F. Albright, "The Psalm of Habbakkuk," *Studies in Old Testament Prophecy*, H. H. Rowley, ed. (Edinburgh: T. & T. Clark, 1950), pp. 1–18.

One should note that one aspect of Habakkuk's message is a striking departure from the earlier prophets. It is the prophet himself who opens the dialogue with God. In the earlier prophets it was always God who began, who called his prophet to question the action of his people. This reversal, in which the prophet begins by asking how God can allow evil to go on, is probably due to the liturgical color of Habakkuk's prophecy. The official cultic prophets were commissioned to take up a case before Yahweh, to present a complaint to him and then mediate his answer. Habakkuk may be doing just this; probably he is simply imitating the forms of the liturgy. Still, it is tempting to call the whole book a liturgical text. Such an assumption would clear up some of the obscurities of the book. The liturgical prophet would be bound to more formal types of discourse and to techniques general enough to be adapted to different situations. This would account for the difficulty in identifying the oppressors in Habakkuk. We have found a sequence of Assyrians punished by Chaldeans who themselves turned into oppressors and so on, but it must be admitted that it would be better if the prophet said it more explicitly. He does not actually mention the Assyrians for us. If we assume that he was bound to the generalized forms of the liturgy the difficulty would be explained.[2]

ZEPHANIAH

The last of this trio of minor prophets, Zephaniah, is the most tradition-minded of them. His central concept of the day of Yahweh depends upon Amos (5:18–20) and Isaiah (2.10–21). He even imitates the language of the earlier prophets. Furthermore, the book of Zephaniah, probably because it was so conventional, seems to have undergone considerable editorial revision. The oracles against Moab and Ammon (2:8–11) were surely added in the time of the exile when these peoples raided a Judah which had been rendered defenseless by the Babylonian conquest. Finally, the language of the promises of hope in 3:9–20 echoes the language of the late exilic prophet, Deutero-Isaiah.

Even the structure of the book is simple and conventional. The first chapter is made up of two descriptions of the day of Yahweh (1:2–13; 1:14–18). This is a threat of judgment on faithless Judah which should respond to this by a return to the Lord (2:1–3). Chapter 2:4 begins a

---

[2] The prophet's taking the initiative is not exclusive to the cult prophet, however, for Jer 12:1–6 shows a prophet who was certainly not an official of the Temple doing it (perhaps in imitation of a cult-prophetic form, it is true).

series of oracles against the nations and 3:1–7 is a renewed condemnation of Jerusalem, followed immediately by a great promise of salvation. The dispersed and conquered people of God will be restored to a new and greater Israel. Thus the structure is the standard one: oracles against the Hebrews, oracles against the nations, and the final promise of hope.

No one can accuse Zephaniah of being overly inventive. However, the essential thing is that he brought his generation and the generations who read him the essential prophetic message of God's lordship. Neither does he lack some modest contributions of his own. In 3:12–13 he adds to the doctrine of the remnant the idea that this must be a humble, lowly people, that is, one utterly dependent upon and fully trusting in God. We cannot end without remarking that the tremendous picture of the day of Yahweh in 1:14–18 is the inspiration of the magnificent poetry of the *Dies irae*. So Zephaniah has not been without his effect upon theology and upon the imagination of the people of God.

JEREMIAH

Jeremiah is one of the most intriguing figures among the prophets, and his book one of the most complicated to interpret. It stands as the longest of the biblical books. However, there is an important difference between the Hebrew text we have and the ancient Greek text, the Septuagint, by far our oldest and most worthwhile independent witness to the text. The Greek text was translated from a Hebrew original well before the Christian era, and it is almost one-eighth shorter than the present Hebrew text. Furthermore, it is much differently arranged. These are but a few indications of the problems of establishing what is truly from Jeremiah and what is the true order within his prophetic preaching. Since these problems exist, we must devote some attention to the makeup of the book.

The first step in modern interpretation was taken by a great Norwegian scholar, Sigmund Mowinckel, in 1914. He distinguished three basic types of material in the book of Jeremiah. The first were the poetic oracles characteristic of prophecy. These are found mostly in chapters 1–25 and in the oracles against the nations in 44–50, which, it should be noted, Mowinckel himself did not include with the other poetic oracles. Then he pointed out that the biographical narratives were especially extensive in the book. These are found in chapters 19, 26, 28, 29, and 36–43. Some of this material is autobiographical, but it is generally conceded that most of it comes from Jeremiah's secretary, Baruch. Strangely, the biographical sections do not occur in the Bible in the actual order of Jeremiah's life. Finally, and very importantly, there is prose in Jeremiah which is not biographical. It has the form of the sermon and reflects the style characteristic of Deuteronomy.

In many ways the poetic oracles offer the least problems. These are like the sayings in the other prophetic books, and once scholars have determined the characteristic Jeremian style and thought they can distinguish fairly easily the poetry of the prophet himself from the other inspired poems which have been included in his works. The biographical material seems to be historical. It does not usually claim to stem from Jeremiah himself, but it is a good source of knowledge about the prophet without claiming to give us his words. The sermons with a Deuteronomic cast are much more difficult. Scholars are in considerable disagreement as to whether anything in them can be attributed to Jeremiah, but at least two of the most significant sayings in the book of Jeremiah belong to these sections. These are the sermon on the Temple in 7:1–15 and the word about the new covenant in chapter 31. What about the authenticity of these passages?

There is no denying the fact. These passages are in the style of Deuteronomy. Can these be the words of the prophet? If not, can they be in any degree faithful reports of his thought? Here one must decide on the basis of one's opinion of Jeremiah. Could he have been sympathetic to the Deuteronomic reform carried on under Josiah? That is the crux of the problem, and if we answer that he could, then Deuteronomic style and concepts could transmit a true message of the prophet himself. Now, in his earliest preaching Jeremiah is dominated by Hosea's idea of fidelity to Yahweh and his worship. This is so close to the ideal of Deuteronomy that it is hardly conceivable that the prophet did not sympathize with the Deuteronomic reform. This is even more likely if we realize that Deuteronomy is not an external law but is an appeal for a religion which is a service of Yahweh in total devotion, a religion in which man gives his whole self — his mind, his heart, and his soul — to God. Jeremiah was primarily concerned with a personal relationship to God very similar to this. Could he have been unsympathetic with the reform guided by ideals so like his own? Moreover, we know now that the style of these prose passages is not archaizing, an imitation of something alien. It is the natural prose style of Jeremiah's time. In other words, the disciples who choose to report Jeremiah's ideas would naturally do so in this style. It is not so much a question of Deuteronomic style as the style of late seventh century

Judah.[3] On this basis, then, we shall accept the basic authenticity of the passages concerning the Temple and the new covenant.

Even if we do distinguish three major types of material in the book of Jeremiah — poetic oracles, biographical reports, and prose sermons — we are still in a quandary when we try to find order in the book. There are smaller collections of sayings about a topic; for instance, chapter 2 is a set of discourses against idolatry; 14:1–15:9 is concerned with drouth; 21:1–23:8, with the kings, and so on. These groupings have been gathered together to form the book of Jeremiah, and beyond this we can hardly see any overall design. This contributes to the problem of summarizing or schematizing the prophet's doctrine, a difficult task in any case. His whole approach was far too personal to leave any topic around which we can organize what he has to say. Jeremiah was a reluctant prophet.

Finally, we should note that in chapter 36 the prophet ordered his prophecies to be written down for presentation to the king and, when the king disdained them, to be preserved so that he would be vindicated when they were fulfilled. The incident occurred in 605 B.C., so that the scroll would have contained some or all of Jeremiah's early oracles. Much effort has been spent on reconstructing this scroll, but with little result. Hence the effort offers as little help in deciding what is authentically Jeremiah's as it does in interpreting his words. The important thing is to note, first, the concern for preserving prophetic sayings in writing even while the prophet lived, for many deny any such concern; and second, the looking to future vindication, for many would restrict the prophet's interest to the immediate here and now without any regard for the future.

If the book of Jeremiah is complicated and full of problems, at least the circumstances of the prophet are quite clear. He belonged to a priestly family of sufficient importance to be a landholder. He was not a Judean, though Anathoth, his home, is only about five miles north of Jerusalem. He was a Benjaminite. Thus, despite the fact that he worked exclusively in Jerusalem and Judah, he had his roots in northern traditions. Hence, no doubt, his evident debt to the one prophet from the kingdom of Israel, and his objective, not to say cool, attitude toward Zion and the Temple traditions.

Furthermore, we can divine something of the prophet's character from his oracles. He was excessively sensitive and introspective. Together with

---

[3] See John Bright, "The Date of the Prose Sermons of Jeremiah," *Journal of Biblical Literature* 70 (1951), pp. 15–35; more briefly *id., Jeremiah. The Anchor Bible* (Garden City, N. Y.: Doubleday, 1965), LXXI–LXXIII.

the literary problems of the book, this makes the doctrine of Jeremiah most difficult to summarize or to schematize. His approach was far too personal to leave a topic around which to organize what he has to say. Jeremiah was a reluctant prophet. If Amos felt compelled to prophecy when the Lord spoke, and Isaiah offered himself instantly when the Lord sought someone to send, Jeremiah tried to avoid his vocation (1:6). Nonetheless Yahweh made this reluctant and uncertain personality his spokesman. It is not only in his reaction to his vocation that Jeremiah reveals his fundamental unsureness. The other prophets often enough speak personally, but none of them speaks of his own inner feelings and problems and doubts in the manner of Jeremiah. His "confessions" (11:18–12:6; 15:10–21; 17:12–18; 18:18–23; 20:7–18) reveal a conflict within the soul of the prophet. He is deeply one with his people, but his message sets him in opposition to them. So his prophetic vocation made him lonely (16:1–4), and he was weak enough to kick against the goad so that he needed conversion and Yahweh's forgiveness (15:19). This was a man who always saw things from his own intimately personal point of view. Naturally, therefore, his message is typically couched in lyric poetry, couched, that is, in terms of his own reaction. Characteristic of this is the famous poem in 8:22–9:1:

> Is there no balm in Gilead?
>   Is there no physician there?
> Why then has the health of the daughter of my people
>   not been restored?
>   O that my head were waters
> and my eyes a fountain of tears,
> that I might weep day and night
>   for the slain of the daughter of my people!

This prophet would proclaim Yahweh's condemnation, but he would always feel pain at what it involved, and he must give voice to his feelings.

It is natural that so introspective a man be bothered by the problem of his mission. Of all the prophets, only Jeremiah is much concerned with the problem of distinguishing between the true and the false spokesman of Yahweh. He tries to find a way to tell true from false. Prophecy which turns the people away from true Yahwism (23:9–11) is easily seen to be false, but error is not always so unsubtle as this. One sign of a true prophet is that he will prophecy hard things, whereas the false prophet insists that there is nothing to fear (23:16–17). Most of all, it is the prophet whose words are actually fulfilled in the history directed by Yahweh who is indeed Yahweh's spokesman. However, neither of these criteria is entirely sufficient. Not all prophecy is prophecy of doom, and future vindication is of no great use in deciding here and now who has the truth. Jeremiah continued to wrestle with the distinction between true and false prophet just as we ourselves must wrestle to discern the good from the bad spirit, and never be completely sure of the answer.

Given the prophet's subjectivism, it is difficult to follow the scheme we have set before us, giving first the prophet's special insight into the nature of God, then demands for men consequent upon this, then the hope that he offers the people, and finally his reaction to the Gentiles. It is best to follow the life of Jeremiah and see the various phrases which were his own education in the ways and meaning of Yahweh as well as the stages of his message.

Jeremiah's call is dated in the thirteenth year of King Josiah, so that his first preaching began around 626 B.C. Directed at Judah, it is largely found in chapters 2–6. It calls the people from the worship of false gods to a return to true Yahwism in terms influenced by Hosea. Like Hosea Jeremiah preaches against the high places, like Hosea he sees the desert as a time of election, and like Hosea he characterizes idolatry as adultery, a vicious and well nigh unforgivable infidelity to the good God.

After this initial activity Jeremiah seems not to have preached for some time. Various reasons have been proposed for this. The most plausible is that he found the reform taking place under King Josiah actually fulfilling his demands, putting down the high places and bringing back pure Yahwism. It may be at this time that the oracles about the return of the northern kingdom (30–31) were given. This would reflect the activity of Josiah, who attempted to recover these lost provinces. In any event Jeremiah did not resume vigorous preaching until after the reign of Josiah, whose death he sincerely laments (22:15–16). The context of the eulogy of Josiah is significant. It is part of a reproach leveled at his successor Jehoiakim. Under this foolish and faithless monarch Jeremiah saw Judah once again upon the road to ruin. This king reintroduced the most vicious forms of idolatry, including the terrible rite of offering the firstborn son to false gods (7:30–31). Moreover, he was guilty not only of idolatry but also of injustice. He built himself palaces, and in order to do so he impressed the poor (22:13–14).

THE FALL OF JERUSALEM

The prophet could see the beginning of the end for Judah. He had preached reform, he had seen Josiah attempt reform, and now he saw that it was hopeless. The new king led the nation back to idolatry and injustice. Moreover, a false reading of the promises of Isaiah and the theology of Zion had given the people an overweaning confidence. They were convinced that in the Temple they had a magic talisman that would protect them against the punishment (7:1–17), forgetting that the God who dwelt in Zion was a God of justice who demanded justice from his people. If they were unworthy of him his holy place would be no protection. Notice that Jeremiah's attack on false confidence in the holiness of the Temple is carried here in one of the Deuteronomic prose sermons, and it is confirmed in an undoubtedly authentic biographical section (26). An abuse and a time of trouble called forth vigorous prophetic preaching in every effective form!

Jeremiah did not leave his audience in ignorance of the sources of danger either. The enemy would come from the north (1:13–16). In the context of the politics of the time the meaning of this was clear. In the struggle to take over the remains of the Assyrian empire Egypt was attempting to renew its hold upon Palestine and Syria from the south, and Jeremiah is warning that they will be unable to do so. This portion of the earth has been given into the hands of the Babylonians who will come from the north to avoid the impassable desert east of Palestine. This prophecy was good political advice, but it was disregarded. Judah joined Egypt and suffered the consequences. In 597 the Babylonian king Nebuchadnezzar laid siege to Jerusalem. The young king who had succeeded Jehoiakim with the almost identical name of Jehoiachin was wise. He surrendered the city to the Babylonians and so won a measure of mercy for himself and for his people. He and thousands of the leading citizens were taken into captivity, but the puppet kingdom of Judah was allowed to go on, with his uncle Zedekiah as king.

One would think that this would be sufficient education for the Judean politicians. Prophet and power both testified that Babylon was superior, and that they must submit to it if they were to survive. Nonetheless they persisted in the folly of courting Egypt. Jeremiah opposed this policy at no little cost to himself. He suffered from his personal unsureness and from loneliness. His family was against him (11:21), and powerful men tried to imprison and kill him. True, King Zedekiah had some sympathy with Jeremiah and even sought his advice (37:3–5), but the king was a weakling. He did not face up to the opposition politicians, and he was drawn into the anti-Babylonian politics which ruined his kingdom. By 587 B.C. Babylonian patience was exhausted. In that year the Babylonian army again laid siege to Jerusalem. Jeremiah constantly warned that the only hope was to give in to Babylon. This was treated as treason and he was imprisoned (37:10–16). Moreover, so foolish were the people that they thought to trick God. They liberated their Hebrew slaves as they were obliged to do according to the law. However, the only motive for this was their fear of the siege, and when an Egyptian army raised the siege for a moment they went back upon their word and re-enslaved their Hebrew brethren. Once more Jeremiah must condemn them (Jer 34:8–22). The interruption of the siege caused by the Egyptians was but momentary. The people must pay for their folly and they did. The Babylonians overwhelmed Jerusalem in 586, captured the king with his family and punished them terribly. They destroyed the city and took anybody who was anybody: nobility, scribes, priests, craftsmen, into the Babylonian captivity. The independent existence of the Hebrew kingdom had come to an end.

Jeremiah's end was as tragic as his life and as senseless as the rejection of his constant good advice. Because he had preached submission the Babylonians did not force him into exile. He stayed in Judah and lived with Gedaliah, a Judean appointed governor of the Babylonian province which had been the kingdom of Judah. However, Gedaliah was murdered by some vengeful anti-Babylonians, and Jeremiah was forced to go with them into exile in Egypt. There he disappeared from sight, to the end apparently a failure.

In what Jeremiah had to say during all these tumultuous events there is little which does not relate to his predecessors. He demanded an absolute fidelity to Yahweh, who after the manner of Hosea he pictured as a lover. He called for strict justice among God's people, and particularly from the people in power toward the less favored, toward the weak and the poor. This was in the tradition from Amos onward. He demanded absolute obedience to the law of Yahweh. Once more this is traditional. If there is any one thing which characterizes all prophecy, it is the absolute demand that Yahweh alone be served and obeyed. All this, then, is not new. Yet Jeremiah brings something new to it. This is his intense personal involvement. He is not the preacher apart from the people, castigating them for their sins and warning them of their punishment. He feels himself a part of the people and their pain is his pain. Equally he is Yahweh's spokesman and he feels the indignation and, as it were, the pained outrage of God.

THE NEW COVENANT

However, the prophet whose name has become a synonym for whining complaint (see *jeremiad*), is most distinctive in the hope which he offered for the future. He saw his nation ruined by its sins and folly. He suffered intensely through this, because he was that kind of person. He could not maintain any distance from what went on. It was all his own very personal experience. And still he is a great prophet of a great hope.

One element in this is the characteristic theme of the fulfillment of the promise to David: "Behold the days are coming, says the Lord, when I will raise up for David a legitimate successor, and he shall reign as king and deal wisely, and shall execute justice and righteousness in the land. In his days Judah will be saved, and Israel will dwell securely. And this is the name by which he will be called: 'The Lord is our righteousness' " (23:5–6; cf. 33:14–16). This is a remarkable bit of prophecy. Jeremiah was not Judean. So he owed no special loyalty to the house of David. Moreover he had lived through terrible disappointments with the descendants of David. He had seen them abuse the people, lead them into idolatry, and bring about their total ruin. Nonetheless he had faith in the promise made to David. It would be false to say that this was central to his theology, but it was an aspect which was there, which he could not and would not avoid. In the promise to David the people of God has a sure reason for hope.

Perhaps some of Jeremiah's confidence in the Davidic dynasty had been aroused by Josiah, for the prophet's hope corresponds to that king's vision of a complete nation reuniting the true people of God separated since the death of Solomon. Still, Josiah failed. He did not reunite the people and his successors show that he did not inaugurate the reign of righteousness. Yet Jeremiah knows that a true Davidic Savior will come. Once again we meet that phenomenon, the preservation of a prophecy which looks to its immediate era but cannot refer entirely to it because it was disappointed then.

Jeremiah also offers to his people a new hope connected with the idea of the remnant. We have seen that in its original military context the remnant was the few people left over after an army attempted to annihilate a defeated nation. Therefore, after the Babylonian conquest the few people remaining in Judah felt that they were the remnant, the custodians of the hopes of the people of God. Not so, says Jeremiah. The exiles in Babylon were the true line which would carry on the people of God (29). This is remarkable in that it separates true Yahwism from any connection with the Promised Land. This confident assertion of the prophet proved to be entirely correct. In Babylon the people learned that they could separate their religion from land and Temple and elaborate cult. They were forced to consider their religion and its meaning, and they found in their law and its directives governing all their lives the means which kept them Yahweh's people. They had to rely on God's word and their fidelity to that word. It was this answer to their circumstances, worked out by the exiled community in terms of the study of God's word and faithful living of that word, which formed the basis on which the people of God restored their nation after the exile.

Jeremiah's great contribution to the message of hope, however, is his concept of the new covenant. He had seen the old covenant fail and the people unfaithful to it punished and almost destroyed. But this was not to be the end. He foresaw a return beyond the physical return of exiled Israel and Judah to the Promised Land. It would be a moral return because they would come back to the true service of Yahweh. This would take the form of a covenant unlike the old one made with the people who had been freed from Egypt. Under the old covenant the people had depended too much on external institutions. They needed cult and teachers and threats to drive them to live according to the law. Not so under the new covenant, when Yahweh would speak directly to his people: "I will put my law within them, and I will write it upon their hearts; and I will be their God, and they shall be my people" (31:33). The latter half of this sentence came to be the very formula of the covenant after Jeremiah, the characteristic way of expressing the special relationship between God and his people. In this covenant God will not have to write his law on tablets of stone; he will write it upon the heart of the individual. That is to say, God will speak to each one within himself so that he will know the right and be ready to perform it.

This is a remarkable conception. It is in some ways the most personal and individualistic view of the relationship between God and his people which the Old Testament presents. However, we must not misunderstand. Jeremiah is not anti-law and anti-institutional. The people of the new covenant will be led by a Davidic prince in the ways of righteousness. This is a simple recognition of the fact that as long as men are men they must have institutions. Neither should we read the passage in the sense that Jeremiah proclaimed that God will dispense with law and directly inspire his people in each special case as it comes up. The law he is to write on their hearts is the Torah. The prophet uses this, the technical word for the law of Moses. The word "torah" probably means, in its original sense, "teaching." It was not, therefore, merely a set of external rules to be consulted but rather something to be learned and acted upon personally. What Jeremiah is really proclaiming here is a more efficient system of education in the law of God so that the people may keep it more easily. He is by no means departing from the traditional Mosaic law when he does so. All in all, then, this hypersensitive individualist, Jeremiah, turns out to be a realist who manages to give hope a depth of meaning it never had before.

We can hardly say the same of his attitude toward the Gentiles. He is certainly aware of their existence. Much of his life was spent on advising the king of Judah that the people should submit to the Gentile powers who were their natural overlords. He sees the Babylonians as the instrument through whom Yahweh will punish his faithless people. In all of this he had advanced not one whit beyond Isaiah who saw the armies of Assyria as the Lord's instrument for the chastisement of his people.

Still, in one place Jeremiah does mark a definite advance. The Babylonians under Nebuchadnezzar are not a mere tool which Yahweh uses in dealing with his people. Yahweh claims power over the whole of the earth and all that is in it, and so he can give this dominion to whomever he wills. Hence Jeremiah's warning that, if one does not submit to the Lord's decree, which has given everything into the hands of Nebuchadnezzar, he sins against the Lord and will be punished (27:1–11). Thus Nebuchadnezzar is Yahweh's positive choice to rule. He is even dignified with the title "my servant" (27:6), which belonged to a Moses and a David. If this does not go so far as to say that Yahweh is positively interested in saving the Gentiles, it is a big step toward affirming his positive interest in them. Revelation still must progress before God's universal will to salvation can be clearly seen, but here in Jeremiah is one of the steps on the way to the realization of this essential doctrine.

Once again, one is embarrassed by Jeremiah's complexity when he tries to sum up the prophet's doctrine. The prophet cries for justice and he speaks of a God of love as did the prophets before him. He is an example of heartfelt involvement in the life of the people. Most of all, perhaps, he demands submission, giving oneself into God's hand without question.

This attitude, rather than any doctrine or idea, is central in him. As for a promise of hope for the future, he reaffirms the promise carried by David's line, and he enriches the concepts of the remnant and the covenant. Finally, his teaching is a step on the road to realizing that God not merely suffers the nations, but that he has a real regard for them.

Chapter 10. Ezekiel

Readings: Ezek 24; 33:21–33; 37; 8–10; 1–3; 20; 16:23; 36:1–37:14

By now we should be used to seeing the prophetic texts as rather haphazard, disorganized collections. At first glance Ezekiel seems not to conform to this pattern. In any modern edition of the Bible one finds the works of the other prophets broken up into short poems marked off by spacing, thus indicating by the external appearance of the page the disunity of the work. The book of Ezekiel, on the other hand, shows long prose discourses with occasional poetry and without the marks of separation found in the other prophets. Even at the turn of the century, in the great days of hypercritical study of the Old Testament texts, it was generally felt that this book was a homogeneous whole, stemming from a single author and organized into a rational scheme.

In biblical studies we can be sure that such a state of quiet will not last. Thus the German critic Hoelscher in 1924 decided that less than one-fifth of Ezekiel was authentic. Arguing from language and style, he considered only those poetic passages which exhibit an extravagant imagination to be Ezekiel's. Some other scholars accepted Hoelscher's views, and the American C. C. Torrey was even more radical. He considered the whole book to be a third-century B.C. fabrication, attributed first to the reign of King Manasseh and soon reworked to appear as the product of the exilic figure Ezekiel. So, despite the considerable appearance of unity in the book, we must again ask how much of it actually belongs to the prophet. And close examination does reveal that the book is not a single literary and logical whole. There is, for instance, the incident of the prophet's becoming mute for an extended period of time. This is reported in three places: 3:26, 24:27, and 33:22, but it was evidently a single incident. Thus we have sure evidence that the book is not a single and orderly whole but is rather like the rest of the prophetic books in construction. On a larger scale, surely the material on the fall of Jerusalem in 33:21 ff. should follow chapter 24, which deals with the city's sins. The intervening matter, a collection of oracles against the nations, has been inserted to give the book of Ezekiel the classic prophetic sequence: oracles against Israel, oracles against the nations, oracles of hope. Finally there are doublets, that is, unnecessary repetitions, for instance, 3:17–21 is the same as 33:7–9; 18:25–29 as 33:17–20 and so on. Evidence of this sort proves the book to be a compilation, not a literary unit cast as a single whole.

In fact, a careful consideration of the contents of the book reveals topical collections just as in the other prophets. Ezekiel's oracles are longer and his style more elaborate so that these collections are not so apparent as they are in the early chapters of Isaiah or Jeremiah, but nonetheless they are there: the vocation of Ezekiel, 1:1–3:15; symbolic acts, 3:16–5:17; idolatry, 6; condemnation, 7; visionary visit to Jerusalem, 8–11 and 21; symbolic actions, 12:1–20; oracles on prophets, 12:21–13:21 with 14:1–11 and 12–23; the sins of Israel, 15:1–16:43 (16:44–63 has been added), 20:1–31 (32–42 also added); against the kings, 17 and 19; oracles about the sword, 21; the sins of the people, 22; the allegory of the two sisters, 23; symbolic actions, 24:1–27; oracles about the neighbors of Judah, 25; oracles against Tyre, 26–28; against Egypt, 29–32; the prophetic office, 33:1–20 (originally also with what is now found in 3:16b–21); the shepherds, 34; Edom, 35; the restoration of Israel, 36–39; and the constitution of the new Temple, 40–48. Note that the latter collections, beginning with the oracles about Gog in chapter 38 and including the constitution of the new Temple, have often been denied to the prophet. Perhaps the story of Gog is too apocalyptic in tone to be from Ezekiel, but the constitution of the Temple is in his style. Moreover, it reflects his overwhelming interest in the cult and the law so that it is reasonable to think that it is based upon the prophet.

If we must, then, deny that the book of Ezekiel is an organized whole, it is nevertheless true that it is outstanding in its homogeneity. The style is similar throughout, the imagery and imagination are the same, and the theology remarkably consistent. This indicates that its contents, if not its structure, are largely from Ezekiel himself. There have been expansions and additions, but these are minor compared to the material based on the prophet's own sayings.

Ezekiel is a fascinating person. With him we meet the first great figure after the collapse of the monarchy. In him we see the Hebrew people beginning to face an entirely new situation. They had lost national sovereignty and gone into exile. In the normal course of events this would have meant the loss of their identity and their religion. It is through men like Ezekiel that God caused it to be otherwise. Religion was detached from its material bases in nationhood and sanctuary and became a personal devotion to Yahweh which was shown in one's readiness to do his will, and concretely this meant keeping his law. An attitude and a course of action — these could be carried and lived anywhere.

There is something of a paradox in Ezekiel's playing so important a part in this, since he was of a priestly family and very attached to the Temple. He was of sufficiently high station to have been taken to Babylon in the first deportation of 597 B.C., and he did all his prophesying in exile according to the opinion presently accepted. At one time it was commonly believed that the prophet had a double ministry, that is, that he preached first in Palestine and then after the exile of 587 B.C. in Babylonia. The reason for this division is the detailed knowledge of Jerusalem and the Temple which is revealed in many of his prophecies. Scholars felt that such knowledge must reflect activity on the spot because it would be impossible in the far off land of exile. However, as a member of a family devoted to the service of the Temple, Ezekiel had ample opportunity to absorb the traditions of the Temple and its city. These were cherished memories among the exiles. Furthermore, Jeremiah (see, for example, chap. 29) confirms the close relation between the earlier exiles and the homeland during the years immediately after the first exile in 597 B.C. These relations were such that the two communities in Judah and in Babylon were aware of intimate details about one another. There is, therefore, no reason to reject the explicit testimony of the book of Ezekiel when it places all the prophet's activity in Babylonia. In fact, he seems to have been an important member of the community of exiled Jews there, for the elders frequently consulted him. His priestly status and his learning in the law would account for this. They also prepared him for his prophetic office and helped make it especially pertinent to a time of great difficulty.

For one thing, Ezekiel saw a further dimension in this office. The prophet had always been God's spokesman. Jeremiah (e.g., 14–15) shows the prophet also to be an intercessor whose prayers can protect Israel. Ezekiel sees the prophet as a watchman (3:17; 33:7). This gives him a tremendous responsibility. Just as the watchman is set over the city at night in order to watch for and warn the people against any surprise attack, so the prophet must foresee the ruin which sin is bringing upon his people and he must cry the alarm. Like the watchman he is liable for the lives given into his care. If he fails to warn as he should, he himself must give an account for those who are lost (33:6).

EZEKIEL THE MAN

So far we have dealt with Ezekiel in his public capacities, as priest and prophet. However, in his case the man does not disappear behind the office. He is very much an individual, and to many he appears a peculiar one. First of all, Ezekiel is subject to visions and ecstatic raptures. He is seized by the spirit of God and odd things happen to him; for instance, he undergoes an extended period of dumbness (3:26; 24:27; 33:22). Such experiences are unusual among the "writing prophets," though they recall the earlier forms of prophetism. Thus, they are by no means unheard of, and they are not signs of mental unbalance as some claim. The only real argument for such a conclusion would be the denial that a man can possibly have mystical experience, that is, some sort of direct contact with the divine. If we admit the possibility of such a contact, and all of religious history indicates that it is a possibility, indeed an indispensable part of religion, we should expect it sometimes to produce overwhelming effects. It is something far beyond the normal human experience and would call for a response beyond the ordinary, but this does not mean the mystic is unstable or abnormal. On the contrary, many have been most astute men and women of affairs.

Part of the appearance of oddness in Ezekiel can be explained by his predilection for the prophetic or symbolic action. This is something which is known throughout the history of prophecy, but among the "writing prophets" Ezekiel uses it far more often than any other. He acts out the siege of Jerusalem (4:1–3), he remains motionless on his side to symbolize the duration of Judah's captivity (4:9–12), and he packs and leaves his house to symbolize the exile (12:1–7). These are but a few of his many symbolic actions (Fohrer in his standard commentary finds twelve such elaborate signs lived out by the prophet). Since these signs apparently were not explained but simply acted out, leaving the people to discern their meaning, such activity perhaps made an odd impression, but it is in the classic prophetic tradition. Like his mysticism it puts him in a class apart, but not in an inferior class.

Finally, the prophet was a complex personality in a complex situation. He is a poet of baroque imagination and a priest who is concerned about the minutiae of the law. He is a member of a proud but defeated nation. As a prophet he must castigate the people whom he loves and the Jerusalem which is the center of his thought. All this would be very trying to a man of sensibility and imagination, and it easily accounts for the various attitudes he displays. But once again, complexity does not prove an abnormal or inferior nature, but rather one which is in tune with all the complexities of history.

Why do we call Ezekiel's imagination baroque? It is wild, extravagant, and pictorial. There is a willingness to build up images one after another without connecting them logically, for instance in the oracle where the Pharaoh is at once a lion, a dragon, and finally a star (32:2–8). Whatever image serves the prophet's purposes he uses even when it verges on the incoherent. In the allegory in 17:1–10 one can hardly distinguish cedars and willows and vines and eagles, but such accumulation and interweaving of images is typical of the imagination which flourishes in the baroque ages of man. We may be grateful for it in Ezekiel. The vision of the throne of God in chapters 1–3, of Yahweh leaving the Temple in chapters 8–10, and of the resurrection of the bones in chapter 37, and many another have become classics in Christian art.

There is a last aspect of Ezekiel which merits attention. He was the last prophet to know an independent Hebrew kingdom. Consciously or not, he seems to have felt this position and to have summed up many of the traditions, prophetic and others, which characterized the older, pre-exilic nation. He harks back beyond the "writing prophets," to men like Elijah and Elisha. Thus he favors the phrase "the word of Yahweh came to me," which was typical of prophecy in Samuel and Kings, but which was not used later. Again, "the spirit of the Lord fell upon" Ezekiel just as it did upon the earlier prophetic bands, but this is not said of the other "writing prophets." Finally, Ezekiel favors greatly the prophetic symbolic act. This, too, characterized the prophets who are recorded in the historical books, before Amos and Hosea and the rest. Ezekiel is going back to the oldest traditions, tying his prophecy into the whole history of Israel. However, he does not disdain the traditions of the classic prophets either. The famous figure of the "coming of the end" or "summer" from Amos 8 is developed exhaustively in Ezekiel 7. Then the marriage theme of Hosea and Jeremiah is extended through Ezekiel's allegories in chapters 16 and 23.

Thus far Ezekiel is the cap to the prophetic traditions, but he uses other tradition as well. He favors a vocabulary which is typically cultic and priestly: "knowledge" and "know," "he is holy," "Yahweh lives," and "I am Yahweh." Obviously the tradition of Zion and its Temple is connected with this. It appears, for instance, in 20:40 and is developed at great length in chapters 40–48. Ezekiel knows another great Jerusalem tradition: in 34:20–24 and 37:24–28 he promises a new David, a true shepherd of his people who will give them lasting peace.

Thus in many ways the older Hebrew nation sums itself up and comes to expression in Ezekiel. He is a bridge between what was and what would be.[1]

THE LAW OF HOLINESS

We may now turn to Ezekiel's special vision of God. If we were to sum this up in a single word it would be the same one that we used for Isaiah. Ezekiel is obsessed by the holiness of Yahweh. However, while not contradictory to the view of Isaiah, the holy one whom Ezekiel sees is quite different from Isaiah's God. Ezekiel is tremendously aware of the transcendence of God, which he brings out in the contrast between the Lord Yahweh and his name for himself: "mere mortal" (literally "son of man," used eighty-seven times of the prophet). Again, he uses the prophetic diatribe (e.g., Ezek 14:4–11), but he does not appeal to his own personal observations to explain the condemnation of the sinners according to what had been the typical procedure of the prophets. Ezekiel prefers to condemn the sins of the people in the impersonal style of the law. This impersonal style emphasizes the apartness, the holiness, of all that pertains to God, including his law. It also seems to imply that the law was a common possession; the prophet need only allude to it and his hearers knew their faults.

It is typical, too, that Ezekiel commonly thinks of sin in terms which

---

[1] For a thorough study of Ezekiel and the prophetic tradition see Georg Fohrer, *Vetus Testamentum* 15 (1965), pp. 515–527.

reflect the cult. Hebrew has a great many words for sin, and many of them are somewhat general, simply meaning "miss the mark," or "transgress," or "be nothing." These words carry no special religious imagery. It is otherwise with Ezekiel's word for sin, which means "spot" or "stain." This is a word straight out of the liturgical tradition, and it refers to cultic impurity. Sin is something which stains a man so that he cannot come close to God. Ezekiel sees his people as being indelibly stained. Unlike almost all the other prophets who preceded him, he does not hold out hope for a national conversion which will ward off disaster before the event. He simply proclaims the state of sin and the punishment which it brings. The chosen people has ceased to be a holy people and must be separated from the all holy God. Hence the magnificent picture of the departure of the "glory of the Lord" (i.e., his special presence) from sinful Jerusalem (Ezek 8–11).

In fact man's sinfulness is at the very center of Ezekiel's picture of the world. He does not see a history which has finally ended in a state of almost universal faithlessness. Rather he sees the history of God's relations with his people as one unchanging story of sin. At the very moment of his choice of the people in Egypt and ever since, the people have responded with sin (Ezek 20). Apart from this direct statement, Ezekiel also uses allegorical tales to make this history of sin graphic (Ezek 16; 23). Preceding prophets had emphasized the sinfulness of the people, but they often felt that this was a later development. Ezekiel is concerned to show that sin has always dominated the people. It is not as though there were a history of growing sin which culminates in the unforgivable infidelity of the later kingdom. The nation has always been sinful. There is no real climax to this history of sin. There is no point at which the volume of sin becomes overwhelming or some great sin finally ends God's relationship with his people. In a sense there never has been a true relationship, because the holy God can never be close to sinners, and the people have always been sinners.

The final break comes as a paradox. Ezekiel has a vision in which God departs from Jerusalem because its sin is incompatible with his presence. But the departure of the Holy One from Jerusalem is but half the story. The sequence actually has been reversed, and the grandiose picture of Yahweh's leaving a defiled Jerusalem (8–10) concludes with his arrival among the exiles in Babylon (1:4–28)! What has happened is that the story has been divided and its conclusions put at the beginning of the book as an appropriate vision to introduce the call of Ezekiel (2–3).

The chronology may be askew, but the theology is not. This is Ezekiel's pictorial way of saying what Jeremiah said: Judah was defiled and God was with the exiles in Babylonia. The exile represented a purification which made the people fit for Yahweh's presence. So his holiness was satisfied.

This, then, is Ezekiel's view of God: a being utterly holy and therefore utterly incompatible with a sinful nation. What sort of demands could such a God have made? As we have mentioned, unlike the other prophets Ezekiel does not hold out hope for a national repentance which will prevent a catastrophe. It is true that the very assumption on which Ezekiel makes his condemnations, namely, that the people have violated a known law, implies that keeping of the law would have prevented catastrophe. However, Ezekiel's position seems to be that whatever may have been the theoretical possibilities, in fact the law was never observed, sin always dominated, and therefore punishment was inevitable.

However, the prophet does develop one important aspect of the human response to the holy God. Jeremiah had already drawn attention to the problem of individual responsibility, but this was a new idea and the old concept of group responsibility remained. One prospered if one's family or one's nation were faithful, and one was punished if the group were unfaithful. This would seem to relieve the individual of his responsibility. He would in any case pay for his father's sins or for his nation's sins. Chapter 18 is devoted to this problem and it points out that it is one's own acts which determine whether one will live or die. One cannot blame one's punishments upon the sins of the father, and one who himself is blameless can be confident that he will not be unjustly punished. However, this latter point is not obvious; one could fairly claim that, whatever Ezekiel may say, the people did suffer as a group. Good and bad suffered the conquest of Jerusalem and the exile. Ezekiel seems not to have considered this problem, or if he did he simply meets it head on with the assertion based on faith that the just will not be punished. It is this insistence upon the correspondence between personal responsibility and reward and punishment which made acute for later Judaism the problem of allotting reward and punishment. The answer did not, in fact, lie within the scope of religion as it had been revealed to Israel up to this point.

There is another element in Ezekiel's view of the relations of man and God which is worth note. The idea that judgment was not merely a punishment or a destruction but a chastisement which would purify the people and enable them to return to the Lord was known before Ezekiel. However, he expressed it clearly and repeatedly (20:37–28; 22:17–22). Thus punishment is not merely arbitrary or vindictive. It is rather the natural result of sin against an all holy God, and it somehow wipes away the stain which separated the people from God and so makes their restoration possible. For there is no doubt that Ezekiel, though he offers no hope of preventing catastrophe, did look forward to a glorious restoration.

THE NEW JERUSALEM

In this as in so many things of the earlier traditions, Ezekiel speaks of the people's new heart, a new spirit to be infused in them so that they will live according to God's ordinances (Ezek 36). This sounds like Jeremiah, but Ezekiel typically adds that the people will be purified from all uncleanness and guarded against it in the future. Thus the renewal is essentially the creation of a holy people fit to associate with God, though even here Ezekiel recalls the promises to the patriarchs and the life on the land which was the essence of that promise (36:28). In the vision of the valley of the bones in chapter 37 he has his own very striking picture of the renewal of God's people.

Again, Ezekiel does not ignore the Davidic tradition. In 34:20–23 God condemns those who abuse his people and proclaims that henceforth he will act as their judge and protector, not directly but through the true David, Yahweh's servant who will be a real shepherd of his people (see also 37:24–28). This is quite strong; it makes the future Davidic leader become God's viceregent upon earth. Nevertheless, Ezekiel avoids calling the new David a king (Hebrew, melek). He is rather a leader (Hebrew, nasi'), though in 37:24 he does speak of David who shall be king. Still, the term "leader" seems favored. It is an old title from the period of Judges, hence honorable, and in the constitution of the new Temple (Ezek 49–48) the leader is given an honored place. Yet he remains leader, not king, and his place is one of honor, not of important participation in nor control of the new Temple community. All this indicates that Ezekiel was not an overenthusiastic follower of the Davidic theology. Perhaps his priestly and prophetic background made him suspicious of the kingship. The prophets had seen that many kings had had an important hand in misleading Israel. The Temple priesthood too, though it owed its original place to the Davidic kings, had learned that the kings were inclined to intrude into and even corrupt the Temple services. Nevertheless, Ezekiel, suspicious as he might be, could not avoid the theological topic of the kingship. So deeply was the theology of the Davidic promise tied into the whole fabric of Hebrew life and doctrine, no one could ignore it. Thus Ezekiel must include in his vision of the future a Davidic prince who would be a true representative of God on earth and a savior of his people, even though his essential interests lay elsewhere.

Finally, we should note that Ezekiel believes so strongly that the true people of God is alive in the exilic community and that it will return from exile that his book finishes with an ideal constitution for the new community of the return (Ezek 40–48). Thus will "the glory of the Lord" return to Jerusalem with the returning, purified community. There is some doubt that these last chapters belong to Ezekiel, but many modern commentators believe that they do. They certainly show a style and trend of thought which are very like his. In them, he looks forward to a restoration where there will be a true community of God's people which will dwell in peace and plenty, with the Temple as the center of its life. There will be true worship of Yahweh and obedience to his greater gift, the law, which is simply the definition of the way man should relate to God. So Ezekiel finds an important element of future hope in the theology of Zion, the theology at the base of this ideal Temple-centered community.

Ezekiel has been called the founder of Judaism. In the sense that he concentrates upon the law (Torah) and upon the ritual which character-ized the community of the return, this is true. However, the statement is often taken in a bad sense, meaning that Ezekiel is the source of the attitude which puts all emphasis upon the minutiae of the law and on ritual and legal purity. This is a travesty of the prophet, as it is a travesty of the Judaism of later Old Testament and early New Testament times. Legalism is subject to abuses, but properly understood the liturgy and the law are a great opportunity. They are the means by which a man can express the convictions of his heart. Yahweh will give his people a new heart and a new spirit, but man does not live in his interior alone. He must express his dispositions, and if he is to do this fittingly in God's community he must have divine direction. This is the attitude of Ezekiel and the true and central tradition of later Judaism. Ritual and law are not empty observance. They are the expression of the chosen people's status, the response of the divinely moved heart and spirit to the divine initiative.

We conclude with the usual topic, the prophet's attitude toward the

nations. In some ways Ezekiel has little to add here. He is quite aware
that the nations are under God. They may think that they are acting
independently, attacking the people of Yahweh and following their own
gods, but it is Yahweh who is in charge even of great kings (cf. Ezek 32
on Pharaoh). God, in fact, has a real concern for the peoples, as appears
in the poem about Tyre in 28:11–19. It describes the prince who represents the pagan Phoenician city as one chosen by God for a lofty position.
The imagery of the passage is of special interest because it reflects the
same background as the story of the beginnings of man in Genesis 2:4b–
3:24. Tyre and Eden are characterized by the remarkable beauty of gold
and precious stones, both the prince of Tyre and Adam are Wise Men,
and each is kept from his garden by Cherubim after his fall. The prophet,
like the Yahwist writer in Genesis, uses elements of popular tradition to
describe a theological fact. In Genesis it is the origin of man and sin;
here it is the special providence of God concerning a non-Hebrew people.
Finally we may note that Ezekiel is the first prophet to condemn a
Hebrew government for failing to live up to its obligations to other nations.
In chapter 17 he condemns Zedekiah for being untrue to his oath of vassal-
hood to Babylon. This is striking indeed, for a prophet like Jeremiah
constantly condemns the same king and his predecessors for their folly
in opposing the Babylonians, but it never seems to occur to him to include
in that condemnation the fact that this folly was also perjury because the
rebellious kings of Judah were going against their sworn word to the
Babylonian overlord. Here in Ezekiel the rights of the gentile overlord
over his Hebrew subjects are recognized, and the Hebrews are condemned
for failing to fulfill these rights.[2] Thus Ezekiel tells us a good deal about
the nations. If we study his attitude attentively we find important implications: all men are in the hands of God, God truly loves and helps them,
and they have rights just as do the chosen people.

To summarize: Ezekiel is very much the priest-prophet. A holy God
must have a holy people, and since his people have sinned they must be
chastised and purified. Then they will be fit to live and worship him as
is fitting: in perfect observance of the law which defines the great privilege
of being admitted to the holy. In this theology even exile is an element
of hope because it can purify, but there is more. God will give a true
Davidic leader to a people with a new spirit and they will return to Zion.
Nor is God concerned with one people alone. All mankind is his charge.

---

[2] See M. Tsevat, "The Neo-Assyrian and Neo-Babylonian Vassal Oaths and the
Prophet Ezekiel," *Journal of Biblical Literature* 78 (1959), pp. 199–204.

Chapter 11. Deutero-Isaiah

Reading: Is 40–55

The second prophet of the community in the Babylonian exile was a man of remarkable religious insight and great powers of expression. Yet we do not even know his name. His writings have simply been added to our book of Isaiah in chapters 40–55, and his name lost. The ancients were little concerned with claims of creativity. For them it was the word that counted. Hence we have an important doctrinal work to which we can only give the long and clumsy name, Deutero-Isaiah, a Greek way of saying Second Isaiah. And why a Second Isaiah? Simply because it has been recognized for a century and more that the material beginning in Isaiah 40 is very different in historical background, doctrine, and style from what precedes. In our own century it has been shown that these chapters are a distinctive work, homogeneous in style and ideas and closely related to events toward the end of the Babylonian exile, that is, about 540 B.C. Chapters 56–66 of Isaiah are a heterogeneous collection influenced in part by Deutero-Isaiah. The date of composition is post-exilic in fact, and these will be treated farther on in this book.[1]

---

[1] In 1908 the Pontifical Biblical Commission decreed that the arguments for a Deutero-Isaiah were not sufficient to compel assent. Since then our knowledge has grown and Catholic scholars agree that Is 40–55 belong to the exilic prophet.

Deutero-Isaiah is evidently speaking to the community in exile in Babylon. He argues against Babylonian idols. He knows that Cyrus the Persian has begun his career of conquest, and he seems to have experienced his capture of Babylon in 539 B.C. Note that this stress on the immediate historical background of the prophet in no way denies that a prophet could and often enough did foresee the future. Theoretically Isaiah could have described in detail events which would occur 150 or more years after his time. However, the fact is that the sayings of the prophets are seldom of this sort. They are messages which speak to contemporary problems, and it would be extraordinary for a prophet to speak so much of events too far in the future to be of concern to his time. Thus when we argue that these chapters of the Book of Isaiah are not the kind of thing which would have concerned Isaiah himself, we do not imply a denial of the possibility of foreseeing the future. This view simply represents a solid scientific conclusion based upon study of the facts of the prophetic phenomenon.

The doctrine of Deutero-Isaiah is also distinctive. In some ways it is a synthesis of Old Testament theology up to his day, but it is a highly personal synthesis. For instance, prophets before him had condemned the service of gods other than Yahweh. Deutero-Isaiah first explicitly formulates monotheism. He argues at length that there is only one god, Yahweh. This sets him apart. So also does his concept of the future hope. He preaches to the exiles and therefore concentrates on the return to the Promised Land. Hence, unlike Isaiah with his emphasis on the promise to the Davidic dynasty, or Jeremiah and Ezekiel with their insistence on a new covenant, he is concerned with the return to the land as a great example of God's salvific will, a new and greater Exodus. This is symbolized by the description of the trip across the desert in which the paths will be made smooth and the barren places flower to a restored Jerusalem which will be a city of marvels.

Finally, Deutero-Isaiah has his own distinctive style. He is a writer of Isaiah's class but very different. Isaiah wrote Hebrew poetry in the classical style, vivid, concise, and emphatic. Deutero-Isaiah favors a hymnic style which produces much longer oracles with a fullness of expression and a solemnity which is unlike the forceful brevity of Isaiah.

EXILE AND RETURN

Such, then, are the characteristics which distinguish Deutero-Isaiah as a unique figure in the history of prophecy. As is the case with most of the prophets, his oracles have been put together in a collection which has little overall form. In fact, with his loose and full style it is often difficult to distinguish the original separate sayings. However, one important division in the book is quite clear. Chapters 40–48 are characterized by hymns to Yahweh and oracles concerning the fallen Hebrews. Moreover, in these chapters the Persian Cyrus appears often as God's anointed, his agent to deliver Israel from the Babylonian captivity, and the impending fall of proud Babylon is emphasized. Chapters 49–55, on the other hand, have nothing about the fall of Babylon and Cyrus does not appear. This section is taken up with hymns to Jerusalem and Zion, a restored and magnificent new "place where Yahweh's name will dwell."

This distinct division has led most scholars to believe that the prophet's sayings are grouped more or less chronologically. Isaiah 40–48 precedes the fall of Babylon to Cyrus. The prophet consoles the exiles and explains that the gentile king, Cyrus, is actually God's chosen agent to free his people. The later silence about Cyrus seems to indicate that he has already arrived and taken Babylon. The prophet would be speaking after 539 B.C., when Cyrus conquered Babylon, to exiles who for one reason or another mostly remained in Babylonia, though they were no longer prisoners and were free to return to Judah. Indeed, it is likely that Deutero-Isaiah's glowing descriptions of the new Exodus and the new Jerusalem aim to encourage the exiles to make the plunge and return to Judah. That some such encouragement was needed is evident from the accounts of the sorry return that we glean from the books of Ezra and Nehemiah and from the prophets Haggai and Zechariah. By 539 two generations of Jews had lived in Babylonia after generations of exile. Surely it is this special circumtry of their captivity. Indeed, some of them prospered there. In one way or another these people had sunk roots in what was originally an alien land of exile, so that they were reluctant to leave it.

Deutero-Isaiah, then, is especially the prophet of the Jewish community in Babylonia after generations of exile. Surely it is this special circumstance which prepared the prophet to receive and his hearers to understand his unique message. It is because he is preaching to the exiles that he finds the great sign of salvation in the imminent return to the promised land; it is because he is dealing with a community surrounded by a rich and powerful pagan people and therefore tempted to turn to the worship of the pagan god to whom this power and wealth were attributed that he makes explicit the monotheism of the Yahwist religion; and it is this constant contact with gentiles and especially with the experience of the gentile Cyrus as deliverer which helps form his attitude toward the non-Hebrew people.

Yet the prophet would surely have been surprised to be called an innovator. His milieu shaped his message and determined his points of emphasis, but his content is a deepening of ancient Hebrew ideas. For one thing, he has explicitly combined and elaborated the ancient beliefs in Yahweh as the creator and as governor of the historical process. Even the combination is not new; it is as old as the Yahwist document from the tenth century where the god of the patriarchs is introduced as creator. However, it is Deutero-Isaiah who provides a nuanced theological synthesis in which the doctrines of creation, God's role in history, Israel's unique vocation,[2] and even the fate of the gentiles are woven into a synthesis where the totality throws new light on the parts which make it up, and which is expressed with a new force and exactness.

A text illustrating most of this is Isaiah 41:1–5:

> Listen to me in silence, O coastlands;
>   let the people renew their strength;
> let them approach, then let them speak;
>   let us draw together for judgment.
> Who stirred up one from the east
>   whom victory meets at every step?
> He gives over nations before him
>   so that he tramples kings under foot;
> he makes them like dust with his sword,
>   like driven stubble with his bow. . . .
> Who has performed and done this,
>   calling the generations from the beginning?
> I, Yahweh, the first,
>   and with the last; I am he.
> The coastlands have seen and are afraid,
>   the ends of the earth tremble,
>   they have drawn near and come.

Apart from the lack of a special mention of Israel's role this oracle is almost a table of contents to Deutero-Isaiah's concepts. There is the opening summons of the people to a trial. The prophet favored this form where the proponents of other gods prove the divinity of their idols. But only the prophet can produce proofs on behalf of Yahweh, Yahweh who has guided the course of history. It is he who has called up "one from the east," that is, Cyrus. Cyrus' army is mighty, and his conquests impressive, but in reality who has done all this? It is Yahweh alone (41:4).

---

[2] Now, with the kingdoms gone, we can follow the prophet and use the name Israel for the people of God without danger of confusion.

His right and his power to do so are proven by the fact that he is of the "first," that is, the one who was before all things and so the one who made all things. Are these not simply the claim of an enthusiast for a particular god? No, Yahweh has enabled us to know who has done all these things by foretelling what will happen: "naming generations from the beginning." This argument from prophecy is Deutero-Isaiah's favorite arm in his polemic against the false gods. Finally, all these facts are visible. Notice that the oracle begins with a summons to the people to come and witness judgment. In a sense Yahweh offers himself to the judgment of many in that he lays before them the claims which establish that it is he alone who has created the world and who guides history. Hence men may see the truth and "draw nearer and come" to the true God. So the gentiles too have their place within the plan.

PROPHET OF REVELATION

Add to this the work which Israel should perform: be a sign to the gentiles, and we have all the elements of the Deutero-Isaian synthesis. However, a synthesis is not simply the addition of its parts; it is an organic whole because it has a central principle of vitality. In Deutero-Isaiah this is the concept of revelation. Hence the importance his argument puts on the demonstration. Chapter 41:21–29 reinforces the interpretation of 41:1–5 on this point. Once more there is the summons to open debate so that men may know the true God (revelation!). Let the devotees of other gods establish their claims. But how is one to do this? Clearly the prophet believes that one shows divinity by doing things (41:23b), but it is not enough merely to act. After the fact any invisible power could lay claim to the act, and who could dispute it when dealing with the intangible? The telling argument is that one can claim the work before it is done. Only the actual agent or one in his confidence can do this (41:25–26), and it is only Yahweh who has done so. Hence only he can speak, not merely to Israel, but to

> . . . the survivors of the nations . . .
> Who has told these things long ago?
> Who declared them of old?
> Was it not I, Yahweh?
> And there is no other God beside me . . . (45:20–21).

Thus the prophet proceeds from the experience of history which reveals the true God because that God reveals his plans and then performs them. Only the all-powerful could do that.

Therefore Deutero-Isaiah does not follow the temporal order, proceeding from the creator God to his activity in the world he created. Rather he proceeds from the realization that Yahweh is the God of history to the fact that the God who guides and controls all activity in the world must be the one who produced that world. This is very clear in texts like 45:1–7. Here the prophet speaking for Yahweh points out that Cyrus is God's chosen instrument. It is not Cyrus and his mighty army who "subdues nations," and "breaks in pieces the doors of bronze." Cyrus is not just another in the long line of conquerors. He is Yahweh's messiah (45:1, "anointed, is the Hebrew *"messiah"*) chosen for the sake of God's people (45:4). It is in this context that the prophet goes on to proclaim that Yahweh alone is God, creator of all things: "I form light and create darkness, I make weal and create woe, I am Yahweh who do all these things" (45:7). Thus it is only after showing that Yahweh is the God who controls the workings of the world because he predicts the coming and the work of Cyrus that the prophet proclaims that he is also the God who created that world. Note here the Hebrew phrases "form light and create darkness" and "make weal and create woe." Hebrew is not an abstract language. Typically it expresses totality in terms of concrete opposite. The creator of light and darkness, good and evil is the creator of all things, for these opposites encompass all things between themselves.[3]

Perhaps the logical sequence from creation to history appears in 45:18–19. God created the earth, but 45:18 emphasizes that he created an orderly universe. Thus the object of the prophet is not to affirm the mere fact of creation but the fact of creation and order, and this implies the idea of continuity. The creator is also the orderer, and so the one who guides all the workings of his world. We find here also the connection with revelation. God created the world to be known for what it was, his ordered work (45:19).

Thus there is a truly organic relationship in the thought of Deutero-Isaiah. The God who creates an orderly universe is one who guides its destiny, though the means of his guidance are often hard to discern. For instance, it was hard for the Jews to accept that the gentile Cyrus was God's anointed instrument. It was hard to see that the splendor of Babylon was the work of Yahweh, not of the Babylonian idols. Yet an essen-

---

[3] See J. L. McKenzie, S.J., "Literary Characteristics of Genesis 2–3," *Myths and Realities* (Milwaukee: The Bruce Publishing Co., 1963), pp. 146–181, for a discussion of this use of all-inclusive opposites to designate totality.

tial part of an orderly world is human recognition that it is Yahweh who has created and continues to control things. Hence the need for revelation and prophecy. It is through these means that men come to God, and so revelation is the key to the theology of the prophet whose office is to bring the two together.

Thus far we have found little role for Israel in all this. It has appeared simply as the recipient of God's salvation mediated by Cyrus. However, the prophet has a far more profound notion of what it means to be the chosen people. First of all, Israel is Yahweh's servant (41:9; 43:10; etc.). It is the business of this servant to bear witness to the Lord among the nations (43:10). However, Israel has been a blind servant and a deaf messenger, that is, a worthless servant (42:19; 48:6–8). Still, Yahweh will not abandon his servant; for the sake of his own honor he will refine and purify the servant and save him (48:9–11). There is a paradox in this. It is precisely because Israel has been faithless and therefore must be punished that it eventually fulfills its function as a witness and brings the nations to recognize the true God. It is when men see the freeing of the chastised nation that they will recognize Yahweh (40:5; 45:6). The end result will be that men from the ends of the earth will come to Israel and recognize that "God is with you only, and there is no other, no god besides him" (45:14). It will be the restored Jerusalem which will do this. It will be "a light to the peoples," that is, a source of knowledge and guidance in the ways of God (51:4). So glorious will be the city of the saved that all must see in it the salvation of God (52:10) and strangers will run to its God (55:5).

Once more in his view of Israel Deutero-Isaiah has integrated his theology. If revelation is essential to the ordering of the universe, he must usually have an instrument through which this revelation will be given. Commonly this instrument is prophecy. However, the concept of Israel as the witness before the nations makes the chosen people also a means of the revelation, which is an essential element in Yahweh's ordering of the universe. Men need not even hear the words of the prophet in order to come to a knowledge of the one true God. If they witness his wonderful ways with his people, they must see who is the God of history and therefore the God of the universe.

Thus the salvation of Israel, the fallen and exiled nation, is an essential element in God's plan for saving not only the chosen people but all mankind. No wonder that the prophet speaks of the salvation worked by Yahweh in such glowing terms. He sees the return from exile as a new, greater exodus (cf. Jer 16:14–15). The Lord himself will lead the majestic procession (52:11–12), and at the passage of Israel's God the desert will bloom (40:3–5; 43:19–20; etc.). At the end of the journey Yahweh will reign as king in Jerusalem (52:7), and the people will enjoy a life of unprecedented peace and prosperity (49:18–23; 52:1–2; 54:11–14) "established in righteousness" (54:14a).

There are those who have been troubled by the magnificent — some would say extravagant — language of the prophet in these matters. As we have remarked, the return from the exile was not really so glorious. An insignificant band of people came back to a second-rate town. How then could the prophet speak so enthusiastically? The answer must lie in the meaning he sees in these events. On the surface they appear to be of little or no importance, but underneath them the prophetic insight sees God in action. This will to save is something magnificent beyond any particular fulfillment of it, and the prophet looks beyond the immediate application to the majestic and loving God who is savior. He sees in the present acts of salvation intimations of that ultimate will to save which must be fulfilled at the end of history.

An element found in all of the other major prophets has been little emphasized in this discussion of Deutero-Isaiah. What about reproaches upon Israel, calls for repentance, and threats of punishment? The prophet reproves the faithless servant, but this is not characteristic. The work of Deutero-Isaiah has well been called the Book of Consolation. Why? First of all, the prophet was speaking to a defeated and chastened people. He did not have to face up to the folly of a faithless king as did Isaiah, nor to the claims of false prophets as did Jeremiah. Presumably the weak and the false had largely deserted the exiled community. What remained was a chastened though not a perfect group, since the prophet must argue continuously against the reality of the Babylonian idols, which he would hardly do unless his people were tempted to join in the false worship. Nevertheless, what this people needed most was the word of hope.

However, the reason for Deutero-Isaiah's book of consolation goes far deeper than this need. Deutero-Isaiah emphasizes that Yahweh loves his people with a great tenderness and compassion. Hosea and Jeremiah also preached a God who loved his faithless nation, but even they are filled with threats and warnings of disaster. Hosea does know a divine love which will break forth and demand that the people be saved in spite of their sins, but this appears more rarely in Hosea than in Deutero-Isaiah. Furthermore, for the exilic prophet no single human analogy can come close to expressing the depth and breadth and strength of divine love. But so great is the divine love that it cannot restrain itself. It allows a certain amount of chastisement, but then it can bear no more and it bursts forth in acts of forgiveness (42:14). This God can say to sinful Israel "thou art precious in my sight . . . and I have loved thee" (43:4; 48:14). The prophet turns also to the Hosean image of Yahweh as the husband of Israel. He may give way to a flash of anger at the infidelity of his spouse, but his love lasts while his wrath is but a fleeting thing (54:5–8). This does not exhaust the prophet's imagery of love. There is the love of the mother for her child, and yet this mighty human bond is as nothing compared as Yahweh's love for his people:

> Can a woman forget her infant child,
>   that she should have no compassion on the child of her womb?
> Even she may forget,
>   yet I will not forget you (49:15).

Yahweh's love for his people may well be compared to the strongest and tenderest of human loves but it far surpasses any of them.

THE SERVANT SONGS

The question of the famous Servant Songs is so complex that we must treat it apart from the rest of Deutero-Isaiah. The basic texts of the Songs admitted by all critics are Isaiah 42:1–4; 49:1–6; 50:4–9; and 52:13–53:12. In addition many scholars believe that 42:5–7 and 50:10–11 belong to the first and third Servant Songs. The matter of the text is far too complex to be discussed in detail here. We can only say that there is evidence of editorial additions which have been made in order to fit the Servant Songs into their present context. This is clearest in 50:10–11 which answers the question raised in the Song proper in 50:4–9. In the second of the Songs, verses 7–12 of chapter 49 are an expansion showing the fulfillment of the promise made to the Servant in the Song itself. Chapter 42:7 adapts the Servant's vocation to Israel to balance the opening verses of chapter 42 which make his proper mission one to the gentiles. Furthermore, 42:5 is in a hymnic style characteristic of Deutero-Isaiah, but not the Servant Songs. This evidence for editorial work fitting the Servant Songs into their context indicates that the doubtful passages are secondary additions so that it is best to deal primarily with the basic Servant Songs. However, this procedure should be understood exactly. When we seek thus to separate out the original Servant Songs we are performing an essentially historical task. We are trying to find out what the original concept was so that we may see its development. It must be emphasized that the editorial adaptions which integrate the Songs into the rest of the book of Isaiah are inspired interpretations of the Songs. For instance, if it is true that the original concept of the Servant was that of someone with a special mission to foster the religion of Yahweh among the gentiles (42:1), the editorial edition in 42:7 shows that this mission extends also to Israel. This is an inspired development of the concept of the servant, making his office more inclusive than in the first versions of the poems.

There is also considerable debate about the source of the Servant Songs. Are they the work of Deutero-Isaiah? Scholars are divided on the point, and we can hardly speak with certainty. The vocabulary of the first two songs is very much the vocabulary of Deutero-Isaiah; that of the last two much less so. This can be interpreted in various ways; for instance, that the poet of the Servant Songs wished to tie his first oracles into the Deutero-Isaian context by this vocabulary, but on the other hand one could hold that the Deutero-Isaian vocabulary stems from the prophet himself. Then the change in vocabulary in the later songs would be dictated by their special subject matter. Similarly the content of the Songs uses many of the basic concepts of Deutero-Isaiah, particularly the idea of witness and mission, but the insight into the redemptive value of the suffering borne by the Servant in the last of the Songs goes beyond anything elsewhere in Deutero-Isaiah.

One can see from all this that the argument can move in several directions. One might argue that the Servant Songs were older than Deutero-Isaiah and that he borrowed their vocabulary and ideas. Or one might hold that the writer of the Servant Songs came after Deutero-Isaiah and learned some of his style and ideas and used them in his own oracles. Finally, one can argue very reasonably that the prophet himself is the author of these poems. It would seem that we have a standoff. In any event the Songs are God's word to us, and no one denies that they are closely related to Deutero-Isaiah in time and in theology. And after all, it is the theology which is of essential interest to us.[4]

Before we turn to that theology of the Servant Songs it may be well to review their contents and structure. In 42:1–4 Yahweh speaks and tells of his commissioning of a Servant to bring true religion (this is better

---

[4] C. R. North, *The Suffering Servant in Deutero-Isaiah* (2nd ed. Oxford: Oxford University Press, 1958), has a thorough study of the Servant Songs surveying the many varied interpretations given them.

than the "justice" of most English versions for Hebrew *mishpat* in 42:1b and 3b) to the nations. In 49:1–6 the Servant himself speaks of his election (in terms reminiscent of Jer 1:5) and of the ill-success which he has met. For his fidelity in the face of difficulty he is rewarded with the assurance that he will eventually be successful in a mission which includes not only the gentiles but also Israel. Note that the Servant seems to introduce himself to the gentiles in the opening lines of this song. He speaks as one unknown who must explain his origin and his office. And yet he speaks of a past failure in his activity. This would seem to imply that he had already started a mission to someone else, presumably Israel, which had been rejected, although there is nothing in the first Song to indicate this. In 50:4–9 the Servant continues to speak of his work as a teacher. But this time he is not met merely with indifference. He is attacked and scorned. Yet he perseveres because of his perfect trust in God. In the last and greatest of the Servant Songs, 52:13–53:12, the Servant no longer speaks. First Yahweh (52:13–15) describes the sufferings of the Servant and the effect it will have upon men. Then in 52:1–10 and 11 an unidentified group of persons speaks of the Servant as their savior. The people here speaking are often thought to be Israel, but there is much to commend the idea that they are the nations, in view of the reference to Gentiles in 52:15 and the fact that the mission of the Servant which is given greatest emphasis is his mission to the Gentiles. In any event, these speakers describe the terrible sufferings and death of the Servant. This is a mystery because he is innocent, but the meaning is revealed: his death is a vicarious atonement which saves many. Finally, he is vindicated in a resurrection (if this is the meaning of 53:12, as it seems to be since the servant, who has suffered death, is offered a present reward which makes sense only if he has returned to life).

These are the contents of the Servant Songs. Such a bare summary does not do justice to their thought, their poetry, nor their dramatic structure, for we do indeed have real drama here. A hero is called, sets forth on his mission, is rebuffed but perseveres in the face of ever-increasing difficulties until he is apparently destroyed, only to be unexpectedly and magnificently vindicated in the end. We are kept in suspense about the true meaning of the Servant and his mission until the very end, and the revelation of the saving value of his fidelity even in the face of death makes a truly dramatic climax.

The identification and the meaning of the Servant are matters of much discussion in points of detail, but the basic theology is sufficiently clear and profound. First of all, there is the very title "servant." The Hebrew can mean "slave," but in the Old Testament it means far more than this. "My servant" is a title of honor often applied to Moses and to David. (Ex 4:10; 2 Sam 7:4; etc.) Thus it is associated with the supreme leader and source of revelation and the model king in Israel. Furthermore, the Books of Kings make Yahweh call the prophets "my servants." In other words, the title "servant" carries prophetic and royal overtones. In the description of the Servant and his office the prophetic elements seem to predominate: he is a preacher, not one who proclaims royal edicts (42:2), his very weapon is speech, not the sword of the king (49:2), and he is a teacher of the word of the Lord (50:4). Still, the spirit of the Lord rests upon him (42:1), and this is a royal trait as well as a prophetic one, moreover, he gives forth judgment and law (42:4), which are royal rather than prophetic prerogatives, and he is a medium of salvation (49:6) as in the royal psalms. The Servant, then, is both prophet and king, and the very uniting of these two offices in itself is remarkable.

More remarkable still is the development of the Servant's work. If he teaches like a prophet and gives judgment like a king, he goes beyond any prophet or king. He perseveres in the face of mounting opposition, he faces up to attacks and contempt, and finally his fidelity leads to a terrible death. There had been men who carried on their divinely appointed office even when it hurt, Jeremiah, for instance, Moses, and many others. However, of none of these can it be said "he made himself an offering for sins" (53:10b). This last phrase represents the technical word for an expiatory sacrifice, that is, the special sacrifice which in certain circumstances alone could absolve a man from sin. Nowhere else in the Old Testament do we find any man who presents himself in the place of others to bear the suffering earned by their guilt and hence to become an offering for their sins. Because the Servant is ready to suffer death even though he is innocent, his offering is accepted and it brings justification to a multitude. Thus the servant in many ways caps Old Testament revelation. He recalls Moses, he recalls the Davidic king, he recalls the prophet, but he goes beyond all this. In him is revealed the paradox that salvation can come only through suffering. The end of life is not suffering, but it is only through suffering that sinful man can come to true life.

An immense amount of ink has been spilled in the effort to identify the actual Suffering Servant whom the prophet had in mind. Many have proposed to identify him with some historical figure of the Old Testament, and if one were to search long enough one could probably find that almost every figure of importance or unimportance from Moses through Jeremiah to the prophet and composer of the Servant Songs himself has been proposed as the Servant. None of these identifications has met with favor, and it seems impossible to identify the Servant with anyone out of the past history of Israel. There is a good deal more weight to the theory that the Servant is a personification of Israel. In 49:3 the Servant even seems to be called Israel. There is some difficulty with this and many authors delete the word Israel in 49:3 — it can be done without changing anything else in the sentence and leaving it with a full meaning — but there is no indication in any of the ancient texts that the word "Israel" was ever absent from the text. The argument for removing the word is that it is an obvious sort of theological interpretation which the earliest scribes favored.[5] The problem with simply identifying the Servant with Israel is that the Servant does not quite fit into the picture of Israel the servant as painted by Deutero-Isaiah. He often speaks of Israel as Yahweh's servant, but a blind and deaf servant who has failed to fulfill his office. Thus the actual Israel is not the Servant who is perfect in his fidelity to the difficult mission Yahweh has given him. One can answer that the poems refer to an ideal Israel, Israel as it should be, and this makes considerable sense. However, it does not quite cover the whole of the data.

On the one hand, since we must now read the Servant Song in the context of Deutero-Isaiah (see above concerning the inspired character of the editorial work which fits them into the prophetic texts), it is impossible to hear the word "servant" without thinking of Israel, since this is one of Deutero-Isaiah's favorite terms for the chosen people. However, as the drama of the Servant progresses he becomes more and more sharply defined as an individual. It were best if we could find a view which would take account of both of these facts, and there seems to be one. This is the concept of "corporate personality" which is deeply embedded in the Old Testament. The essentials of the idea of corporate personality are these. On the one hand the ancients felt themselves to be much more parts of a unit than we moderns do. They were less conscious of their individuality and more conscious of their collective existence as members of a family, a clan, or a people. This does not deny that they were and knew themselves as individuals, but it does point out the truth

---

[5] It is also possible to make the word "Israel" the predicate: "You are my servant, my Israel (i.e., my chosen one), in whom I will be glorified." This is sound Hebrew, avoids arbitrary textual emendation, and keeps the Deutero-Isaian concept of Israel as servant consistent.

that in comparison with us they were far less conscious of their individuality. The corollary is that the head of the group, its chief and its representative, could and did represent the people as a whole. In these circumstances, it is possible for thought and expression to move back and forth between group and the eminent individual who represented it since they shared the same character and experiences.[6]

We may conclude with the words of two eminent English scholars who have devoted themselves to the problem.

> Nevertheless, if the songs are by Deutero-Isaiah, or, failing the absolute certainty of that, by a very near contemporary who copied his style and entered deeply into his thought-world, it is clear that we must take as our starting point the equation that the servant equals Israel. But in view of the anonymity of the servant in the songs, accompanied as it is by a more distinct individualization, the mission of the servant to Israel and the heathen, together with other theological differences, it would seem as if we must narrow down the definition of the servant. . . . The higher the task of the servant becomes, the less is any community capable of fulfilling it. There is expansion and contraction as the corporate personality theory urges . . . "in general I believe the author was personifying Israel, but in the fourth poem that personification is carried to a point where it is hard to escape the feeling that he really thought of an individual, so supremely the servant of Yahweh that within the servant's community he stood out as a representative and leader, carrying its mission of service to a point no other could reach."[7]

Thus ultimately we come to a Servant who sums up and represents all that is best in Old Testament revelation and carries it forward to a new concept of salvation. As we have seen, there is no evidence that the prophet was thinking of any figure from the history of Israel in speaking of the Servant. He must have been looking to the future. His future view is obscure, as the human view of the future must always be, but it contains profound insights into the meaning of God's choice and the salvation it brings.

It is time to sum up the theology of Isaiah 40–55 according to the divisions we have been following. First of all is his special view of God. He teaches a God whose activity in history is demonstrated through the prophets whom he sends to foretell what he will do. Only the effective agent could foretell. And because he is ultimately the only effective agent in history he is ultimately the creator of all things. So we have a God who is creator and guide of history. This view of God immediately indi-

---

[6] Jean De Fraine, S.J., *Adam and the Family of Man* (New York: Alba House, 1965), chap. 1, has a good explanation of "corporate personality."

[7] C. R. North, *The Suffering Servant*, pp. 206–207, quoting at the end H. H. Rowley.

cates what is to be demanded of man. Essentially this is fidelity to the mission of witnessing to the true God. The prophet actually devotes little time to inculcating this positively, but he implies it in his condemnation of Israel as the servant who failed to bear witness. Positively we learn the value of fidelity from the Suffering Servant. What is strikingly new, however, is that the mission both of Israel and of the Servant is universal. It is through Israel that the nations are to come to know the true God, and the primary mission of the Servant is to bring religion to the Gentiles.

As for future hope, Deutero-Isaiah is full of it. He develops themes which are not unique to him, but the manner of his development lends them new force and meaning. He sees in the return from the exile a sign of God's will to save which surpasses even the Exodus. He sees in the restoration of Jerusalem the sign of a new and perfect kingdom of righteousness where God will be honored as he should be. Most profoundly, it is this book which reveals that even suffering is a reason for hope. It is only through a fidelity which faces up to and passes through the fire of opposition and suffering and even death that salvation can come. Finally, Deutero-Isaiah does not entirely ignore the hopes placed in the Davidic line. It is a reason for hope and a promise for restoration (55:3). However, one cannot but feel that it is perfunctory. Once again it is an item which an Israelite theologian had to discuss, but for Deutero-Isaiah it was hardly at the center of his theology.

Our last topic is the prophet's attitude toward the Gentiles. We have already seen the essential matters here. First of all, God gives a pagan king like Cyrus a true mission of salvation. This gives a Gentile a position far higher than anything previously seen in the Old Testament. Moreover, the prophet looks to a conversion of nations. They will see the salvation wrought by Yahweh and will come themselves to worship him (50:4; 45:6, 14; 52:10; etc.). Thus Deutero-Isaiah is far more of a universalist than his predecessors. However, he does not get entirely away from a certain condescending attitude toward the nations. If they are to be converted, they are to be the servants of a true Israel (49:22–23).

THE SERVANT AND THE NEW TESTAMENT

It is not within the scope of this book to detail the further interpretation of the Servant Songs in later Judaism and the New Testament. However, the Songs and their theology were so important to the early Church and so basic to an understanding of the New Testament that it seems desirable to note a few of the important elements which the Servant Songs contribute to an insight into the life of Jesus. But first a word of caution is in order. One should not take any reference to "servant" as a reference to the Servant of the Servant Songs. As we have seen, the simple title "servant" was a title of honor given to many in the Old Testament, and many references to a servant in the New Testament go back to these antecedents and not to the Servant Songs. Nevertheless the Songs did contribute a basic framework to New Testament theology.

The public life of our Lord begins with his baptism, and the very words used by John to describe this are a quotation from Isaiah 42:1 (see Mk 1:11; Mt 3:17; Lk 3:22). In other words, the beginning of our Lord's ministry is explained for us as the coming of the true servant of God on a mission of preaching and bringing salvation. This interpretation of our Lord's actions and preaching before his passion is re-enforced by Matthew. In 12:18–21 this Gospel repeats the interpretation of the Lord's life as a fulfillment of the description of a servant given in Isaiah 42:1–4. However, it is in the interpretation of the passion that the Servant Songs are most used. Before the fact the disciples are warned that the savior must suffer ill treatment at the hands of those who reject him (Mk 9:12; Mt 17:12). The realization that the Christ must suffer and die to save many from their sins becomes part of the earliest Christian creed (see 1 Cor 15:3–5; Rom 4:25). It is widely held that the words "for many" in the Pauline formula for the Eucharist (1 Cor 11:23–25) is another reference to the Servant Songs (cf. Is 53:11–12), thus making clear the connection between the Eucharist and Christ's death as a sacrifice which saves the world.

The use of the Servant Songs in the earliest Christian preaching and apologetics is illustrated in Acts. The story of Philip and the minister of the queen of Ethiopia in Acts 8:26–40 makes the claim that Christ's sufferings and death had fulfilled the prophetic oracle of Isaiah 53. The Christian community had come to understand that "it was necessary that the Christ should suffer and so enter into his glory" (Lk 24:26). And the first Epistle of Peter could describe the death of Christ and its meaning in a collection of references to the Servant Songs: Christ has suffered for his people, he suffered though he was innocent, he did not answer back when he was reviled and so bore our sins that we might die to sin and live in righteousness (1 Pet 2:21–25; see Is 53 and probably 50:6).

We can do no better in explaining the meaning of all this than quote the words of Father John McKenzie:

> It is not too much to say that the conception of the atoning and redeeming death in the NT is a development of the idea of the Servant.
>
> This development is not to be regarded as the work of the apostles themselves. The witness of the Gospels is that this essential feature of the life and mission of Jesus is one which they, with the mass of Judaism, found most difficult to understand and accept. The identification of Jesus with the servant is best attributed to Jesus himself. The title and the conception . . . permitted Him to assume a role which fell into none of the existing categories of charismatic leader and savior. This brought out the novelty of his character and at the same time presented Him as the fulfillment of all the elements of Israel's gifts and missions. It furnished a biblical basis for His teaching on the atoning passion and death, and on the meaning of suffering and death in human experience.
>
> The identity of the Servant and Israel is paralleled by the identity of Jesus and the Church. Jesus is the Servant who brings Israel to fullness; He is the true and perfect "corporate personality," one with the Church which is His body. This great conception has many roots in the OT and one of them is the conception of the Servant who suffers in his own person and who sanctifies the sufferings of the group which he represents.[8]

We will understand the difficulties which the apostles and other Jews had in understanding the suffering of Christ if we realize that at the time of Christ Jewish theology had not finally come to terms with the interpretation of the Servant Songs and particularly the concept of the Suffering Servant. Later on Judaism developed the noble concept of itself, Israel, as the servant whose sufferings keep the world safe. Although there are scattered references to suffering on the part of the Messiah, earlier Jewish literature simply does not treat the idea of a suffering Messiah.[9]

---

[8] J. L. McKenzie, S.J., *Dictionary of the Bible,* pp. 793–794.

[9] See Joseph Bonsirven, S.J., *Palestinian Judaism in the Time of Christ* (New York: Holt, Rinehart & Winston, 1964), pp. 192–194, for the few early references to a suffering messiah in Jewish literature.

Chapter 12. Post-Exilic Prophecy

Readings: Hag; Zech 1–8; Is 56–66; Mal; Jl; Ob; Jon; Is 24–27, 34–35; Zech 9:14; Dan 7–12

Prophecy did not die out with the end of the exile and the beginnings of the new Judean state, but it showed a very different character. First of all, this was a community of returned exiles, and like most such groups it was determined to reproduce the old conditions, not innovate. Thus it was an age concerned with the study of the old ways and an effort to restore them in their entirety. It was an age of the codification and commentary upon the law rather than an era in which a law was produced. So also with prophecy. The first post-exilic prophets, Haggai and Zechariah, are concerned entirely with applying Ezekiel's program for the Temple and Temple state, and, as Ezekiel had emphasized the visionary aspect of prophecy, so Zechariah's prophecy must be a "night vision." One feels that these prophets of the restoration had to insist on their continuity with the past, and they picked the last great traditional prophet, Ezekiel, as guide and model. The impression is confirmed when one reflects that Ezekiel multiplies angels as mediators of God's will. Beginning with Zechariah the post-exilic era took this up and produced an elaborate angelology — for instance, this age has furnished the traditional angelic names like Gabriel and Raphael.

This is not to say that the era of the return was merely derivative and unproductive. It was active but in spheres rather different from the old Israel. For instance, the Wisdom schools flourished as never before. They took up one aspect of prophecy, the emphasis on individual responsibility which appears in Jeremiah and Ezekiel. How was it, if the good man was sure of his reward and the bad man of his punishment, that in fact it was often the bad who prosper and the good who suffer in this life? These are questions which are raised by books like Qohelet and Job. They do not find an answer, although Job concludes with a magnificent act of faith in the God who created the world and guides it, a faith which transcends the whole problem in its confidence in the creating God.

The other great development in the later Jewish community is eschatology, the hope for a definitive deliverance, often expressed in the tremendous, if confused and conventional imagery of apocalyptic. This is the age which developed ideas like that of the return of Elijah as prelude to the new age to come (Mal 4:5), the age which emphasized the final judgment in which the good and the wicked would receive their ultimate reward (Zech 12–14). One fruit of this apocalyptic ferment was the doctrine of the resurrection of the just as an answer to the problem of the apparent failure of the good to receive the reward they deserved (Is 26:19; Dan 12:1–3).

Actually most of this eschatological ferment belongs to an age after all prophecy has ceased, but we must have some idea of what it was if we are to understand the post-exilic prophets. On the one hand they were men very much rooted in the past, concerned with a restoration which was often somewhat wooden in its insistence on old forms; on the other hand, precisely because the old forms had so solidified they stood at the threshold of a new age which had to find new forms to express itself and its problems. Indeed, as we shall see, these forms, especially the ideas of apocalyptic literature, do appear in our post-exilic prophets.

HAGGAI

We know nothing of this post-exilic prophet besides his name which means "feast," an unusual name but verified in extrabiblical sources. We can date his activity precisely. He delivered his oracles between August and December of the year 520 B.C. to encourage the community of the return to finish rebuilding the Temple. When he spoke the first people of the return had been back for some eighteen years and, while they had begun building a Temple immediately upon their return, their fervor cooled and the work begun was never finished. Haggai and Zechariah now appear to urge the complete construction of the Temple as an indispensable religious and cultural rallying point for the people of Yahweh.

This preoccupation with the Temple and cult has led many to believe Haggai to have been a prophet officially associated with the worship, whose office apparently was to deliver formal answers to formal questions. An example of this sort of thing is contained in Psalm 60 where we have a ritualized complaint that the enemies of Israel are overwhelming her and, beginning in verse 6, a prophetic-sounding reply proclaiming that God is with his people. Such a reply probably came from the prophets associated with the cult. However, we have in Haggai the classic example of the teaching office of the Old Testament priest. It was his duty to know and explain to the people the conditions, both moral and ritual, under which they could join in the community of those who worshiped Yahweh, as we find him doing in a matter of ritual purity in Haggai 2:10–13. But the prophet uses this opportunity to belabor his point: build the Temple! This is hardly formalized prophecy, it is living response to a situation.[1]

The Book of Haggai is unusual among the prophetic books in that it is entirely in the third person. This may indicate that someone else compiled the book from Haggai's words. In any case there is nothing in the book which is inconsistent with the prophet and the whole may be ascribed to him. We should simply read 2:15–23 after 1:13 because these verses should come before the completion of the Temple.

Haggai's doctrine is summed up easily. Basically he attributes the troubles of his age to the fact that the people have not fulfilled their obligation to rebuild the Temple. He sees in the completion of this task a sign of the new era which God has promised to bring. He is sure of this because a member of the line of David (Zerubbabel, a Davidid) will lead the new age (1:14 and 2:23, which seems consciously to reverse Jeremiah 22:24). We can see already in Haggai elements which become popular in apocalyptic circles. There is the theme of overturning heaven and earth (2:6, 21) and the destruction of enemy kingdoms by God's direct intervention (2:22), all of which will result in a new and remarkable peace (2:9). All this is conventional. Other prophets had great

[1] See A. R. Johnson, *The Cultic Prophet*, pp. 64–65.

hopes for the Temple, the place where Yahweh's name dwelt, and the Davidic line.

ZECHARIAH 1–8

We limit ourselves to these eight out of the fourteen chapters of Zechariah because it is universally admitted that chapters 9–14 are from a much later date than the oracles in the earlier chapters and are rather apocalyptic than prophetic. Like Ezekiel, Zechariah seems to have been a member of an important priestly family (cf. Ezra 5:1; 6:14; Neh 12:16) who favors the form of visions for his prophecy. There are eight of these visions: (1) the four horsemen and the end of the peaceful sway of the empires over Judah (1:7–17); (2) the four horns — note that the horn was a symbol of strength in Hebrew: those who have scattered the people of God will themselves be destroyed (1:18–21); (3) the man with the measuring line to protect Jerusalem (2:1–9); (4) the investiture of the high priest Joshua who was to greet the Davidic prince (3:1–10). Note that as it stands now this oracle mentions only the priest Joshua, but in 3:8 there is reference to the Branch, a messianic title belonging to the Davidids (Jer 23:5; 33:15; Ps 132:17). Hence in 3:9 we should read Zerubbabel in place of Joshua. The fifth vision (5) is of the seven-branched lamp and the olive trees which symbolize the unity of the people in the cult and the two powers which supervise the cult, the priestly and the kingly (4:1–6a plus 10b–14); the sixth (6) is of the scroll with the curses which passes over the land and destroys the infidels among the Jews (5:1–4); (7) the basket with the woman who signifies wickedness which is carried to Babylon to call down punishment upon it (5:5–11); (8) the four chariots which will carry destruction to the empires (6:1–8).

Thus far the visions of Zechariah. The rest of the material has been inserted or appended to the visions with some logic. Thus the song of rejoicing in 2:10–13 fits after the promise of a restored Jerusalem. The question concerning the fast in 7:1–3 is not answered until 8:18 because the intervening portion on the contrast between mere fasting and interior religion seems appropriate after the question about fasting. It is in the spirit and manner of the prophet that we feel a notable difference. He inclines to formulate his doctrine almost exclusively in visions, and these visions are both elaborate and obscure in their symbolism. In this he has gone a long way toward the manner of the later apocalyptic literature. Nevertheless we must not confuse this with the authentic eschatology of later Judaism. Zechariah does not look forward to a completely renewed and entirely different world in the final era to come. This is indicated by the fact that he expects a succession in the messianic office (6:12), an idea which implies an ongoing world and not the definitive end of all things as in true eschatology. The important thing is that the prophet is supplying material which was the very stuff of later eschatological ideas and apocalyptic imagery: the defeat of the nations (2:1–4), the new and greater Temple (1:16; 8:3), the coming of God to his holy city and the conversion of the nations (8:20–23). The prophetic word, not a vision, in 6:9–15 is rather special. As it stands it tells of the coronation of the high priest Joshua. However, we have a substitution, just as in 3:8–9. The reference to the Branch is again Davidic. This indicates that the prophet is speaking of Zerubbabel, the current carrier of the Davidic hopes.

The theology of Zechariah can be summarized fairly simply. For one thing, it is evidently very priestly in its orientation. He emphasizes the place of the high priest near the messiah, he is much concerned with ritual purity, he emphasizes the transcendent holiness of God. All this doctrine is familiar from the priestly traditions or from Ezekiel.

TRITO-ISAIAH

The material in Isaiah 56–66 apparently comes from Palestine itself (Isaiah 57:5–9 describes pagan practices characteristic of Palestine and not Babylon), at a time when the Temple is standing (56:5–7; 60:7), but Jerusalem has not yet been rewalled (60:10). Thus these chapters, which are marked by the vocabulary and theology of Deutero-Isaiah are not exilic but reflect the era of the return. Some feel that certain elements in these chapters are the work of Deutero-Isaiah who would certainly have participated in the return if he lived long enough to do so. However, most of the book departs so much from the lofty theology of Deutero-Isaiah that it is easier to believe that these chapters are a collection of oracles from various men, some of whom were influenced by the great exilic prophet. Admitting that the poems stem from various authors makes it impossible to place and date the whole collection exactly, except that the signs of Deutero-Isaian influence (56:1; 57:14–19; 58:8–12; 65:15–25), and the fact that prophecy seems to have ceased within a century and a half after the return set certain limits. The poems must come from the fifth century B.C.

Though it is an anthology, "Trito-Isaiah" has a certain characteristic theology which sets it off among the prophets. There is a marked consciousness of national guilt, a guilt which retards salvation (58:8–10; 59:1–4; 65:1). Chapter 56:1–8 shows a compassionate universalism, a concern for the Gentile and the deprived, in fine, for the salvation of all, which is the equal or superior of anything of the sort in the Old Testament. However, in accord with the attitudes of the post-exilic community there is a certain insistence upon external cult, for instance the Sabbath (58:13; 66:23). Then the new Jerusalem and its Temple are described in chapters 60–62 as so grandiose as to imply a concern with ritual, not to mention a nationalism, unlike Deutero-Isaiah or even Ezekiel. Still this is the Temple and the city of the true God, and we must never lose sight of this fact, as also in reading the terrible picture of judgment on the nations in 63:1–6. Finally, one of the poets who is represented in Trito-Isaiah expands the picture of the great new age to come, the picture which is the dominant theme of this collection, beyond the reconstitution of Jerusalem to a recreation of the universe, a new and glorious paradise (65:17–25).

Some find these various features incompatible or even contradictory, as though a concern for religious observances, which are necessarily arbitrary and, in the ancient circumstances of difficult communications, even provincial, must interfere with a concern for one's fellow men. This is to read inattentively. In fact, the splendid passage offering hope to all mankind in chapter 56 relates this hope with observance of the Sabbath and with the cult. In fact, of course, religion will never be able and will never even wish to rid itself of external worship, and it is this truth which is recognized here. We have had several occasions to note the prophetic insistence on the holiness of God, that is, the complete strangeness or otherness of the divine which strikes man with awe. Since man feels in contact with something alien in this area, he always marks it off from everyday life, and since he is dealing with mystery, such marking off cannot be entirely rational for it is concerned with something not entirely understood. Hence the necessary element of the arbitrary in all religion. Feast and fast can never be entirely explained for they are human response to the holy which says: "Thus far and no farther" without explanation just because it is holy and mysterious. On the other hand, the religious is never purely cultic, purely arbitrary. It is always concerned with moral conduct too, i.e., with relations with men. Thus to find a concern with observance of cultic regulation at odds with a concern for charity is to fail to understand the character of religion as such.

MALACHI

Actually this book is anonymous since the traditional name, Malachi, is simply the Hebrew phrase "my messenger" and is taken from 3:1 and turned into a name for the prophet in the introduction to the book. Still, the background of the prophecy can be fairly well established. It is largely concerned with the proper carrying out of the Temple cult. So it comes from a time after the rebuilding of the Temple in 516 B.C., while the fact that the prophet must insist so emphatically upon the proper observance of the cult indicates that he is preaching before the reforms of Ezra and Nehemiah had become effective, that is, before the last quarter of the fifth century B.C.

In the prophecy itself we find an attack upon Edom (1:2–5) which reflects the dislike of the Jews for the people that had turned on Judah in 587 B.C. Then come accusations against priests who fail to observe the proper ritual in sacrifices (1:6–2:9) and a proclamation against mixed marriages (2:10–16). Chapters 2:17–3:5 describe the day when the evil will be properly punished and the good rewarded. Chapter 3:6–12 returns to the cult and condemns fraud in the payment of tithes, while with 3:13–4:3 we return to the description of the day of judgment. Evidently this is not the logical order. Scholars often attempt to regroup the material on more logical lines, but such attempts have cast little light on the prophet's message.

Except for the attack upon marriages with non-Jews which reflects the legislation imposed under Ezra and Nehemiah against foreign wives, this material is homogeneous. Hence it is not doubted that it is from Malachi. The very end of the book has been graced with some added notes. Chapter 4:4 is an admonition in the style of the Deuteronomic writers to keep the law. More interesting is the following bit of exegesis on the messenger of Yahweh mentioned in 3:1. He is said to be Elijah who will return before the final days of the world. This figure captured the imagination of Judaism and there was much concern to find out who this returned Elijah, the precursor of the messianic age, was (see Mt 17:12; Mk 9:12–13; Mt 16:14 and parallels; Lk 1:17; Jn 1:21).

The theology of Malachi is very Deuteronomic. He sees the high point of religion in the liturgical service of God. Hence his concern with the minutiae of the cult. This may seem trivial, but a preoccupation with the proper worship of God is not without its nobility. Moreover, the priest is not merely concerned with rubrics. He must "guard knowledge . . . for he is the messenger of the lord of hosts" (2:7). Here we have the great duty and privilege of the priest to be a teacher of his people. Furthermore, this interest in the cult is used to express a wonderful universalism in 1:11, where the recognition of the true divinity of Yahweh by all mankind is seen as a pure offering among the nations.[2] Hence Malachi can proclaim that Yahweh is king of all the world, not just of Israel (1:14).

The prophet also can speak feelingly of the true bases of morality. The fatherhood of God is brought out as the motive for brotherly love in lines like: "Have we not all one Father? Has not one God created us? Why then are we faithless to one another?" (2:10), and 2:13 shows that with all his concern for rubrics the prophet is acutely conscious of the need for true interior dispositions of worship. Another notable feature in Malachi is his condemnation of divorce (2:14–16), a condemnation which opens the way to an ideal of marriage higher than anything expressed before him.

When we look to the prophet's concept of the future hope we find it in his idea about the day of Yahweh, and this is essentially a day for cultic purification. The new Israel will perform the true worship of Yahweh, and this is the end and object of its creation (3:4).

JOEL

The Book of Joel has two clearly distinguishable parts. First there is a prophetic liturgy lamenting a plague of locusts (1:2–2:27). There follows a collection of apocalyptic sayings in 2:28–3:21 (this is the numbering of our English Bibles; in the Hebrew text our 2:28–32 constitutes chapter 3, and our chapter 3 is chapter 4).

The portion of the book concerned with a plague of locusts is an illustration of a Temple service in a period of calamity. There are descriptions of the locusts interspersed with lamentations and calls for repentance and penance and the whole concludes with an oracle. This latter represents the work of a cultic prophet who replies to the lament with an assurance of the people's deliverance (2:18–27).

The apocalyptic poems in the latter half of the book begin by describing an outpouring of the spirit upon the people of Israel which recalls

---

[2] This is a widely accepted interpretation of the text, but the opinion that it refers to the Jewish diaspora about the world who offer prayer (often "the sacrifice of praise" or "of the lips" in the psalms) also has weight. However, the fact that the prophet could utter an oracle against a near and bitter enemy does not prove that he must reject gentiles in general, yet this argument is a main prop of the restrictive interpretation.

Ezekiel's idea of a new heart and the revivified bones and Jeremiah's concept of the new covenant in which God would deal directly with his people (2:28–29). There follows in typical apocalyptical fashion a description of the tremendous portents in the heavens and on the earth which will mark the terrible day of Yahweh (2:30–32). Then there is the terrific judgment of the nations in 3:1–14 and the final triumph of Israel (3:16–21).

The two parts of Joel are very different, and this difference has led critics to deny unity of authorship. Still the very marked differences in style can, to a considerable extent, be accounted for by the marked differences in subject matter. It was customary to describe the day of Yahweh in terms different from those used of a locust plague. Moreover, there are elements of apocalyptic in the description of the locust plague. Hence this part of the book probably stems from the same general era as the latter part, that later age in which apocalyptic was a natural form of expression. Furthermore, the Hebrew is marked by Aramaisms, things characteristic of the Aramaic language which was spoken in Israel after the exile rather than Hebrew, and it presupposes a daily offering (1:9; 2:14), a practice which develops only in the later post-exilic Temple. These affinities in style and the closeness in date between the two portions of Joel are good reasons to take the book as the product of a single author. A fairly late dating for the book is confirmed by the mention of Greeks in 3:6. This takes us into the fourth century since Judah hardly had contact with the Greek people earlier than that.

If we hold that Joel is a unity, this influences the interpretation which we put upon it. The locust plague surely refers to a historical event, the subject of a special liturgical prayer. Such attacks by huge members of insects were and are common in the Near East, and in a subsistence economy they represent a disaster of great magnitude since the loss of a single crop means famine for many. Hence the forceful language which Joel applies to the plague of the locusts is not out of place. If he speaks of them in terms which the earlier prophets applied to the terrible armies of Assyria and Babylon he was speaking of something which could in its way be as destructive as those armies. Now, if we admit that the two parts of the book are the work of a single author we can see a deeper meaning in all this. The prophet has taken the historical experience of the locusts and made it into a type or a sign of the day of Yahweh. Prayer and penance enable Israel to escape the plague. The same means will save it on the tremendous day of Yahweh when he comes to judge all men.

Finally, we should note the concept of the Day of Yahweh. On that day, God will vindicate the true Israel and punish the sinful. The new world which will result is a world centered upon Zion (3:17), that is to say a world centered upon the liturgy worshiping the one true God, and from this worship of the true God will follow a paradise-like prosperity (3:18).

OBADIAH

This shortest of all Old Testament books has nonetheless given rise to the standard questions: Is it from one author or more? When was it written? and so on. It represents in miniature all the questions that can be raised about the prophetic literature. Nonetheless, the contents are simple. After a title and introduction, verses 2–14, 15b contain curses and threats against the Edomites, the hated southern neighbors of Judah. Verses 15a and 16–21 are a proclamation of hope of restoration for the people of God.

Some see verses 2–9 as a separate poem referring to a time in the fourth century when Edom was attacked by its neighbors.[8] In fact, in 312 B.C. the former territory of the Edomites had been entirely overrun by the Arab tribe known as the Nabateans, and Obadiah 2–9 may refer to the continuing attacks which led up to destruction of the nation in 312. The oracles against Edom apart from 2–9 could be older. They could refer to any of the various attacks made by the Edomites upon Judah when it was helpless during its struggle with the Babylonians and after the Babylonians had laid it waste. The following poem about the restoration of God's people in 16–21 consists of familiar themes. The enemies of the people of God are destroyed and that people returned to its proper place, and saviors reign in the holy city on Zion.

Many, perhaps most, interpreters have found Obadiah unworthy of the name prophet. His book seems exclusively nationalistic. It lacks any concern for the gentiles, and its picture of the restoration shows no originality. It hardly advances beyond the destruction of the enemy and the restoration of material prosperity. Out of the total biblical context this would have little meaning. However, a people like the Edomites represented a serious danger for the people of God. Their enmity threatened the very existence of that people who were the chosen channel of grace for mankind. Hence it was natural enough that the Jews wish that they be kept

---

[8] Obad 2–9 also appears in Jer 49:7–22, but the verses surely are later than Jeremiah. They belong to the imprecations against Edom common in exilic and post-exilic literature (cf. Lam 4:21–22; Ezek 25:12–14; Mal 1:2–5).

in hand. On the one hand, the enemies of the people of God are to be put down; on the other hand, the people of God are to prosper. The one and the other are aspects of hope. For the sorely tried people of the exile and the centuries following the exile, people living in the midst of so many enemies, such a message of hope could be useful.

JONAH

Here we have one of the most interesting little books in the whole of the canon of minor prophets, but we must begin with a question. Is this prophecy at all? The answer seems to be "no." Our decision in this matter has nothing to do with the problem of the giant fish or anything of that sort. We are confronted with a number of anomalies in the book which indicate that it was not intended to be taken as prophetic literature.

We may recall first of all that the prophets generally reflect the political and other circumstances of their time. Not so Jonah. The prophet of the book is represented as being Jonah, the son of Amittai, a prophet mentioned in 2 Kings 14:25 as working under Jeroboam II, the eighth-century king of Israel. Such a dating is appropriate enough because the prophet in the book of Jonah is concerned with the Assyrians. The difficulty is that the prophet is sent to Nineveh, which was not the capital nor the chief city of Assyria at the time when the prophet is supposed to have lived, and yet the king of Assyria is represented as having his palace there. Then the immense size of the city, three days' journey across, is more folklore than history. Finally, the miraculous conversion of all Assyria is a miracle greater than Pentecost, not to mention an effect which all God's dealings with his own people in the Old Testament could not produce. As a matter of fact, we are dealing with the elements of popular story-telling. The great storm, the fish, the immense size of Nineveh, and the immediate effect of Jonah's short speech on the king and people of that pagan city are marvels, and men are always interested in marvels. Such things have been used to make a story interesting and to enforce a point time out of mind. This is an easily recognizable and quite respectable literary category, a story with elements of folklore used to make a point. Thus, while it is true that the prophets sometimes used symbolic actions to communicate God's message without words, prophets were essentially preachers, and Jonah is something quite other. He is a figure in a parable, a story teaching a truth, not a speaker of words proclaiming the truth.

Finally, and probably most important, the message of Jonah was most desperately needed not in the eighth century B.C. but in post-exilic times.

What is that message? It is very simple and very important. Yahweh is the God of all the world. He is concerned to save all mankind and not some chosen few upon whom he lavishes all his regard while allowing the rest to go to ruin. The point is driven home in a variety of ways. Thus the Hebrew Jonah is quite willing to refuse the task offered him by Yahweh, but the Gentile sailors are aghast that they should be connected with one who would ignore Yahweh, the God of the Hebrews (Jon 1:9–10). They exhibit a faith greater than Jonah's (1:14)! So also Jonah needs but mention, "Yet forty days, and Nineveh will be overthrown," and the whole of pagan Nineveh gives itself over to penance. Once more the Gentiles are readier to listen to the word of the Lord than the Hebrew. But Jonah is nothing if not obstinate. In the face of all this insistence that Yahweh loves and is determined to save all men, Jonah is petulant because God insists on saving the Gentiles. He himself, a true Hebrew, will have nothing to do with these mere outsiders and cannot even bear the sight of their salvation. And so once more the Lord must explain carefully that he has pity upon all men (Jon 4).

This is effective and emphatic storytelling with an important point for later Judaism. It is easy for the chosen people, as it is easy for the favored in all times, to look upon themselves as the only important ones. They arrogate to themselves the entire concern of the Lord and cannot even muster pity for the outsiders. They have nothing but contempt for them, and often enough look forward to the joys of watching them suffer. This was an attitude common in the apocalyptic literature popular in later Old Testament times. Jonah and the men of his time and indeed all of us have need of this message: we are all God's children and God loves and wills to save us all equally.

APOCALYPTIC LITERATURE

The type of literature which goes by the name of apocalyptic is not the direct concern of this book. Apocalyptic is not prophecy, even though it is much concerned with predicting the future. As a matter of fact, as we have seen, it is not characteristic of prophecy as such to be concerned with the distant future, while apocalyptic literature delights in detailed pictures of remote eras of time. This gives apocalyptic a similarity with prophecy as defined popularly, but it actually sets apocalyptic off from the truly prophetic.

Nevertheless, the origins of much of apocalyptic thought lie in the prophets. In addition, apocalyptic is the legitimate successor of prophecy in its constant affirmation that it is God and God alone who governs the course of history, and in its consequent interest in the course of a history which is a revelation of God's will. Finally, we have seen imagery in the books of the prophets which is definitely apocalyptic in color. Hence there would be a certain incompleteness if we ignored the subject entirely.

In fact, quite apart from the themes and motifs and imagery which have apocalyptic or eschatological or messianic overtones, found in all the prophets (but especially in the post-exilic prophets who use modes of expression and ideas which belong to true prophecy while moving over toward the apocalyptic), passages of out-and-out apocalyptic have found their way into the prophetic books.

Among such passages are the so-called Apocalypses of Isaiah (Is 24–26 and 34–35). The first of these presupposes a diaspora, a Jewish people widely scattered throughout the world. This condition obtained only in the latest Old Testament times. Then there is the punishment of the angels (24:21), and the idea of the resurrection of the dead (26:19). These too are late ideas. The shorter apocalypse in Isaiah 34–35, with its visionary character, its vigorous oracle against the nations, and its obvious dependence upon exilic literature (especially Deutero-Isaiah), must also be dated later and attributed to the apocalyptic school. Besides these passages in Isaiah there are two pieces of apocalyptic writing in Zechariah: the collection introduced as an oracle in 9–11 and the new oracle introduced in 12–14. These are two separate collections characterized by the apocalyptic spirit. There is no agreement about unity of authorship here; probably most scholars would be inclined to think that the two sets of oracles are separate collections from varied sources. These two apocalyptic oracles are also late. Zechariah 9–14 does not know even the Persian period. Chapter 9:13 speaks of Greece, and we assume that the oracles date from the time of the Greek hegemony in the east. The references to Egypt and Assyria are cryptic signs behind which lurk the Ptolemaic and Seleucid empires whose struggles dominated the period. Such cryptograms are typical of the apocalyptic way of writing. Finally, the affirmation in 13:2–6 that no more true prophets will arise can only stem from a date after prophecy had ceased to be an effective element in Jewish religion. In addition to these sections from the prophetic books we have already seen and which can be identified as apocalyptic there is Daniel 6–12. This is the classic example of the form in the Old Testament.

We have seen where we can find apocalyptic; now we must ask what it is. In some ways this question can be answered most easily by a comparison with prophecy. In the merely external aspect of the form of writing there is already a difference. Prophecy is usually given in short poetic oracles which speak to the immediate situation. Typical apocalyptic writing is in prose. Its compositions are lengthy and complicated. Even when it imitates prophecy in using verse it is long, complex, and esoteric. These are sure signs that apocalyptic is literary in its origins, not, like prophetic literature, essentially oral. The typical matter for apocalyptic writing is a long review of history projected into the future. Far from attempting to speak immediately and clearly about current concerns, as did the prophet, the apocalyptic writers delighted in the esoteric, in cryptic numbers, obscure symbols, and secret names. Furthermore, prophecy typically presented history as conditioned by human choice. The Hebrews are offered the chance to repent and become faithful. If they do so the course of history will be different. Thus the prophets saw history governed by God but through the means of human agents, whether they be the kings of Assyria or Babylon or Persia or Israel and Judah. This idea, indeed, carried on into the latest Old Testament times and beyond in the form of the belief that it was Israel's fidelity to the law which would bring about the final great new age, and it was its infidelity which was delaying the breaking in of the new times to come. However, the basic attitude of apocalyptic tends to be deterministic about history. A mysterious time has been appointed by divine decree and when this time comes God will intervene automatically and himself produce the new world. Thus there is determinism, and the constant preoccupation with the future is governed by the effort to discover the divinely appointed time.

Such are the characteristics of apocalyptic literature. What are its major ideas? Again we may begin with its borrowings from prophecy. For one thing there is emphasis on "that day" or "the day of the Lord." As far back as Amos we heard of the day of Yahweh in the prophets. Now it has come to be the technical name for that mysterious time that God has appointed for his own intervention and the final determination of the new era. Another prophetic idea much developed in the apocalyptic literature was that of the remnant. It was not enough simply to belong to the nation Israel to be saved. Rather it was the saints, the faithful, within the nation who were to be saved. Such an idea is the evident result of experience. Clearly not all Jews were faithful; for instance the Maccabean revolt was brought about by antipathy to the higher priestly families who had gone over to a semi-pagan Hellenism in imitation of their Greek overlords. Again, the prophets, especially Isaiah, spoke of a new golden age of peace in which the world would be remade and paradise restored. This idea that the new world which God would bring about by his direct intervention would be a return to the conditions of paradise is another popular theme of apocalyptic. Interestingly enough apocalyptic literature is not characterized by enthusiasm for a Davidic messiah. This is not to say that it ignores the messiah. Zechariah 9:9–10, for instance, speaks of the king who will come and achieve universal domination. Clearly this is the messiah but there is a striking development: This is the messiah of the pure and the humble. Though he is "triumphant and victorious," he comes "humble and riding on an ass, on a colt, the foal of an ass." Other non-canonical literature like the Book of Enoch which, though not inspired, gives us information about the ideas of Judaism in the centuries before Jesus are more explicit and more enthusiastic about the messiah who will be super-human, a mighty warrior and terrible judge. On the other hand, an apocalyptic work like Daniel plays down the messianic aspect of the hoped for end. Such an attitude may be the result of the disappointments of the return and the apparent lack of a Davidic successor.[4]

However, prophecy is not the only source from which apocalyptic grew. It was also influenced by things from outside Israel, and especially by certain concepts borrowed from Iranian religion. This religion had a wealth of mediating spirits or powers between its higher gods and the world, and it is beyond doubt that contact with these ideas influenced the interest in angelology displayed by apocalyptic. Furthermore, the Persian religion looked forward to the consummation of this world by fire and its replacement by a new and better world. This theme also found favor with many of the apocalyptic writers and we find it often repeated among them.

The major purpose of this form[5] of literature seems to have been to console the faithful who were troubled in times of doubt and persecution. For instance, Daniel was written for the people who were suffering under the persecution of the Greek kings from Syria whose tyranny brought about the Maccabean revolt. Typically the apocalyptic form is a vision in which the history of the world is presented as a vision of the future,

---

[4] In Dan 7:13–18 the singular Son of Man could be a messiah, but this interpretation is given up in favor of an application to the people of God as a group (v. 18).

[5] On Apocalyptic literature see H. H. Rowley, *The Relevance of Apocalyptic* (2nd ed. London: Lutterworth Press, 1947). The best collection of eschatological and apocalyptic texts is R. H. Charles, *The Apocrypha and Pseudepigrapha of the Old Testament* 2 vols. (Oxford: Clarendon Press, 1963–1964) (unaltered reprint of the 1913 edition).

though actually it is drawn from the past and used to explain the present (spoken of as though it were the future). Then it goes on to offer a hope for the future through divine intervention. In outline a typical vision of this sort shows God allowing things to go on according to their natural course or under the influence of evil until the fixed time comes. Then ordinarily he will intervene directly to bring about a totally new world, a new age, a new eon quite separate from this present world. Sometimes, but by no means always, he uses as an instrument for this the messiah who will lead the forces of good in the destruction of evil and the bringing about of the wonderful new era. Commonly this turning point at the time set by God is called the "day of the Lord" or "that day" and is pictured as a cosmic cataclysm: the stars fall, the mountains shake, and the sun grows dark, while among men there is a mighty battle in which the nations who represent the forces of evil are conquered. Then there is a judgment which metes out payment to the good and the evil according to their deserts. In this way God imposes the new era upon the world. The new world so created will be a new paradise centered on a Jerusalem and especially its Temple described as built of gold and precious jewels. Finally, in order that the just who have died may see the reward of their justice, there is a resurrection in which the good will return to life and enjoy the new age. Sometimes in the very latest forms there is even a resurrection of all men, evil as well as good, so that the evil can be punished as well as the good rewarded (Cf. Dn 12:1–3).

The reader should not be deceived by a summary like this. It represents the elements in which apocalyptic literature pictured its hopes for the millenium, but it is synthesized from many sources. In fact the elements of apocalyptic could be and were combined in every possible way, though a hope for a restored moral purity and national revival of Israel is universal in the literature. Some hopes stopped with this minimal renewal. Others looked for a new paradise, some with and some without a messiah. Often this was to be brought about by a battle, but often again by God's peaceful fiat. Sometimes the hope centered on a new and purified Temple state. But often too the nearness of God in the new age was taken to mean that no liturgy would be needed. Personal prayer would suffice. And so on.

Apocalyptic kept alive a future hope in Judaism, and so performed an invaluable service. But it could also be a source of confusion and disquiet, of sectarianism and wild revolutionary hopes. One can understand the disdain of Zechariah 13:3–4: "And if anyone again appears as a prophet, his father and mother who bore him will say to him, 'you shall not live, for you speak lies in the name of the Lord'; and his father and mother who bore him shall pierce him through when he prophesies. On that day every prophet will be ashamed of his vision," if the writer was thinking of these seers who saw only confusion. Still men thirsted for the word of the Lord, and 1 Maccabee 4:45–46 is poignant. When Judas Maccabee had retaken the Temple from the Greeks who had profaned it, "They tore down the altar, and stored the stones . . . until there should come a prophet to tell what to do with them." And so many found it a relief and a fulfillment of ancient hopes when the apostolic Church laid claim to the prophetic spirit (Acts 2:17–21 referring to Jl 2:28–29) and saw reproduced in its life God's dealings with the prophets of old (Acts 8:39; compare with 1 Kgs 18:12 and 2 Kgs 2:16).

Select Bibliography

Introduction

(For the dating and authenticity of texts)
Otto Eissfeldt, *The Old Testament: an Introduction* (New York: Harper and Row, 1965).
Peter Ellis, C.SS.R., *The Men and the Message of the Old Testament* (Collegeville, Minn.: Liturgical Press, 1962).
Aldo J. Tos, *Approaches to the Bible: The Old Testament* (Englewood Cliffs, N. J.: Prentice-Hall, 1963).

History of Israel

(For more background detail, especially in regard to the kings)
John Bright, *A History of Israel* (Philadelphia: Westminster, 1959), Parts 3–5.
Martin Noth, *The History of Israel*, 2nd ed (London: Adam and Charles Black, 1960), Part 2, chap. II Part 3, chap. II.

Royal Ideology

(For the theology of kingship and messianism)
Jean De Fraine, S.J., *L'aspect religieux de la royauté israélite. Analecta biblica* 3 (Rome: Pontifical Biblical Institute, 1954).
Henri Frankfort, *Kingship and the Gods* (Chicago: University of Chicago, 1948).
The Catholic Biblical Quarterly 19 (1957), No. 2. (An issue devoted to essays on messianism).
Sigmund Mowinckel, *He That Cometh* (Oxford: Blackwell, 1954).

The Prophets

Johannes Lindblom, *Prophecy in Ancient Israel* (Philadelphia: Fortress Press, 1962).
Jean Steinmann, *Isaïe, sa vie, son ouvre, et son temps,* 2nd ed. Lectio divina 5. (Paris: Cerf, 1955).
Jean Steinmann, *Jérèmie, sa vie, son ouvre, et son temps. Lectio divina* 9. (Paris: Cerf, 1952).
——— *Le prophète Ezéchiel et les débuts de l'éxile. Lectio divina* 13. (Paris: Cerf, 1953).
Bruce Vawter, C.M., *The Conscience of Israel* (New York: Sheed & Ward, 1961).
C. Westermann, *The Basic Forms of Prophetic Speech* (Philadelphia: Westminster, 1967).

Subject Index

Ahaz, king of Judah, added altar to Assyrian gods in Jerusalem Temple, 44; sought alliance with Assyria, 44

Amos. authenticity of 9:11–12, 100 f; justice, 95 ff; life and times, 93 f; note of hope, 99 f; promise of Davidic restoration, 100 f; remnant, 99; teaching on God, 74 ff

Apocalyptic literature, 88 f, 188 ff

Ark of the Covenant, brought to Jerusalem by David, 27; importance of, as unifying factor, 15 f

Assyria, collapse of, 46; rise of, 43 f

Baalism, 97, 103; in kingdom of Israel, 37 f

Babylon, rise of, 47

Balaam, 4

Bethel, sanctuary for kingdom of Israel, 38

Chronicler, and Davidic covenant, 62 f; theology of, 12 ff

Covenant, in Jeremiah, 145 f; and king, 56 ff; notion of, 57

Cult, and prophecy, 77 f

Dan, sanctuary for kingdom of Israel, 38

Daniel, example of apocalyptic literature, 88 f

David, capture of Jerusalem, 27; character of, 23 ff; covenant with, 36; military victories, 26 f; promise of dynasty, 27 f; promise to (covenant with), 58 ff

Deutero-Isaiah, creation and God of history, 165; oracles of hope, 166; a prophet of Jews in Babylon, 160; Servant Songs, 168 ff; themes in, 161 ff; theology of, 163; times of, 161

Deuteronomic History, 6 ff; discovery of under Josiah, 46; theology of, 6 ff

Deuteronomy, theology of, 50 ff

Elijah, 80, 81; stories about, 84 f

Elisha, 80, 81; stories about, 84 f

Emmanuel prophecies, in Isaiah, 122 ff

Eschatology, meaning of, 65; and messianism, 65

Ezekiel, attitude toward prophets, 159; character of, 151 f; law of holiness, 154; and Judaism, 158; the new Jerusalem, 157 f; personality of, 152 ff; and Priest-Messiah, 64; purifying power of punishment, 156 f; sins in, 154 f; structure of book, 150 ff

First person narratives, 90

Habakkuk, summary of book and problems connected with it, 135 f

Haggai, messianism in, 62; summary of book, 178 ff

Hezekiah, king of Judah, defied Assyria, 45

Hoelscher, and Ezekiel, 149

Holy war, in Isaiah, 120 f; notion of, 16

Hosea, attitude toward Gentiles, 109; book of, structure, 102 f; on God, 103 f; on God's will, 107 f; hope for future, 108; Israel as God's pride, 106; key notions in, 103 f; symbolism in, 104 f

Hoshea, last king of Israel, 43; life and times, 101 f

Isaiah, attitude toward Gentiles, 128 f; book of, divisions within, 111; Davidic monarchy, 121 ff; Emmanuel prophecies, 122 ff; God as holy, 113 ff; holiness and cult, 117 f; and holy war, 120 f; life and times, 110 ff; messianism in, 61; morality and holiness, 115; on political alliances, 118 f; remnant notion in, 127 ff; theology of Temple, 119 ff

Ishbaal, temporarily succeeded Saul, 26

INDEX OF SCRIPTURAL REFERENCES

OLD TESTAMENT

New Testament